Culture and Society in
the Dutch Republic
During the 17th Century

Culture and Society in the Dutch Republic During the 17th Century

J. L. PRICE

Charles Scribner's Sons, New York

Printed in Great Britain
Library of Congress Catalog Card Number 73-8274
ISBN 0-684-13589-2

Contents

List of Illustrations

Acknowledgments

The Author and Publishers would like to thank the following Museums and Collections for permission to reproduce the illustrations appearing in this book:

Rijksmuseum, Amsterdam (Plates 1, 2, 5, 8, 11, 16, 18, 22, 27); Boymans-Van Beuningen Museum, Rotterdam (Pls 24 & 28); Frans Hals Museum, Haarlem (Pls 4 & 6); The Mauritshuis Museum, The Hague (Pls 9, 15, 23, 30); The National Gallery, London (Pls 3, 12, 25); Wallace Collection, London (Pl. 14); Altere Pinakothek, Munich (Pl. 7); Kunsthistorische Museum, Vienna (Pl. 17); Dresden Museum (Pl. 19); Altman Bequest, Metropolitan Museum of Art, New York (Pl. 13); Ferens Art Gallery, Kingston-upon-Hull (Pl. 10); Gardner Museum, Boston, Mass. (Pl. 21); Nationalmuseum, Stockholm (Pl. 20); Louvre (Pl. 29); Herzog August Library, Wolfenbüttel (Pl. 26). Thanks are due to The Mansell Collection for Pls 3, 15, 19, 29.

Preface

To venture into the complex subject of the relationship between culture and society requires a certain temerity, not to say rashness. Indeed the very use of the term 'culture' in the rather old-fashioned sense employed here will be objected to in a number of quarters. However, the term is at least useful, and the investigation of the connection between a culture and the society producing it is an important and necessary task, whatever the pitfalls. The central focus of this book is the contrast between Dutch art and literature in the seventeenth century; to consider why the Dutch in this century were able to produce a school of painting remarkable both for its outstanding quality and for its marked independence of the general movement of artistic taste in Europe, and yet were unable to produce a literature that was more than a minor offshoot of European literature. This theme has determined the main lines of the book, but other aspects of Dutch culture in their Golden Century have been dealt with, not only for their inherent importance, but also for the light they shed on the central issue. This cannot hope to be a definitive work, but if it helps to focus attention on an important, and neglected, problem, the author will be more than satisfied.

I am glad to be able to take this opportunity of thanking those whose help has eradicated at least some of the weaknesses in this work: Mr A. C. Duke and Miss R. Jones who read an early version of the typescript and gave considerable encouragement and useful advice; my friend Mr P. R. J. Hainsworth who helped to remedy some of the failings in my treatment of literature; and my friend and colleague Dr J. J. N. Palmer who not only read and criticised the whole of this work in typescript but also read the proofs. Finally, I should like to acknowledge my debt to Prof. J. R. Hale, the general editor of this series, for his constructive criticism of the penultimate draft of this book.

The University, Hull   J. L. Price

THE DUTCH REPUBLIC
in the 17th century

NORTH

SEA

Ameland
Terschelling

GRONINGEN

Vlieland
Groningen
Leeuwarden
Heiligerlee

Texel
FRIESLAND

Helder
DRENTHE

Steenwyk
Coevorden

Hoorn • Enkhuizen
ZUIDER

Alkmaar •
ZEE
Zwolle
OVERYSSEL

Edam
Oldenzaal

Haarlem •
Amsterdam
Deventer
Entschede

Muiden

Rhine
Amersfoort Zutphen
Leiden
UTRECHT
GELDERLAND
Dieren
Groll

The Hague •
Delft Gouda
Utrecht
Arnhem
Breedevoort
Lek
Duisburg

Schiedam Rotterdam
Schoonhoven

Brill
Waal Gorinchem
Nijmegen
Rhine

Dordrecht

Den Grave
Schouwen
Bosch

ZEELAND
Zevenbergen
Walcheren
Breda • Boxtel
Middelburg •
OF THE GENERALITY

Flushing
S. Beveland Bergen
op Zoom

Sluys •
LANDS

Antwerp
BISHOPRIC
OF LIÈGE
Meuse

Ghent
Cologne •

Maastricht

Liège

——·——·—— Boundary of the United
Provinces

———————— Provincial boundaries

•••••••••••••••• Boundary of the Spanish
Netherlands

0   25   50
|————————————————| miles

one

The Dutch Republic and Europe

The Republic of the United Netherlands had its origins in the Eighty Years War with Spain, which was only ended by the Treaty of Münster (1648) in which Spain resigned its claims to the territory controlled by the rebel provinces. This treaty signalled the final and formal recognition by the rest of Europe of the existence of the Republic as an independent state, but it was little more than the official confirmation of a fact which had been established by the beginning of the seventeenth century.

By 1600 the war with Spain had been in progress for some 30 years: the traditional date for its beginning is 1568, but it would probably be more realistic to take the year 1572, when the Sea Beggars seized control of most of the towns of Holland and Zeeland. The revolt thus initiated was both protestant and anti-Spanish, and within a few years it had become clear that only military conquest could bring these two provinces, which were to form the core of the Dutch Republic, back to obedience.

The years between 1572 and the end of the century did not see a steady strengthening of the position of the rebels. As late as 1588–9 a decisive victory for the Spanish forces under Alexander Farnesa, prince of Parma, seemed to be imminent, and it is possible that only the diversion of Parma's army to intervention in France saved the North from defeat. In the event, the 'Ten Years' made so famous by the Dutch historian Robert Fruin,[1] 1588–98, saw the definitive establishment of the Dutch state. The most obviously important events of these years were the military successes of the Republic's armies under Maurice of Orange and his cousin William Louis, and by 1600 the Dutch were in control of nearly all the territory which was to be the Republic's for the following two centuries. Yet the internal developments which took place during these years had perhaps an even greater importance for the future of the state. The Union of Utrecht (1579), which united the rebellious provinces, was essentially a military alliance which made the very minimum of provision for centralised government. Even William the Silent (1533–84) had found it difficult to make this system work with anything approaching efficiency. After his death, in particular during the earl of Leicester's period in the Netherlands (1585–7), it seemed for a few years that internal dissension would cause the collapse of the embryonic state even if the Spanish armies did not. However, with the appointment of Johan van Oldenbarnevelt as *Advocaat van den Lande*[2] in 1586 and the departure of Leicester began a process which was to convert a near-anarchy of warring elements into a viable political community. Leaving the political structure unchanged in form, Oldenbarnevelt radically transformed the way in which the system worked. In his first years of power he established the leadership of the province of Holland and, as in practice chief minister of this province, he brought the central direction of the Republic's policies, especially foreign affairs, into his own hands. A relatively stable and efficient form of government had been constructed by 1600, a form which was to remain basically unchanged while the Republic lasted, whether directed by a grand pensionary or a stadhouder.

With a firm territorial basis and a sound political system, the Republic was already a viable state by the beginning of the seventeenth century. Its position within Europe, however, had yet to be defined. Acting as an independent state and making treaties with its allies as a sovereign power, the Republic was still regarded by its enemies, formally at least, as an impudent rebel fiction. This uncertainty meant that some of the spirit of the Revolt was carried over into the first half of the seventeenth century: there was an awareness that the Republic, unlike its enemies, was fighting not for political, territorial or economic advantage but for its existence. Dutch successes made this awareness less immediate and less pressing but could not eradicate it completely.

Moreover, until the middle of the century war was the normal condition of life for the Republic. Other states might wage war frequently, the Republic was able occasionally to suspend hostilities. Part of the opposition to the Truce with Spain, which was signed in 1609 and lasted till 1621, sprang from the fear that the Republic might disintegrate in peace-time; the war with Spain was part of its life and no one was quite sure what would happen if it ended. Before its conclusion in 1648 the Eighty Years War was only suspended for the 12 years of this truce, and even at this stage it was at no time clear that the truce would be allowed to run its full term.[3] Thus even when the Republic was not actively pursuing the war with Spain it remained in a beleaguered state—psychologically at least. The army had to be kept in readiness, alliances had to be maintained and refurbished, and the international situation watched carefully. The constant threat of a Spanish attack and the fear of a change in the diplomatic or military situation in Europe which would favour Spain meant that the Dutch had to be as wary in foreign affairs during the truce as they had been in wartime. This uncertainty brought the necessity of intervention, even military, in the affairs of their neighbours—as in the question of the succession to Jülich, Kleve and Berg—and therefore a great part of the resources of the country had still to be diverted to military purposes.

The economic strain of this constant warfare, or readiness for war, led to the growth of a peace party in the Republic, particularly among the regents—the political rulers—of the towns of Holland. This was not a party in the modern sense, but was more a movement of opinion among men of similarly pragmatic views. As the war dragged on and the gains from it became less and less tangible or evident, such men became increasingly impatient with the inflexible and dogmatic attitudes to the war which were held by many politicians and by orthodox Reformed ministers in particular. The peace party had little interest in freeing the South from Spanish rule, nor had it much sympathy for the view that the war was essentially a crusade against the power of Catholicism in Europe.

Oldenbarnevelt shared these views and early in the first decade of the seventeenth century he put himself at the head of the peace party. He was able to negotiate the Truce in 1609 and afterwards worked persistently to turn it into a lasting peace. He had, however, to contend not only with the intransigence of Spain (for he would only have accepted a peace which recognised the full independence of the Republic,[4] while the Spanish stood out for at least a formal recognition of the sovereignty of the king of Spain), but with the equally stubborn opposition to peace of powerful forces within the Republic.

Prince Maurice favoured the continuation of the war for a complex of reasons, in which self-interest, dynastic ambition, and the conviction that the war was necessary to preserve the unity of the state, were inextricably mixed. He found support among a wide range of groups, from the penurious nobles who officered the army and saw peace as a threat to their careers to the more fanatical of the ministers of the Reformed Church with their confused vision of Spain as the mighty tool of Anti-Christ which had to be fought without let. Oldenbarnevelt had prevented the setting up of a West India Company because of his peace plans, so those merchants of Holland and Zeeland who expected great material gains from an attack on the Portuguese and Spanish possessions in the Americas resented the Truce and opposed a lasting peace. At this stage the war with Spain could still be seen by at least an influential section of the population of the Republic as the most effective way of increasing the prosperity of the state. Thus religion and trade came to the support of the war party.

Despite the uncertain situation in Europe and the troubles within the Republic culminating in the execution of Oldenbarnevelt in 1619, the Truce did in fact drag out its full length, and only in 1621 did the cold war again turn into a hot one. From this point until 1648 the war maintained a fairly straightforward character and the European position of the Republic similarly clarified. Throughout this period there was never much doubt that the conflict between Spain and the Republic would be resolved in the latter's favour—at least in so far as Spain would be unable to bring the Dutch back to obedience. On the other hand it became increasingly clear that powerful interests in the Republic were opposed to squandering its resources on any serious attempt at large-scale conquests in the Southern Netherlands. Consequently, for long periods the war appears pointless with few major successes for either side. After about 1626 the military initiative moved to the Dutch, but the limited nature of their aims is illustrated by the lack of any serious attempt to capture Antwerp.

The Republic remained on the fringes of the great conflicts expressed in the Thirty Years War, but the struggle between Habsburg and France was of direct importance to the position of the Republic. France was the Republic's most important ally: not only was it probably already the most powerful state in Europe, but it was in its interest that the strength of Spain should be broken, especially in the Netherlands. Indeed, it was the Republic which first found it convenient to abandon the alliance and make a separate peace with Spain, leaving France to fight on alone for a further 12 years. Yet, however much the Republic tried to concentrate on the war with Spain, its leaders could not ignore the struggle taking place in Germany. Just as the absorption of a large part of the Spanish army and much of Spain's resources in the Netherlands aided the anti-Habsburg cause in Germany, so the war in Germany prevented a concentration of Spanish and Austrian Habsburg forces against the Dutch Republic. A decisive victory for the catholic Habsburg power in Germany might have changed the whole course of the war in the Netherlands. However, even in the years of his greatest successes, Ferdinand II's chances of restoring the power of the emperor in Germany remained very slim. It would have required an astonishing reversal of a situation which had been developing in Germany for centuries for the emperor to become a serious threat to Dutch independence.

The half century up to the Peace of Westphalia was marked by increasing Dutch confidence. The signing of the Truce in 1609 can now be seen as a decisive moment, though this was not clear at the time. If there were still some grounds for pessimism in the early 1620s, by the end of the decade the question was no longer whether the Dutch would be able to hold their own, but how much of an impression they would be able, or wish, to make on Spanish power in the Southern Netherlands. If the Republic had lacked self-confidence before 1609, feeling itself dependent on one or other of its great allies, France and England, by the 1630s there could be no question of its ability to stand on its own. There was no longer any question of a dependent relationship with any other power, not even with France which continued to pay subsidies to the Dutch, but only as the most convenient way of opposing Spanish power while remaining formally neutral. The Republic was approaching the position of a great power and began to realise this fact after 1621.

At the Treaty of Münster Spain recognised the independence of the Republic, and the extent of the new state's territory was fixed. The conquests made by Frederick Henry since the end of the Truce, the most important of these being the area around 's-Hertogenbosch (the *Meierij*), were ceded to the Republic, which in return abandoned its claims to the southern provinces of the Netherlands. One claim affecting the Southern Netherlands was maintained by the Republic and finally accepted by Spain—the blockade of the mouths of the Scheldt and Zwin. The closure of these rivers to trade was considered by the Dutch to be essential to the continued prosperity of the trading towns of the North—Amsterdam in particular felt this matter to be vital to her interests—and on this point they refused to make any concession.

In the second half of the century the Republic played a very different rôle in Europe. Until 1648 the task facing the Republic had been a straightforward one: it was fighting for its existence and its independence against Spain. Differences of opinion over foreign policy were largely concerned with means rather than ends. The peace party, which had been strong since the Truce and had grown stronger in the 1630s and 1640s, was marked by the belief that satisfactory terms could be obtained from Spain rather than by a belief that the war was unnecessary. The chief difference between the peace party and the war party was that the former could see the ending of the war as a desirable objective, while for the latter peace with Spain was undesirable either for political or religious reasons.

With the Peace of Westphalia this relative simplicity as far as the foreign policy of the Republic was concerned came to an end, and with it went the comparative unanimity with regard to the state's objectives. The Republic had to work out a new foreign policy, and, given the differing interests of the chief forces within the state, this task was far from simple. The serious conflicts which arose during the stadhouder- ship of William II (1647–50), leading to the crisis of 1650 and the threat of civil war, may have been essentially over the distribution of power within the state but they crystallised around decisions concerning foreign policy. William II, young, rash, and ambitious, was determined on an aggressive military policy in alliance with France aimed at ter- ritorial expansion in the Southern Netherlands at the expense of Spain and at the restoration of the Stuarts in England. It is clear that this policy was dictated by the dynastic interests of the house of Orange and not by those of the Republic.[6] William wished to make his mark as a military leader and, moreover, had more material ambitions to pursue. His eagerness to renew the war against Spain was greatly encouraged by the French minister, Mazarin, who offered him the prospect of independent possessions in the Southern Netherlands and, rather more vaguely, help in winning for himself a sovereign position in the Republic. William's attitude to English affairs was a conse- quence of his marriage to a daughter of Charles I. The Republic had nothing to gain from taking sides in England, especially at this late date, but the interests of the house of Orange called for intervention on the side of the Stuarts. Little concrete came from these plans for interven- tion in England, but the known attitude of the stadhouder was enough to make relations between the Republic and the new English govern- ment very difficult.

The centre of the opposition to these adventurous policies was the states of the province of Holland. The signing of the peace in 1648 had been a triumph for the political leaders of Holland, and they were determined to prevent the prince from undoing their work so swiftly. As far as they were concerned the war with Spain had achieved its object, and they could see no profit in renewing it. Whatever their attitudes towards the East Indies and the Americas, the States of Holland were by now convinced of the necessity of a pacific policy in Europe. Not only could the Holland regents see no economic advantage in either the Spanish or the English project, they were also concerned about the finances of their province. Holland had emerged from the Eighty Years War with a disturbingly heavy load of debt and retrenchment rather than an expensive foreign policy seemed to be called for. Moreover, any further conquests in the South would bring up the problem of Antwerp again, and the merchants of Holland were determined that this once-great commercial centre should not be allowed to rise again. Intervention in England would not only be expensive and probably unsuccessful, but also disastrous, at least in the short term, to Dutch trade with that country. Thus the leaders in the States of Holland were beginning to develop a foreign policy which ran directly contrary to that of William II—they aimed at peace to allow the Republic to retrench its finances which had been strained by the long years of war and also to encourage the full development of the country's trade.

The crisis of 1650 ended in deadlock with an apparent victory for the prince after his imprisonment of six prominent regents from Holland and his attack on and threatened siege of Amsterdam. Amsterdam and with it Holland backed down over the minor matter of the number of troops to be paid off, but the States of Holland still blocked in the States General any attempt to push through a renewal of the war with Spain. The death of the prince later in the year brought this impasse to an end and allowed a total victory for the States of Holland and the policies it favoured.

For the next 20 years or more the leading politicians of the Republic, and Johan de Witt in particular, attempted to realise the pacific foreign policy of the States of Holland. The Republic's trade, industry and fisheries were so well-developed and depended so heavily on foreign markets and on a very complex system of commerce that its prosperity could only be damaged by any disturbances of European peace. Not only was the Republic concerned to avoid war itself, but it also felt that its interests were best served by the preservation of peace in Europe as a whole.

The chief problem which faced the Republic in these years was the steady resurgence of both France and England after the troubles of the Civil War and the Fronde. Under Cromwell England once again began to play the rôle of a major power in Europe, and after the Restoration this development continued. In the late 1650s and during the personal rule of Louis xiv France began to pursue an expansive foreign policy which disturbed not only its neighbours but the whole of Europe. Both England and France found the Republic an obstacle to the realisation of their ambitions, and the Dutch were involved in wars with them both, despite their best efforts to maintain peace and a balance of power.

With England conflicts arose mainly out of a clash of economic interests: in trade, industry and fishing Holland was the power in possession and English expansion could only be at its expense. The economic rivalry between the Dutch Republic and England had been apparent from the beginning of the century, centring on clashes over fishing rights in the North Sea and Dutch domination in the East Indies. In the third quarter of the century these rivalries became so acute that war broke out between the two states three times—and on each occasion England was the aggressor.[7] The wars with England of 1652-4 and 1665-7 show how difficult it was for the Republic to maintain its remarkable prosperity, especially its economic dominance in Europe built up during the first half of the century, without having to fight for its preservation against those states, and in particular the rising mercantile power of England, which resented Dutch pre-eminence.

If English rivalry threatened the prosperity of the Republic the aggressive policy of France seemed to endanger its very existence as an independent state. While Colbert's economic policies, which included heavy tariffs on Dutch manufactures, were damaging to Dutch trade and industry, French military strength posed a much more serious threat. The preservation of the Spanish Netherlands as a buffer between the Republic and France became a fundamental aim of Dutch foreign policy. It was feared that if France were able to annex the Southern Netherlands the Republic would soon be absorbed into France or at least become a political dependency. Even without going to such extremes of pessimism it could be argued that if France came into the possession of Antwerp the closure of the Scheldt, which was felt to be so important to the prosperity of the Republic, could hardly be maintained for long.

With Spain in full, and now apparent, decline it often seemed that only the Republic stood in the way of French conquest of the Spanish Netherlands. Dutch military power alone could not hope to contain that of France, and De Witt had been the prime mover and organiser behind the triple alliance between the Republic, England and Sweden which prevented France from benefiting from its military successes in the Southern Netherlands in 1668. To Louis xiv it seemed clear that if the Republic were defeated the way would be clear for French ambitions in this region. The French attack was well prepared both militarily and diplomatically, and when it came in the spring of 1672 the Republic was without powerful allies and its army was unprepared. Within a few months the French armies had broken through the almost unresisting landward defences and occupied most of the Republic's territory outside Holland and Zeeland. As the French had secured England as an ally, the Dutch were attacked by sea at the same time, and by the summer of this year it seemed that the Dutch Republic as an independent state was about to cease to exist. The French armies were poised for the final attack on the province of Holland, and the English and French fleets were occupying all the energies of the Dutch navy. The plans of France and England for a partition of the Republic between them, leaving only a small and dependent principality for the young prince of Orange, seemed at the time realistic, particularly as the inhabitants of the towns of the yet-unconquered provinces were rising against their rulers. This internal disorder seemed to fit all too well into the picture of a state in dissolution.

However, the Republic did survive: its fleets defeated those of France and England, and the armies of France were slowly driven out of Dutch territory. William III became stadhouder and captain-general, restoring the power of his house in the Republic, and internal order was re-established.

From this point William III was the dominant influence in Dutch foreign policy, and this introduced a new phase in the Republic's rôle within Europe. While De Witt's policy had been to work for the maintenance of peace in Europe, to avoid entangling alliances, and to try to hold the balance between France and England, William turned his energy and the resources of the Republic into a crusade against France. De Witt had served what he felt to be the interests of the state, which in practice meant those of the economy and in particular those of the merchants of Holland; William III in contrast also felt himself to be serving the interests of the Republic but he saw the threat of French dominance in Europe as the chief danger and was consequently prepared to subordinate the interests of the economy to those of his foreign policy. In some sense this return to a more active and aggressive foreign policy was a reversion, not unexpected in a prince of Orange, to the traditions of his house. But, whereas the aims of his father, William II, had chiefly been the furtherance of the dynastic interests of his house, he devoted himself to checking the expansion of France. If the Holland regents had tended to equate the interests of the Republic with those of its trade, William III could only really comprehend the imperatives of international politics. For the prince opposition to Louis XIV was not only a political necessity, but also a moral and religious imperative. He felt that he had a mission imposed upon him by God to hold France in check, for the latter represented not only a threat to the balance of power in Europe but seemed also to be the spearhead of militant catholicism.

Here we meet again the religious element in Dutch politics. For many of the Dutch the Eighty Years War had been primarily a war of religion, and in the last decades of the seventeenth century the threat posed by France could as easily be seen in religious terms. The defence of the European balance of power against French ambitions was also regarded, especially by William III, as the defence of European protestantism against the aggressive catholicism of Louis XIV. The revocation of the Edict of Nantes in 1685, which followed a period of persecution of the Huguenots and heralded a yet more severe persecution, lent some weight to this view, for it seemed to stamp the French king as the unmistakable champion of catholicism. Moreover, the accession of an openly catholic king to the throne of England in the same year appeared to put in jeopardy the protestant cause in the whole of Europe. This religious motif in William's foreign policy brought him the backing of the old allies of Orange—the ministers of the Reformed Church and their followers among the common people. He represented not only the European, political tradition in Dutch foreign policy as opposed to the more passive, trade-oriented approach of the Holland regents, but also the militant protestant concept of the significance of the Republic as opposed to the latter's secular and pragmatic attitude.

William's power in the Republic was very considerable. His constitutional position was to a remarkable extent undefined, and this circumstance gave him the opportunity to wield more de facto power than many constitutional monarchs. His influence was perhaps even greater after the success of his English enterprise, and he appears to have had more difficulty in forcing through his will in his kingdom than in the Republic, where he was formally a servant of the state. Despite the reluctance of the States of Holland, led by Amsterdam, to continue to pay for any war which did not seem to be absolutely necessary, William was in general able to impose his foreign policy on the Republic after 1672, and there were fifteen years of war with France between 1672 and the end of the century (1672–8, 1688–97).

It can be seen from this short sketch that throughout the seventeenth century the Dutch Republic was under constant pressure from without. For more than half the century the state was involved in serious wars in Europe (not to mention the wars and armed conflicts inseparable from the development of a trading empire on a world scale). In the first half of the century the Republic was fighting to establish itself as a recognised independent state; in the second half to preserve the position, both political and economic, which it had gained in the first. In a real sense the Dutch were fighting for the existence of their state in all these wars. This fact is clear, of course, with regard to the war of independence against Spain, but French aggression in the later part of the century clearly endangered this dearly-won independence, while English economic rivalry and the naval wars which sprang from it also threatened to undermine Dutch prosperity.

The tensions within the Republic which resulted from these outside pressures and the continuous battle for survival forged a national self-consciousness and a sense of national purpose. Both of these ideas were closely associated with a Calvinist concept of mission and separateness. The Dutch consciousness of nationality and political unity was weak— each province referred to the others in official documents as 'the Allies' —and the sense of a common religion, particularly a religion which was under threat, helped to bind the separate provinces which composed the state more firmly together, combating the worst effects of the provincial separatist tendencies more powerfully than an imperfect community of economic interests could do. The Eighty Years War did foster the development of a patriotic spirit inspired by the Republic as a political unit, but for large sections of the population this patriotic idea was, as the crises of 1618 and 1672 show, incomprehensible without the religious element. In both years loyalty to the state was confused in the popular mind—and perhaps not only there—with Reformed orthodoxy. This concept of the religious *raison d'être* of the state brought with it the idea of a religious mission for the state: the preservation or spreading of protestantism not only within the Republic but in the rest of Europe. While the war with Spain continued the interest of the state appeared more easily reconcilable with this protestant mission than it was to become later, when rational self-interest and purely political motives became more clearly the motor behind policy. Part of William III's success came from his ability to add once more a religious motivation for his foreign policies to the rational calculation that France was an immediate political threat to the Republic.

Warfare in the first half of the century brought greater political unity to the Republic and also economic success. The orthodox Reformed ministers, the merchants and the *politiques* could all support wholeheartedly a struggle which aimed at political independence, the defeat of the catholic champion in Europe, and the establishment of Dutch commercial strength. A serious clash between these various motives came in the Southern Netherlands, and to some extent in the Americas. With regard to the South, economic self-interest combined with the political leaders' views as to what was practicable to defeat the urge to conquer the Southern provinces of the Netherlands for the Reformed faith.

In contrast the wars of the second half of the century brought with them severe strains on the economy of the Republic and often encouraged domestic disunity. The wars with England were direct attacks on Dutch trade and caused serious economic disruption at least in the short term. Moreover, in the 1660s and particularly in 1672 the English were able to make good propaganda use of the family connection between the house of Stuart and the house of Orange. A large number of the supporters of Orange in the Republic found it possible to believe that England was only fighting in order to secure the promotion of the young prince of Orange to the offices of stadhouder and captain-general. Consequently they felt that these wars were not being fought to protect the interests of the Dutch state, but only to consolidate the power of the States party. The French wars produced similar if less intense disagreement over what should be the objectives of Dutch foreign policy: for those who lacked the prince's religious motivation, it was far from clear that William III's anti-French policy was in the best interests of the state. In the long term England was a greater threat to Dutch power than France, in that its development undermined the very basis of that power—economic dominance in Europe. It was all too clear to many in Holland that William's insistence on giving absolute priority to the problem of France would benefit England rather than the Republic in the long run. The issues involved in Dutch foreign relations in the later part of the seventeenth century were much less straightforward than in the simple, heroic days of the Eighty Years War, and the fundamental divisions in Dutch society could emerge more easily.

The period of the Eighty Years War, which saw the establishment of national independence, also witnessed the development of a specifically Dutch culture. Before the Revolt it is difficult to discover a separate identity in the Northern Netherlands, either in painting or in literature. In painting Holland at least had been a lively centre of activity, but it had been an offshoot or dependency of the more highly developed and artistically powerful provinces of Flanders and Brabant. Only with the Revolt and the creation of a new state in the northern Netherlands did a clearly distinct form of art begin to develop here, a process which, to a lesser extent, is also evident in literature.

One aspect of this development was an obvious and almost inevitable consequence of the Revolt and the war for independence: Dutch writers responded to the challenge of the war by producing propagandist works of a more or less subtle nature. From the militant songs of the Sea Beggars and the hardly less militant psalms translated by the protestants to Grotius's *De antiquitate reipublicae batavicae*[8] a large number of works appeared in print justifying the Revolt on religious or political grounds. If a religious emphasis was more necessary in the early, desperate years of the struggle, by the beginning of the seventeenth century Grotius's argument that sovereignty had always rested with the states of the provinces and thus that the Revolt had not been a revolution but armed resistance by sovereign states to the Spanish king's attempt at usurpation was more useful to the leaders of a state which was busily trying to make itself respectable in the eyes of the rest of Europe.[9] Such works also laid the groundwork of a Dutch national consciousness, whether with a religious basis—the Republic as a protestant state—or through the idea of the Dutch state as the direct descendant of the Batavian republic of Roman times which had, so it was argued, maintained its essential independence throughout the Middle Ages.

The society which formed during the Eighty Years War was in many ways distinct from any other in Europe; not least was this difference shown in the cultural achievements of the Republic. The speed with which an independent and distinctive culture grew up in the Republic during the Eighty Years War is one of the most surprising aspects of Dutch history in this period. If the ability of the Republic to resist the apparently massive power of Spain was a source of wonder to contemporaries, it is perhaps even more surprising that so small a country could in so short a time have freed itself to such a considerable extent from the cultural dominance of southern Europe. For the weaknesses behind the imposing façade of Spanish power are now evident, and the economic strength of the young Republic as well as the relatively favourable international situation in which it found itself are more obvious, and so the success of the Republic's fight against Spain is less astonishing. If the Dutch success was less complete in the second battle —particularly in literature—and less lasting, so the strength of general European influence and tradition was far greater on the cultural plane than the power of Spain on the political and military. Moreover, on the political level the enemy was clear and the objective plain, while on the cultural there was little conscious stimulation of a native and distinctive tradition and imitation of foreign modes was commonly seen as the proper way to develop a worthwhile civilisation. In such circumstances for the Dutch to have built up any form of distinctive culture would have been a major achievement: that they were able to produce great art in the process is a sign of the remarkable strength and vitality of Dutch society in this century.

The extent to which the Dutch were able to develop a culture which was unique in Europe will be discussed in much of the rest of this book. The political system of the Republic, with its powerful survivals of provincial particularism and decentralisation was looked upon by most outside observers as an aberration in a century which saw the development and the adulation of absolute and centralised monarchies, and the Dutch cultural development was in many ways, particularly in painting, equally opposed to general European modes. In painting this difference from the rest of Europe was so marked that it is only relatively recently that the greatness of the Dutch achievement has been fully realised. The dominant style in Europe for much of the seventeenth century, usually, though not with particular clarity, termed baroque, was closely associated with the celebration of royal power and with the Counter-Reformation Church, while in the Republic both the idea of royal power and catholicism were opposed to the most powerful elements in society. These circumstances allowed Dutch art to follow an independent course, though they cannot explain the high quality of the achievement thus rendered possible.

However, the development of a really independent culture was a difficult task and was only partially achieved outside painting, and its preservation in the later seventeenth century was much more problematical than the preservation of political independence. If the attacks of France and England were successfully resisted—at least as far as the political survival of the Republic, if not its position as a great power, was concerned—the situation was very different with regard both to the nature and to the quality of Dutch culture. The French attack failed on the military and political plane, but succeeded on the cultural. French influence in manners, art and literature had always been strong at the court of the stadhouders, but in the last decades of the seventeenth century it spread throughout Dutch society and undermined the vitality of the peculiar Dutch tradition. Painting was especially vulnerable to such influences and by the beginning of the eighteenth century there was little left either of the originality or the vitality of Dutch art. The Dutch Republic was unable to play an independent rôle either in politics or in culture after the end of its golden century.

Notes

[1] R. Fruin, *Tien jaren uit den Tachtigjarigen Oorlog, 1588-1598* (Amsterdam 1861)

[2] *Advocaat van den Lande* or *Landsadvocaat* was the office which later became known as *Raadspensionaris*—or, to the English, Grand Pensionary. This office evolved from the post of pensionary (legal adviser and spokesman) of the nobles in the States of Holland. In the course of the Revolt the *Landsadvocaat* became the chief minister of the States and thus, in effect, of the Republic

[3] A. Th. van Deursen, *Honni soit qui mal y pense? De Republiek tussen de mogenheden (1610-1612)* (Mededelingen der Koninklijke Nederlandse Akademie van Wetenschappen, afd. Letterkunde, nieuwe reeks, deel 28, no. 1) (Amsterdam 1965), pp. 28, 76-7

[4] J. den Tex, *Oldenbarnevelt*, vol. II (Haarlem 1962), p. 540

[5] Maurice's half-brother who succeeded him as stadhouder and captain-general in 1625

[6] See P. Geyl, *Orange and Stuart* (London 1969)

[7] For these wars, see C. Wilson, *Profit and Power* (London 1957)

[8] See below, p. 184

[9] Grotius wrote his work in Latin with his eye on a European as much as on a Dutch audience

two

The Dutch Republic and its Internal Tensions

The constant pressure from without which the Republic had to face during the seventeenth century was accompanied by conflicts and divisions within Dutch society which at times appeared to threaten the state with disintegration, and which in times of crisis weakened its ability to resist foreign attack. The main divisive elements were provincial separatism, the struggle for power between the urban oligarchs of Holland and the princes of Orange, and conflicts over religion. These factors were always present and could at any moment become a threat to the unity or coherence of the state. The problems raised by the conflicts between these various forces within the Republic were never insoluble, and in fact even the great crises of the seventeenth century were overcome with a notable lack of violence and bloodshed —though on occasion, as with the sudden death of William II in late 1650, luck played an important part in making a peaceful solution possible. Further, these inner conflicts can be seen as a source of vitality in Dutch society, giving a boost to political and intellectual activity. Certainly the failure of any one of the contending forces to gain a complete and lasting victory, particularly in the field of religion, is one of the chief reasons why the Dutch Republic was able to become the most tolerant society in Europe in the seventeenth century. A high price had to be paid, however, for this vitality and tolerance in recurring crises and frequent periods of serious political instability.

The Dutch Republic (also known as the United Provinces) was composed of seven provinces—Holland, Zeeland, Utrecht, Friesland, Groningen, Overijsel and Gelderland[1]—each with a separate government centred on the states of the province.[2] Each province looked upon itself as sovereign and the Republic can be better regarded as an alliance of independent states than as a single political unit.[3] The central government was very limited both in its practical power and its formal competence. The chief federal institution was the States General composed of delegates from the provincial states who were ambassadors rather than plenipotentiaries: matters of any importance had to be referred back to the provincial states for decision before the delegates in the States General could give an opinion. The States General was chiefly concerned with the formulation of foreign policy and with military matters. Even here, however, important decisions required unanimity. The States General had no power to levy taxes, though it drew up the military budget through the Council of State, and each province collected its own taxes according to its own system. Each province paid a fixed proportion of the federal budget, but no province could be compelled to pay for any policy of which it disapproved. Thus each was to a large degree self-governing and there was no way of imposing even a majority decision on a dissident province. While patient negotiation could usually bring about agreement or compromise, it was exceedingly difficult except in the most critical of situations for the States General to reach a decision quickly.

This survival of medieval particularism in the form of provincial separatism was fundamental to the political system of the Republic. This system has found many adverse critics, but it should be pointed out that it worked in practice, and well by the standards of the time. On the other hand it did bring to the surface conflicts between the various provinces—the most important being those between the prosperous commercial and industrial province of Holland and the others.

Holland was by far the most important single province. It provided well over half of the total tax revenue of the Republic, and it was, moreover, frequently the only province to pay its quota promptly and completely. Consequently, it normally had a decisive influence on the government of the Republic as a whole. In fact for long periods the policy of Holland was to all intents and purposes that of the Republic. Because of the necessity for unanimity Holland, like any other province, could exercise a veto in important matters, including finance, but its economic power meant that it also had the most influential voice in the States General as no policy was really practicable without the wholehearted support of this province. The political predominance of Holland was a source of both weakness and strength for the Republic: on the one hand Holland's leadership gave a purpose and a coherence to the politics of the Union and enabled urgent decisions to be pushed through much more quickly than might have been expected considering the cumbersome nature of the machinery involved; but it also stimulated inter-provincial jealousies and resentment from the less powerful provinces. There was a conflict between the formal political system, where equality of rights, power and influence between the provinces, irrespective of size or wealth, was carefully preserved, and the way in which the system worked in practice, with Holland using its financial power to impose its leadership on the other provinces.

Conflict between Holland and the rest of the Republic arose especially over foreign and military policy. The political leaders of Holland were primarily concerned with the economic interests of their province. This is shown both by the general foreign policies which they pursued and in their concern to maintain a powerful navy, which was necessary to protect Holland's trade and great merchant fleet. In contrast, the land provinces, which were more open to invasion and less interested in trade, felt that a higher priority should be given to the army. As the position of the Republic as a major power depended primarily on the wealth of Holland the attitude of the regents of this province was justifiable on the grounds of national interest, but it is understandable that the other provinces suspected that their interests were too often sacrificed to those of their more powerful partner.

Such disagreements could only be exacerbated by the contrast between the extraordinary prosperity of Holland and the relative penury of the other provinces. Zeeland, Friesland and, to a lesser extent, Utrecht shared in the general economic growth of the Republic, but their prosperity was always overshadowed by that of Holland. Gelderland, Overijsel and Groningen remained largely agricultural and took little part in the commercial expansion so characteristic of the rest of the Republic. Similarly, the size and political influence of the towns of these provinces was much less than in Holland, and the influence of the nobility in the provincial estates much greater. In social structure as in economy these provinces contrasted strongly with Holland, and it was to be expected that their attitude to politics would be markedly different.

The position was similar with regard to culture: here Holland was even more dominant than in politics. The great Dutch artistic achievement of the seventeenth century was not exclusively, but very largely, a product of the province of Holland, and the situation was not very different in other fields of culture. In literature as in painting the leading figures were either born in Holland or were drawn to it at an early stage in their lives and produced their best work there. It is true that there were outposts in other provinces—the school of painting in Utrecht, a modest production of poetry in Zeeland—but these were of very minor importance compared with the achievement of Holland.

It was the political system of Holland, with the domination of the towns and the urban regents, which was most clearly distinct from those existing in the rest of Europe; and it was the artists, writers and men of learning of this province who produced the finest and most distinctive of Dutch works in art, literature and scholarship. This predominance of Holland in the life of the Republic aggravated the jealousy of the other provinces and underlined the difference dividing them from their more powerful partner. As far as the development of a national feeling is concerned, the cultural flowering of the seventeenth century certainly produced something that was specifically Dutch, but its influence as a force for unification was weakened by its close association with one province, Holland. The Dutch cultural achievement all too often appeared to be only a success for Holland, just as the great Dutch prosperity of this century often seemed essentially limited to that province.

Provincial separatism, which showed itself particularly in the fear of the lesser provinces of domination by Holland, and their resentment of the power of this province in the Union, is an important factor in the major continuing political conflict of the seventeenth century: the struggle for power between the States of Holland and the house of Orange.

This conflict first came to the fore in the years immediately preceding the signing of the Twelve Years Truce with Spain in 1609, and it became a constant theme in Dutch politics throughout the seventeenth century. This first appearance was typical of the way in which it was to underlie many later political and religious disputes; a disagreement over foreign policy revealed fundamental uncertainties in the constitution of the Republic. The regents of Holland believed that a truce would be in the best interests of their province, which carried the chief financial burden of the war. To avoid being forced to stay in the war against their better judgement, Oldenbarnevelt and his supporters emphasised the doctrine of provincial sovereignty, which in effect meant the dominance of Holland in the Union. For if the central, federal institutions, especially the Council of State, were kept weak, Holland could use its economic power to compel the other provinces to accept its leadership.

In contrast the war party, fearing that peace might lead to the disintegration of the state, called on the forces of provincial separatism— somewhat paradoxically—to strengthen the central institutions of the state. The overwhelming influence of Holland caused the other provinces to look to these central institutions of the Republic to provide checks on its power and to safeguard their interests. The stadhouders, especially Maurice who held this office in five out of the seven provinces, the Council of State, and the States General were to be used to deprive Holland of her leadership of the Republic. Thus Maurice could rely to a considerable extent on the support of the lesser provinces in his opposition to the policies of Oldenbarnevelt and the majority in the States of Holland, and this support was indispensable as a legitimation of his actions.

It needs to be stressed here that the constitutional system of the Republic was still uncertain in the first decades of the seventeenth century. Oldenbarnevelt and his supporters based their actions on the principle of provincial sovereignty, while their opponents stressed the powers and prerogatives of the States General and the other central organs of government. The situation of the stadhouders was particularly ambiguous. This office stemmed from the provincial governors appointed by the sovereign in the Burgundian and Habsburg periods. After the Revolt the stadhouders became formally subject to the states of their provinces, but—a peculiar and fundamental illogicality of the Dutch political system—they retained some sovereign attributes, such as the power to appoint certain magistrates in the towns. The princes of Orange from William the Silent to William III were stadhouders in the majority of the provinces, members of the Council of State, and commanders of the army of the Republic, thus they could play a very important rôle in the state. The stadhouders of Friesland (who usually held this office in Groningen and Drente also) came from another branch of the house of Nassau and were much less influential.

After the signing of the truce, in April 1609, the war party's fear that the end of hostilities would bring serious domestic discord, and possibly the disintegration of the Republic, proved to have been far from baseless. The years after 1609 saw such an intensification of the disagreements within the Reformed Church that a civil war began to appear a distinct possibility. If Oldenbarnevelt and his supporters in the States of Holland did not always give active aid to the Arminians in this dispute, they were certainly consistently ready to protect Remonstrant ministers from the attacks of the orthodox.[4] They were convinced that the power and authority of the state had to be upheld against the claims of the church to political influence. Oldenbarnevelt never tired of recalling the way in which the fanatical Calvinists in Ghent had, according to his interpretation, caused the loss to the Revolt of much of the Southern Netherlands.[5] The Remonstrants, as a minority group within the church, were well aware of their need for support from the state. Consequently they actively sought an alliance with the States of Holland, offering as bait an erastian formulation of the position of the church within the state, giving the civil authority the final decision even in matters of doctrine. At the same time they pointed out the ambiguities in the arguments of the orthodox champions when it came to the matter of the relationship between civil and ecclesiastical authorities. As the Remonstrant movement was to all practical purposes confined to Holland it was to the states of this province that its arguments were directed, and especially to its chief servant, Oldenbarnevelt, whose views were well known. The Remonstrant question also became involved with the doctrine of provincial sovereignty so dear to the hearts of the political leaders of Holland. The orthodox ministers and their supporters looked to a national synod for the solution of the religious dispute, as they could be sure that such a body would condemn the Remonstrants. A national synod, however, if its decisions were to be binding on the individual provinces, would represent an infringement of provincial sovereignty, as according to this doctrine the religious affairs of an individual province were the concern of its civil and ecclesiastical authorities alone.

While political uncertainties made it more difficult to find a solution to the religious conflict, religious considerations aggravated the political disagreements. The orthodox in the Reformed Church knew that they would have to break the opposition of Holland before they could secure a national synod, and for this they would need the help of Prince Maurice, the other focus of political power within the Republic.

As the dispute within the Reformed Church became more intense, and disorders in the towns of Holland arising from it more frequent, Maurice after much hesitation finally threw in his lot with the opponents of Oldenbarnevelt. In 1618, in a carefully organised *coup*, the stadhouder first arrested Oldenbarnevelt and his leading political associates, and then made a tour of the voting towns of Holland expelling from the town governments the Remonstrants, their sympathisers, and the supporters of Oldenbarnevelt, and replacing them with Contra-remonstrants and men on whom he could rely for support. The legality of these actions was highly dubious, but Maurice could claim to be acting on the authority of the States General. Only his control of the army and widespread popular support, however, enabled him to succeed. The national synod was held at Dordrecht in the following year. As expected it condemned the Remonstrants. Early in the same year, 1619, Oldenbarnevelt was executed, and Maurice took over in practice the leadership of the Republic.

Despite the religious terms in which the conflicts during the truce had been expressed, at the crisis the issue had been political—whether the urban oligarchs represented in the States of Holland, supported by allies and clients in the other provinces, would enjoy the leadership of the Republic, or the prince of Orange, backed by the majority party in the Reformed Church and the nobility, who were still powerful in the land provinces.

Maurice's victory in 1618 was, however, far from decisive in the long term. He made no real changes in the political system: the only major break with the past was that for over 30 years the stadhouder and not the grand pensionary of Holland was the directing hand in Dutch political life. The struggle for the political control of the Republic continued, but with the States of Holland—or at least the dominant groups within it—in opposition. Holland showed little enthusiasm for the war after its resumption in 1621, opposing high military expenditure, agitating for peace, and becoming increasingly suspicious of the interest shown by Frederick Henry, who succeeded his half-brother Maurice as stadhouder in 1625, in the Southern Netherlands. Similarly, the triumph of the Contra-remonstrants at the Synod of Dordrecht could not force religious orthodoxy on Dutch society: liberal theology was expelled from the Reformed Church, but the strength of tolerance among the leading politicians, from Frederick Henry to the Holland regents, was far greater than that of rigid orthodoxy. The Remonstrants suffered a period of persecution immediately after 1619, but by the end of the 1620s they were finding it possible to set up their own churches. Although they were now a sect, they were very influential especially among the regents, and the wealthier classes in general, of the towns of Holland.

By the mid-century the nature and composition of the two major political groupings in the Republic were becoming clear. The Orangists believed that the Republic needed at least a semi-monarchical head—an *Eminente Hoofd* as it was called—to provide a focus of loyalty and a final constitutional authority to an otherwise all-too-fragmented state. The practical strength of this party lay largely in the position and powers of the prince of Orange: as head of both the army and navy he had considerable powers of patronage, and as stadhouder in most of the

1 Michiel van Miereveld,
Johan van Oldenbarnevelt
(Rijksmuseum,
Amsterdam)

2 Michiel van Miereveld,
Prince Maurice (Rijks-
museum, Amsterdam)

3 Gerard ter Borch, *The Swearing of the Oath of Ratification of the Treaty of Münster*, 1648 (National Gallery, London)

4 Frans Hals, *Regents of the Old Men's Home, c. 1664* (Frans Halsmuseum, Haarlem)

5 Rembrandt van Rijn, *The Syndics of the Cloth Drapers' Guild*, 1661/62 (Rijksmuseum, Amsterdam)

6   Frans Hals, *Officers of the Militia Company of St Hadrian, c. 1633* (Frans Halsmuseum, Haarlem)

7 Jan van Goyen, *View of Leiden*, 1643 (Altere Pinakothek, Munich)

provinces he had considerable influence on affairs of state. The prince was especially powerful in Zeeland where as First Noble, marquis of Vere and Lord of Vlissingen, he controlled three out of the seven votes in the states of the province. Even in Holland his influence was great, as in most towns—including those represented in the States of Holland —he had, as stadhouder, the right to appoint from a double nomination the magistrates who changed yearly, and in some towns he could even appoint out of a triple nomination members to the council (*vroedschap* or *raad*) of the town. The princes of Orange could also rely on a large clientage among the impoverished nobility of the land provinces, who had much influence in the states of their provinces, and who were avid for commissions in the army and the other important and lucrative posts at the disposal of the prince. In addition, the princes of Orange could generally rely on the support of the ministers of the Reformed Church, who regarded them both as the champions of orthodoxy and as protectors of the church against the attacks of the town regents on its independence. Not all ministers were Orangists nor was their Orangism without nuances,[6] but the connection between Reformed orthodoxy and support for the princes of Orange was very strong and could be decisive at times of crisis.

The princes of Orange could be, both symbolically and in fact, an important unifying force in the Republic, standing above and apart from provincial interests, but their interests were not always identical with those of the Republic. Under Frederick Henry and his son, William II, the house of Orange became increasingly concerned to promote the interests of the dynasty at the expense of those of the state they were supposed to serve.[7] During this period their control of the policies and politicians of the majority of the provinces steadily deprived the latter of their ability to exercise any independent judgement in politics. Only Holland, whose political vitality had been only peripherally affected by the system of influence maintained by the princes of Orange, retained sufficient independence to oppose their policies.

Opposition to the power of the princes of Orange came from the Republican tradition, working chiefly through the States of Holland. Its fundamental beliefs were, at one level, the sovereignty of the individual provinces and, at another, the rights and privileges—the 'freedom'—of the towns and the town oligarchies. The Republicans (or the States Party as they became known in opposition to the Orangists[8]) believed that the Revolt had been the result of political rather than religious grievances, i.e. that it had been a reaction to the attempt of the Spanish king to undermine and destroy the liberties enjoyed by the provinces, the nobility and the towns in the Netherlands. This emphasis on the rights and privileges of certain groups and institutions was a legalistic and limited view of liberty, but it was entirely satisfactory to the regents of the towns of Holland. The Republicans wished to keep the reality of power in the hands of the provincial states, allowing them autonomy as far as their internal affairs were concerned, and with decisions on matters of mutual concern—foreign affairs, the army and navy, the administration of the Generality Lands—taken by free agreement between the provinces. In addition a policy of general religious toleration was an integral part of their programme. Among the educated classes in the Republic the influence of the tolerant, Erasmian tradition was very strong, and the regents of Holland in particular were tenacious defenders of a degree of religious toleration unknown elsewhere in Europe. Many of them had been attracted to the Remonstrants, and although after 1619 only members of the Reformed Church were officially eligible for places in the town governments, by the middle of the century this rule was far from being rigidly applied. A considerable number of regents were connected in some way with one or other of the unorthodox religious movements which flourished in Holland around the mid-century, notably the Collegiants.[9] The regents were determined to prevent the Reformed Church from interfering in political matters, and they recognised a high degree of toleration as a practical political necessity. Even the most orthodox of the regents were more concerned to preserve order than to promote conformity in religion.

The Republicans recognised that the princes of Orange could be useful as *foci* of loyalty and that, as men of prestige without direct ties to any particular province, they could help to bring about those compromises so essential to the workings of the Dutch political system. However, they feared the monarchical tendencies of the stadhouders and distrusted their policies, which too often seemed designed to further their own private and dynastic ends rather than those of the Republic. It has been common for historians to see in the house of Orange the champions of the unitary state and to castigate the Republican regents for their narrow-minded and anti-national particularism,[10] but despite their undoubted narrowness of vision the Holland regents pursued policies which were frequently more truly in the general interest of the Dutch state than those of the princes of Orange. Particularly in the middle years of the seventeenth century the dynastic emphasis in the policies of Frederick Henry and William II, after the marriage of the latter to the daughter of Charles I of England in 1641, became dangerous to the Republic, threatening renewed war with Spain and involvement in English civil strife.

The triumph of Holland in 1648 in forcing through the Peace of Westphalia against the opposition of William II appeared to be the climax of the long struggle between Holland and the stadhouders over the question of peace or war, but it was in fact only the prelude to an even more serious conflict. William II refused to accept the *fait accompli*, except formally, and proceeded to intrigue with the French who were still at war with Spain, with the hope of dragging the Republic back into the conflict. He also hoped to aid the Stuart's cause in England and he was not unmoved by Mazarin's hints that French help might be forthcoming to establish him as a monarch in the Dutch state. With such prospects in mind William did his best to keep relations with the new régime in England in a strained state, and used all his influence to prevent any major reduction in the size of the Dutch army.

On both these matters he was firmly opposed by Holland. This province's trading connections with England were important, and legal problems arising from trade were piling up. They could only be solved if relations between the two countries improved. Holland was even more determined to preserve the peace with Spain. Yet again although the conflict was apparently over foreign policy, the question at issue was in fact whether the prince of Orange and his supporters or the States of Holland would be master in the Republic. The position was particularly difficult for Holland as the prince was able to use his influence on the lesser provinces to ensure that no move was made to improve relations with England and that no agreement was reached over the reduction in the size of the army.

The crisis of 1650 grew out of this question of what proportion of the army was to be paid off.[11] From the conclusion of peace Holland had been pressing for major reductions in the military establishment, spurred on not only by its opposition to the prince's aggressive foreign policy, but also by the need for economy in view of the size of the debt accumulated by the province during the late war. There had been a considerable reduction in the size of the army in 1648, but Holland continued to press for further economies while the prince used his influence to ensure that the lesser provinces blocked its proposals. The conflict came to a head in 1650 when Holland, baulked once again of the economies it felt to be necessary, proceeded to pay off a number of the troops assigned to its repartition.[12] Holland's situation was difficult: as long as no agreement was reached in the States General the army remained the size it was, which meant in practice a defeat for Holland. Only the Council of State, on the orders of the States General, was empowered actually to dismiss troops, so Holland informed some of the troops which it paid directly that it intended to cease these payments. The province argued that it was only bound constitutionally to pay for measures which it had approved in the States General, therefore as it had refused to accept the Staat van Oorlog—the military budget—for 1650, it had no obligation to meet its share of the financial burdens imposed by the budget.[13]

In response to this unusual move, the States General—by a majority vote in a very incomplete session[14]—empowered William to visit formally the voting towns of Holland individually to try to bring them over to his point of view. This visitation was a constitutional irregularity (the States General could send a deputation to the states of one of the provinces, but to send such a deputation to the individual members of the states of a province was an interference in its internal affairs);[15] it was also unsuccessful, being received coolly by most of the towns, and being refused a hearing by some, including Amsterdam. However, discussions were reopened between the States of Holland and the prince and concessions were made on both sides until they came very close to agreement—finally there was only a difference of about 300 foot and 300 horse between the proposals on either hand.[16] Here the compromises ended: it seems that both sides saw the matter as one of principle. Moreover, there is good reason to believe that William was less concerned with reaching an agreement than with establishing a pretext to justify action against Holland.[17]

On 30 July William arrested six of the leading politicians of Holland, and attempted to take Amsterdam by surprise with troops led by William Frederick, the stadhouder of Friesland. This coup failed: Amsterdam was warned in time and, after a half-hearted siege lasting a few days, an agreement was reached between the town and William. The troops were dispersed and the prisoners released. Although Amsterdam accepted the prince's proposals concerning the army and removed from its government two of the most determined opponents of the prince, the central problems remained undecided. The prince had hoped to change the government first of Amsterdam and then of the other intransigent Holland towns, and so break the opposition of the province to his plans. After the failure of the attack on Amsterdam and the arrest of the six regents to intimidate Holland, this province continued to oppose the prince's policies and to dispute with him the leadership of the Republic. Only the timely death of William in November of the same year brought an end to this impasse which was still threatening to cause civil war.

William's death—he left only a posthumous son—opened the way for the complete triumph of Holland and the anti-stadhouder party. Holland decided not to appoint a stadhouder and most of the other provinces followed suit.[18] Holland took over the leadership of the Republic and her grand pensionary became—as in the great days of Oldenbarnevelt—the chief political figure and de facto head of the executive of the state as a whole as well as Holland. This situation lasted for over twenty years, and for most of this period the grand pensionary was Johan de Witt (the son of one of the regents arrested by William II), a statesman of outstanding ability who stamped his impress on the policies of the Republic as no one had been able to do since Oldenbarnevelt. In many ways this time—the so-called First Stadhouderless Period (1650-72)—marked the high point in the Republic's history. Not only was the Dutch state at the height of its power and prosperity, but the regent régime, unfettered by the presence of a stadhouder, allowed full development to some of the most individual traits in the Dutch State: it was mercantile, republican and tolerant. The weaknesses of the system only began to appear when the son of William II approached maturity.

Towards the end of the 1660s pressure from the Orangists was so great—aided not a little by continuous and skilful English propaganda[19]—that the young prince (the future William III) was admitted to the Council of State and given the prospect of the highest military command. How far his career would have been able to go and how much power he would have been able to amass in the long term are interesting but hypothetical questions, for the situation was changed decisively in 1672 by the collapse of the Dutch defences before the invading French armies.

The consequent panic and suspicion of treachery in Holland and Zeeland, almost the only unoccupied territory in the Republic, gave the Orangists the opportunity they needed. Aided by the strength of Orangist feeling in the middling and lower classes, and by the popular influence of the generally pro-Orange ministers of the Reformed Church, the supporters of the prince were able to turn this wave of fear and mistrust against the Republican regents. William had already been appointed captain-general, on restricted terms, earlier in the year, and in the summer of 1672 popular pressure forced the States of Holland to make him stadhouder with all the rights and privileges which his father had enjoyed. This revolution was completed by the assassination of Johan de Witt and his brother, Cornelis, by a mob in The Hague, and by the replacement of the States-party regents in the voting towns of Holland by Orangists—a change accompanied by severe popular disturbances.[20]

So the pendulum swung yet again, bringing William III (1650-1702) a position of greater power than perhaps even his father had enjoyed. The prince was satisfied to accept his place within the constitution of the Republic; properly manipulated this gave him sufficient power for his purposes. In the 1670s he did show signs of a desire to strengthen his formal position in the state by securing the sovereign title in each of the provinces of the Republic. But when his creatures engineered the offer by Gelderland of the sovereignty of this province with the title of duke in January 1675, the opposition to this move in most of the other provinces was so strong that William felt constrained to refuse the offer.[21] The death of William III in 1702 without issue showed that the Republican tradition was far from dead—no successor was appointed and the second stadhouderless period covered most of the first half of the eighteenth century.

These internal conflicts may have sapped the strength of the Republic at times of crisis—in 1672 the violent clashes between Orangists and Republicans threatened to cause the collapse of the state—but they certainly ensured that the political life of the Dutch state remained vigorous. Almost from the very beginning of the seventeenth century two separate and opposed political traditions had developed until by the mid-century they had become more or less fully-articulated political theories, supporting on the one hand the position of the house of Orange in the Republic, and on the other providing theoretical justification for the actions of the States-party. The conflict between these two traditions may have helped to preserve the health of the Dutch political system in a yet more direct way: by preventing the ossification of the oligarchic system in the towns of Holland. The besetting sin of the governments of the Holland voting towns was the tendency towards the formation of closed oligarchies, but the recurring crises of 1618, 1650 and 1672 brought with them considerable changes in the composition of these oligarchies. In each case just as the town governments were beginning to close up, and offices of power and prestige to be reserved for the members of a small number of families, a political crisis intervened and new blood was introduced into the oligarchy. This process is clear in 1618 and 1672, when large-scale changes were made in the personnel of most of the town governments —by the intervention of Maurice in the first case and in response to carefully organised popular pressure in the second—and new families brought to power, but there is reason to believe that something similar occurred after 1650 also. Here the process was certainly less dramatic, but it does seem that in many towns new men were able to force their way into the town governments in the decade after 1650. The triumph of the Republicans and the establishment of the stadhouderless system weakened the position of the regents in power in a number of towns and allowed many families which had lost power and office in the upheaval of 1618 to make their way back into the oligarchy at the expense of Orangists. These restored families were often able to bring with them into the town government other families allied to them either by marriage or through political conviction. The result was that the renewal of the regent élite was perhaps as drastic at this time as at either of the other occasions, although it took place much more slowly. These three critical periods helped to make the oligarchies of Holland relatively open during the seventeenth century. The political élite, in Holland at least, was far less stable, and far less isolated from the rest of the population in this period than has often been suggested. While a small number of families were able to maintain their positions in the élite throughout the century, there was in general a large turnover in the composition of the urban oligarchies, in response to political and social changes in Holland.

★   ★   ★

A further source of disunity in Dutch society was religion, which was never far removed from politics. The existence of a very large catholic element within the Republic should always be remembered when the religious disputes within this apparently protestant state are being considered. The population of the Generality Lands was almost completely catholic, having experienced the Counter-Reformation before being brought under Dutch rule. These catholics, however, were only part of the problem. Even in the nominally protestant provinces—particularly Holland and Utrecht—a considerable minority was still largely untouched by the Reformation until at least the late seventeenth century. Large areas of the Holland countryside remained over-whelmingly catholic, and even in the towns a substantial minority was to remain catholic throughout the history of the Republic. While the war with Spain continued many protestants could see these catholics not only as an alien element within the state but also as a potential fifth column.

By the end of the sixteenth century it had become possible to forget the important rôle played by catholics in the Revolt and to regard the catholics as a group as unreconciled to the state set up as a consequence of the break with Spain—and the pope. This attitude remained strong until after the end of the Truce at least and, although they were viewed with less suspicion later, catholics continued to be officially barred from all public office. Fear of catholic subversion was especially strong during the Truce: indeed, much of the virulence of the quarrels within the Reformed Church in the first two decades of the century can be explained by the unease and insecurity of the Reformed protestants, who felt that the Republic had still to be won for their faith and that any relaxation of rigid orthodoxy would be the first step on the road back to catholicism.

The Reformed Church saw its position attacked on three fronts: firstly, catholic Spain was its open enemy, fighting to bring the Dutch back to the dual domination of Madrid and Rome; secondly, the catholics and crypto-catholics within the boundaries of the Republic were a threat to the grip of the Church on the state; and finally, and most insidiously, the Remonstrants seemed to be working to under-mine the Reformed Church from within. The suspicions of the ortho-dox with regard to both the Remonstrants and Oldenbarnevelt seemed to be confirmed when the latter negotiated the Truce with Spain and began to support the former. They began to suspect a plot to weaken the Republic and its protestant faith and deliver it into the hands of its enemies, and specifically that Oldenbarnevelt was a conscious tool in the hands of the Spanish. Thus what had at first seemed an insignificant difference of opinion over the precise definition of Reformed dogma split first the Reformed Church and then the Dutch State.

A further complicating factor was the uncertainty in the relationship between church and state at all levels. The Reformed Church was only a state church in a very limited sense. Its members were supposed to have a monopoly of all governmental and administrative posts, but this rule was applied only very inefficiently, at least until the last decades of the seventeenth century. Also, in contrast to the situation in England for example, there was no general obligation to attend the services of the Reformed Church, and in the middle of the seventeenth century at least one-half and perhaps as many as two-thirds of the population were either catholics or belonged to one or other of the protestant sects. Town governments claimed the right to a large measure of control over the appointment of ministers to the Reformed Church within their towns; the states of the provinces wished to have supervisory authority over the Reformed Church within their provinces; and civil authorities at every level wanted to prevent the Church from interfering in politics. The ministers of the Reformed Church did not challenge the right of the civil authorities to supremacy in the state, and they always insisted on the religious responsibilities of the state, namely that provincial and local governments had a duty to preserve and promote the Reformed faith. The various secular authorities never repudiated explicitly this theory, but in practice they were primarily concerned to avoid any disturbances arising from religious disputes and to restrict the political influence of the Reformed Church.

The Arminians were, and remained, in the minority among the ministers of the Reformed Church, and their strength lay in their ability to attract many of the better educated and politically powerful laymen. The States of Holland included many regents who sympathised with the Remonstrant position and rather more who felt that a comprehensive church would contribute more to the rest and quiet of the state than an exclusive one. Furthermore, the Arminians, recognising their need for support from the States, developed a theory of church/state relations which was particularly explicit in recognising the final supremacy of the civil authority. Sure of a sympathetic hearing they addressed a Remonstrance (from which they got their name of Remonstrants) to the States of Holland setting out their point of view and asking for protection from the persecution of their opponents within the Church. Under the firm leadership of Oldenbarnevelt, the States took the Remonstrants into their protection by attempting to silence the disputes within the Church, and by continuing to oppose the calling of a national synod except on terms which the Contra-remonstrants found impossible to accept.[22]

In this way the regent oligarchy of Holland was drawn into the religious dispute, partly through a genuine sympathy for the Remonstrants but largely for political reasons. The situation became critical when Prince Maurice chose to support the Contra-remonstrants. His reasons for this move are not completely clear, but they must at least in part be sought in his growing disagreements with Oldenbarnevelt over political questions. In particular the signing of the Truce had undermined his trust in the wisdom and sincerity of Oldenbarnevelt, and the latter's handling of the religious conflict only increased his suspicions of the statesman's motives, as it appeared, in Maurice's view, to be leading rapidly to civil war. For the prince the only solution to the Republic's internal disorders was to accept the fact of the strength of orthodox opinion and to accede to its demands.

This decision of Maurice's was the beginning of the alliance of the house of Orange with the forces of Reformed orthodoxy which was to last throughout the century. The Synod of Dordrecht in 1619 condemned the Remonstrants and expelled them from the Church: some years of persecution followed, but the Remonstrants survived. In time they found that they had, in general, the sympathy of the town regents, at least in so far as these were prepared to protect them against the attempts at persecution set in train by the Reformed Church. The Remonstrants thus looked to the regents for support, while the orthodox looked to the stadhouders. In this way the religious division took on political overtones, with the States-party associating itself with tolerance and the protection of the Remonstrants and other dissident sects, and the princes of Orange being regarded—rightly or wrongly— as the champions of orthodoxy. In consequence, the Orangism of a large section of the population below the regent élite was inseparable from their devotion to orthodoxy, and this connection was encouraged in sermons and pamphlets by many ministers of the Reformed Church. At times of crisis the confusion of patriotism and orthodoxy which had played so important a rôle during the Truce again came to the surface. The regents who were forced out of office by popular pressure in 1672 were singled out as much for their lack of sympathy with Reformed orthodoxy as because of their support for the States-party. The ministers of the Reformed Church looked to the stadhouders to protect their interests against the local political authorities in town and countryside, and the princes of Orange, however lukewarm their religious feelings may have been, recognised the political utility of orthodox support. They were always prepared to use Reformed slogans to gain orthodox backing for their policies, and they had considerable success among the middling classes in the Holland towns, though here they benefited from the circumstance that only the stadhouder had any power to set limits to the authority the regents could exercise over their subjects.

THE DUTCH REPUBLIC AND ITS INTERNAL TENSIONS

Although the Synod of Dordrecht was on the surface a triumph for Reformed orthodoxy, it can perhaps better be seen as the last major, and unsuccessful attempt to make the Dutch Republic a truly Reformed state. From the earliest days of the Revolt the political nation had been opposed to the pretensions of the Reformed Church in the political field and at best half-hearted in its support of its efforts to impose religious orthodoxy. By the 1620s the regents of Holland at least had recognised that a large degree of religious liberty was a political necessity: given the large proportion of catholics and protestant dissenters in Holland the forcible imposition of religious conformity would have caused serious internal disorders or at least serious economic disruption. Moreover, religious nonconformists were in effect a valuable bulwark of social and political stability, as they were only too ready to support the regents in return for toleration in practice. Against such opposition the ministers of the Reformed Church could have only a very limited success in turning the Republic into a protestant state somewhat on the Genevan model.

After the Synod the Reformed Church made some progress in increasing its influence in the Republic. It was able to ensure that in theory at least only its members were eligible for public office. The regents of most towns had formally to be members of the Reformed Church, and there were many laws and ordinances banning dissenters from official positions, but the States of Holland and many town governments were not prepared to impose such regulations effectively. Indeed in a number of the towns of Holland the regents themselves included men who were not even nominally orthodox. During the first stadhouderless period particularly, many Remonstrant families were able to make their way back into the town governments, and other dissident sects found sympathisers among the Holland regents.

Even the laws against the exercise of the catholic faith were very generally evaded, especially in the second half of the century. A sort of unofficial tax was widely levied by police officials on catholics in return for allowing them more freedom in the exercise of their religion than they enjoyed in any other protestant country. Indeed, the understanding between police and catholics could be closer than this bald statement suggests—the Reformed Church council of Rotterdam complained in 1658 that the 'papists' in the town had become so shameless that they were using the servants of the *baljuw* (i.e. the lesser police officials) to guard the doors of their 'pope-church'. The problem of poor relief was another area where fruitful and mutually beneficial arrangements could be arrived at between the catholics and the local authorities. It became convenient for many town governments to allow the catholics to organise their congregations, particularly for the provision of poor relief. Although the poor relief dispensed through the Reformed Church has been (and to some extent still is) seen as one of the most effective means at the disposal of the church for putting pressure on the catholics to induce conversion to protestantism, and although the organisation of a system of poor relief undoubtedly helped to strengthen the unity and sense of community among Dutch catholics where it was allowed, such considerations were relatively unimportant to most of the town governments of Holland. The deacons—the members of the Reformed Church councils especially concerned with the administration of poor relief—were regularly forced to apply to the town governments for subsidies, as the demands on the system were too great for the resources of the church. The financial advantage to a town government if the catholics looked after their own poor was far from negligible, and easily outweighed any considerations arising from religious prejudice—particularly after 1648, when the end of the long war with Spain meant that the catholics could no longer in normal circumstances be looked upon as a fifth column.

*   *   *

The struggle for dominance in the Republic between the States of Holland and the princes of Orange was reflected to an extent in a distinct clash of artistic taste. This difference was most marked with regard to painting. The Dutch style in painting which developed during the first half of the seventeenth century was a reflection of the tastes and requirements of the dominant social group within the Republic—or at least within Holland, for it was in this province that most of the leading artists worked and it was also in this province that the biggest market for paintings existed. The regent oligarchy and large sections of the middling classes—merchants and tradesmen—constituted the market at which Dutch painters aimed. The regents were particularly important for the growth of the group portrait of town militias and similar official bodies, but the widespread distribution of wealth in the Republic meant that, given the generally low price of paintings, large numbers of people below this rank in society could and did become the chief market for paintings. This public encouraged above all a realistic and restrained style of painting—most pictures were destined for private houses and had to be comfortable to live with. Moreover, pictures were seen as decorations or furniture rather than as works of art; they were bought according to their subject rather than their artist. Such an attitude stimulated among painters a thorough-going specialisation in particular types of painting: the artist could rely on a steady sale for landscapes, genre-pieces, still-lifes, seascapes and, later in the century, church interiors and architectural pieces. Such works reflected the everyday-life and surroundings or their buyers in a realistic style. Even the greatest artists accepted the restrictions on subject and treatment imposed by the market; the most striking of Jacob van Ruisdael's landscapes remained within an already well-established tradition, their originality made acceptable by the reassuring conventionality of the form.[23]

In contrast, the court of the stadhouder showed no appreciation of this restrained and modest art. Particularly under Frederick Henry—the only stadhouder who showed much interest in art—the court patronised a more magnificent and allegorical style. In the political system of the Republic the monarchical element represented by the stadhouders introduced what might be seen as a foreign influence. In a similar way the princes of Orange favoured styles in art very different from the native Dutch product. In fact they chiefly patronised foreign painters—especially those from the Spanish Netherlands—for their large-scale commissions. The artistic style of the court was the international baroque, and while there may have been baroque elements in Dutch art they were far from being dominant and its mood was far removed from that of the baroque proper. The only Dutch school favoured at all extensively was that of Utrecht, which specialised in history paintings and Italianate landscapes and, being more influenced by international developments in style, suited better the taste of the stadhouders' court. The stadhouders were too busy trying to represent themselves as true princes in the eyes of the rest of Europe to have much appreciation for the most typical products of Dutch art. Their needs were for an art which would emphasise the prestige and power of their house—the international baroque, and later French classicism, could answer these needs, while the Dutch School, with its concentration on everyday subjects in a realistic style, could not.[24]

The political conflicts of the century were reflected even more directly by the literature of the period. Some of the finest works by Dutch writers were inspired by one or other of the crises of the century. One of the most obvious examples of this immediate response to political events is Vondel's play *Palamedes* (1625), which is a thinly-disguised comment on the trial and execution of Oldenbarnevelt. The sub-title of this play, *Murdered Innocence*, is sufficient to indicate the somewhat simplistic line taken by the poet. Its lasting political relevance is illustrated by the consequences of a performance in Rotterdam as late as 1665. A minister of the Reformed Church was so incensed by the play that he preached a sermon in which he attacked not only the memory of Oldenbarnevelt but also the régime of De Witt, arguing in favour of the restoration of the powers of the house of Orange. For this act the minister was deprived of his salary by the States of Holland. Also many of the early writings of the jurist Grotius were concerned to propagate the point of view of the States of Holland, and more particularly to support the actions of Oldenbarnevelt. On the Orangist side Hooft dedicated his history of the Revolt to Frederick Henry, the troubles during the Truce having taught him the importance of a leader who could stand above party and so preserve peace and unity within the state.[25]

The stadhouders' court had little influence on Dutch painting, its patronage being too limited compared to the size of the total market for art, and Orangist influence in literature was not an act of the court but was a consequence of the large number of Orangists among the educated and wealthy. Here there was no question of direct patronage but of a reflection of political attitudes (though these may obviously in individual cases have been influenced by the career opportunities open to those in favour at court or with Orangist regents), nor was there any difference in style between Orangists and Republicans, only in content. These political differences gave rise to a very considerable body of pamphlet literature, and at their best these polemical writings contain some of the most original political thought of the century. The controversy over the stadhoudership in the 1660s, for example, was the occasion for the publication of the radically republican works of the brothers Pieter and Johan de la Court,[26] and Spinoza's political theory can also be seen as a fruit of this polemic—both through his reading of Johan de la Court's *Politike Weegschaal*[27] and through his concern to defend the Republican régime of De Witt.

Not all the leading writers supported the Republican cause, of course, but it is hardly surprising that the most original writers tended to choose the sides of the States, who in practice ensured a considerable degree of freedom of speech and publication for new ideas, and oppose the pretensions of the princes of Orange. To balance this Republican tendency it should be noted that most of the outstanding poets—Hooft, Huygens, Cats—were either associated with, or sympathetic to, the house of Orange. One explanation of this sympathy is that these poets were in close contact with the international literary culture of the time, and had absorbed much of the admiration for princes—and even the obsequiousness before monarchs—which stamped such circles so clearly. Their heads were turned towards the stadhouders' court rather than towards the regent society from which they had almost without exception sprung.

In the other great conflict of the century, the failure of the Reformed Church to gain control of Dutch society allowed a freer development to thought, art and literature than would otherwise have been the case. There was some sporadic persecution: Socinians and others who were considered to be dangerous atheists were pursued by the law, and Spinoza was careful not to publish much during his lifetime. On the whole, however, Holland was the safest place in Europe for such men, and only the dissemination of their ideas could get them into trouble; they were free to think what they liked and to develop their ideas in peace.

The clash between the regents of Holland and the dominant, intolerant element in the Reformed Church undoubtedly helped to stimulate and preserve the diversity and vitality of Dutch intellectual and literary life. In practice, the Holland political élite was prepared to extend its protection over unorthodox writers and to save them from any censorship demanded by the Reformed Church. Consequently a tradition developed which was sympathetic to the unorthodox in religion and Republican in politics. It had its roots in the 'libertine' champions of tolerance of the late sixteenth century such as Coornhert, and was very powerful in the seventeenth from Grotius and Uyttenbogaert in the first decades to Brandt and Oudaen in the second half of the century. Uyttenbogaert was the leading Remonstrant controversialist during the troubled years of the Truce and immediately after, and later his *Ecclesiastical History*[28] effectively presented the Remonstrant case over the conflicts of this period. His example was followed by Brandt whose *History of the Reformation*[29] was very largely concerned with a detailed study of the Remonstrant/Contra-remonstrant disputes, and whose liberal views were shown even more clearly in his biography of Vondel. Grotius in his later years turned to arguing the case for an ecumenical, latitudinarian view of the church and Christianity, but he had to write in exile. He had been arrested with Oldenbarnevelt but escaped after a couple of years. He was never able to live in the Republic again: he was too closely associated in politics as well as religion with the defeated party for even the many sympathetic regents to secure his pardon. The Amsterdam regents, however, were able to save the doubly unorthodox and bellicose poet and playwright Vondel from serious trouble.[30] Joachim Oudaen was a lesser poet, but a rather better representative of a specific tendency in Dutch letters. He not only praised the virtues of the States-party and its leaders, but his religious unorthodoxy—he was closely involved in the Collegiant movement[31]—brought him into contact with many of the regents of his home town, Rotterdam, who were also interested in this movement.

It must be added, however, that the town governments and the States of Holland could also act as persecutors when faced with publications which they felt to be subversive of their authority. They were tolerant of attacks on the Church or on the powers of the stadhouder, but they were rarely prepared to allow attacks on themselves or on the oligarchic system in general. When such attacks came from the side of the orthodox protestants or the Orangists, the Reformed Church or the stadhouder could be relied on to do what they were able to protect the authors. They were perhaps not as successful in such matters as the town governments, who were exceedingly difficult to restrain, but their influence was far from negligible. Moreover, a number of towns were under the control of more or less orthodox, more or less Orangist regents, and these could provide havens for those in danger from the other party. Again, the influence of the ministers of the Reformed Church over their congregations was so great that town governments on the whole were chary of pushing them too far, for fear of popular disturbances. The power of the stadhouder could also be used to restrain the governments from an over-arbitrary use of their powers. These various centres of power and influence, each ready for its own ends to protect different groups, ensured that there were large areas of freedom for writers in the Republic in the seventeenth century—areas which in practice were larger than they would have been had any one power been dominant.

It is significant for the nature of Dutch culture in its great period that few of its achievements took Reformed orthodoxy as their foundation or inspiration. One exception is perhaps religious poetry, where the Reformed tradition produced Huygens and Cats, but their poems never reach the heights of those of Vondel, and Camphuysen, clearly one of the best lyric poets of specifically religious inspiration, was a religious radical. In literature generally the poems and plays of Hooft, Vondel and Bredero were far from reflecting the attitudes of the Reformed Church. In the writing of history the greatest figure, P. C. Hooft, was the son of a 'libertine' regent of Amsterdam and there is little trace of a Reformed inspiration in his work. Similarly, if we consider political thought and philosophy, the outstanding names—Grotius, Spinoza, the brothers De la Court—are all representatives of various types of heterodoxy. In painting, where Holland's greatest contribution was made, it is difficult to discover even the nominal religious affiliation of most artists and impossible to read orthodoxy into their works. Rembrandt was deeply religious, but had no contact with the Reformed Church in his maturity and was possibly attracted to the Mennonites. In the one field where the Reformed Church could hope to exercise most influence, i.e. music, the great period for the Dutch had already passed by the early seventeenth century—and the Calvinist suspicion of church music helped to make it certain that Sweelinck's influence would bear most fruit outside the Republic.

Notes

1 There was an eighth province, Drente, but this was not normally counted as one of the 'United Provinces' as, although it was part of the Republic, it was not represented in the States General and played very little part in political life. It was small, very poor, and very thinly inhabited

2 The states (or estates) were the supreme authority in each province, having risen to fill the gap left by the collapse of royal power during the Revolt. Their composition varied from province to province, but in effect (with the possible exception of Friesland) only the town oligarchies and the nobility were represented

3 R. Fruin (ed. H. Colenbrander), *Geschiedenis der staatsinstellingen in Nederland* (2nd ed., The Hague 1922), p. 179

4 Or rather, that majority in the Reformed Church which considered itself to be orthodox. What was orthodoxy for the Dutch Reformed Church was never clear. The Arminians took their name from Jacob Harmensz (Arminius), but also became known as Remonstrants after they had delivered a remonstrance to the States of Holland. Similarly, the orthodox party were known as Gomarists after their champion Franciscus Gomarus, and then as Contra-remonstrants after they had delivered a protest—counter-remonstrance—to the States against the Arminians

5 J. den Tex, *Oldenbarnevelt*, vol. III (Haarlem 1966), pp. 22, 295–6, 396–7, 417,

546

[6] M. Th. Uit den Bogaard, *De gereformeerden en Oranje tijdens het eerste stadhouderloze tijdperk* (Groningen 1954)

[7] P. Geyl, *Orange and Stuart* (London 1969), chaps 1 and 2

[8] They were given this name because their centre of power was the States of Holland and they supported the power of the provincial states against that of the stadhouder

[9] See below, p. 176

[10] See P. Geyl, 'Historische appreciaties van het zeventiende eeuwse regenten-regiem', in *Studies en strijdschriften* (Groningen 1958)

[11] On the crisis of 1650, see G. W. Kernkamp, *Prins Willem II* (Amsterdam 1943) and J. A. Wijnne, *De geschillen over de afdanking van 't krijgsvolk in de Vereenigde Neder-landen in de jaren 1649 en 1650* (Utrecht 1885)

[12] The 'repartition' system meant that each province was assigned a certain number of troops, according to the proportion of Generality expenditure it normally bore, and paid these directly without the money having to go through central institutions

[13] J. A. Wijnne, *op. cit.*, pp. CLXXI–CLXXVII

[14] *Ibid.*, pp. L–LIV

[15] *Ibid.*, pp. CLXXVII–CLXXIX

[16] G. W. Kernkamp, *op. cit.*, p. 117

[17] J. A. Wijnne, *op. cit.*, pp. CXCIII–IV

[18] Friesland already had a stadhouder, William Frederick, and Groningen and Drente appointed him their stadhouder also. The other four provinces followed Holland's example

[19] Charles II hoped that if the house of Orange were restored to power his nephew would show gratitude and ensure that the Republic supported the interests of the Stuarts rather than pursue an independent policy

[20] For these events, see D. J. Roorda, *Partij en factie. De oproeren van 1672 in de steden van Holland en Zeeland, een krachtmeting tussen partijen en facties* (Groningen 1961)

[21] S. B. Baxter, *William III* (London 1966), pp. 123–6

[22] J. den Tex, *Oldenbarnevelt*, vol. III (Haarlem 1966), pp. 123–57

[23] These ideas are worked out in more detail below, pp. 119–34

[24] See below, pp. 123–5

[25] See below, pp. 191–2

[26] See below, pp. 198–203

[27] E. H. Kossmann, *Politieke theorie in het zeventiende-eeuwse Nederland* (Verhande-lingen der Koninklijke Nederlandse Akademie van Wetenschappen, afd. Letterkunde, nieuwe reeks, deel lxvii, no. 2) (Amsterdam 1960), p. 50

[28] *De Kerkelijke Historie, vervattende verscheyden ghedenckwaerdige saecken, in de Christenhyt voor-gevallen* (1647)

[29] See below, p. 194

[30] See below, pp. 107–8

[31] See below, pp. 175–7

three

Economic Expansion and
Commercial Dominance in Europe

The Netherlands had by the sixteenth century long been one of the most important centres of industry and trade in Europe. The most important areas in this respect had been the county of Flanders and the duchy of Brabant. In the later middle ages the great Flemish towns —Ghent, Bruges, Ypres—had been outstanding centres for the production of textiles and their trade connections had extended throughout Europe. In the fifteenth and sixteenth centuries these towns experienced a serious decline in prosperity, but the 'rural' textile industry of the small towns and villages of West Flanders, and the great expansion of the trade of Antwerp served to a large extent to balance the depression in the old centres, and to preserve the overall wealth of the region. By the middle of the sixteenth century Antwerp had become the entrepôt of Europe, a staple-market whose resources, particularly financial, were essential to European trading activity. At this time the northern provinces of the Netherlands were still overshadowed by Flanders and Brabant—the textile industries of Leiden and Haarlem were suffering from the same depression which had hit the Flemish towns, and no port in the north could rival Antwerp in size or prosperity.

However, even at this time there were signs indicating the considerable economic potential of these northern regions. The phenomenal economic expansion of Holland after the Revolt clearly had its roots in developments which took place in the earlier years of the century. Amsterdam, for example, was already becoming the most important trading centre in the Northern Netherlands and, significantly, it was already building up those aspects of its economic system which were to be the foundations of its later greatness—the trade in Baltic grain and its very large merchant fleet. For, in contrast to Antwerp, the economic power of Amsterdam was to lie, at least in part, in the size and efficiency of its trading fleet. Antwerp attracted the trade of Europe, but the goods handled there were carried in foreign ships; Amsterdam was served very largely by the ships of its own merchants. Again, unlike Antwerp which had built its wealth on trade in luxury goods such as spices, the 'mother-commerce' of Amsterdam was the trade in bulk in grain between the Baltic and southern Europe. Other indications of the growing economic importance of Holland in the early sixteenth century can be found in the rapidly expanding shipping activities of the small towns and villages of north Holland, and in the importance of the herring fisheries of the province as a whole. The latter activity was also to be one of the most important bases of the later wealth of the province.

Nevertheless, although these pointers to the future economic development of the North were already present in the middle of the sixteenth century, it was only after the Revolt that the Northern Netherlands began to overtake the South in wealth and economic vitality. Of course, for the first ten or twenty years after the beginning of the Revolt the economies of both the North and the South suffered considerably from the disturbances inseparable from such a war, but as the political situation became more stable and as the fleet of the rebel provinces made the sea safer for their own trade than for that of their enemies, the merchants and shippers of the Republic slowly began to take a grip on European trade which was not to be broken for over a century. An important event in this connection was the fall of Antwerp to the prince of Parma in 1585—the rebels controlled, and continued to control, the mouth of the Scheldt (which gave access to the town from the sea) and were able to deprive the town of a great part of its European trade. Much of the international commerce which had used Antwerp was now diverted to the trading towns of the North, and many merchants followed the same course bringing with them the capital which had been the great strength of Antwerp, and which was to become the basis of Amsterdam's financial dominance in Europe during the following century. The importance of Amsterdam as a financial centre was in fact to last until almost the end of the eighteenth century, long after the peculiar importance of the town as a centre of trade had passed.

The great expansion of Dutch trade came in the first half of the seventeenth century, and reached its peak round about the middle of the century. After this point, the economy began to suffer from the disturbances of war and the protectionist policies of neighbouring states.

During the long war with Spain Dutch trade had been able to expand unchecked, as the Spanish had never been able to challenge Dutch maritime supremacy; only the Dunkirk pirates had presented a serious threat to the security of Dutch shipping. The wars with England in the second half of the century, however, showed how vulnerable Dutch trade was to the attack of another maritime power with a favourable strategic position.[1] These wars hit the herring fisheries even harder, as the Dutch fleet was not powerful enough to take on the burden of protecting the fishing fleets—or rather to do so would have been too great a strain on naval resources and would have diverted much-needed ships from more immediately urgent tasks. In consequence during the Anglo-Dutch wars the herring fleet was simply ordered not to sail, and this was a serious blow not only to the owners of the boats and those directly involved in the trade in herring. Herring was an important item in Dutch trade with many areas, notably northern France, as it could be used to help keep trade in balance. The commercial policy introduced systematically by Colbert in France also damaged Dutch trade immediately, but its long term consequences were even more serious, particularly for Dutch manufactures.

However, though signs of decline can be found after 1650, especially in the last quarter of the century, the Dutch Republic retained much of its economic predominance in Europe until well after 1700.[2] Throughout the seventeenth century the Republic was the foremost trading power in Europe: the merchants of Holland acted as the intermediaries between northern and southern, eastern and western Europe, and Holland also acted to a considerable extent as the distribution centre for goods coming from the Americas and Asia. Not only was a great part of this international trade in the hands of Dutch merchants, it was also carried in Dutch ships.

Contemporaries were so impressed by the size and ubiquity of the Dutch trading fleet that they completely overestimated its numbers. The French minister Colbert in the second half of the century thought that the Dutch had 20,000 ships, a figure already given by an English observer in 1609. In fact, the Dutch merchant fleet numbered possibly about 2,300–2,500 ships in 1636, plus about 2,000 herring-busses (specialised fishing-boats).[3] Besides their number, Dutch merchant ships were remarkable for their good design and efficient operation. The flute (*fluit*) was the most successful merchant ship of the age, being designed especially for easy handling and the carriage of bulky cargoes such as grain and wood. The Baltic grain trade was dominated by

Dutch merchants and Dutch shipping to a notable degree: until the middle of the seventeenth century about half the ships passing yearly through the Sound to reach the Baltic ports were Dutch. This proportion fell in the second half of the century and this change was one of the most important signs that the end of Dutch commercial hegemony was approaching.[4] Because of the importance of this trade the Dutch were ever sensitive to political disturbances in the Baltic region, and one of the first indications that the Republic was beginning to play the part of a great power in Europe was its intervention in the war between Denmark and Sweden in 1645—a fleet was sent to protect the interests of Dutch traders and to give weight to the arguments of the Dutch envoys who were attempting to arbitrate between the combatants. In the circumstances it is hardly surprising that the peace which was signed contained clauses which were particularly favourable to the Republic, although it had not been formally involved in the war. (A sign of the singular strength of the Dutch presence in the Baltic is that the fleet which the Swedes sent against Denmark had been assembled and fitted out in the Republic by the Amsterdam merchant Lodewijk de Geer, whose Swedish interests were enormous.[5])

Perhaps of less fundamental importance, but still very significant for the expansion of the Dutch economy was the trade with France and southern Europe. This branch of trade was associated with the 'mother-commerce', of course, as one of its staple items was grain, exported to Spain especially as this country, like much of southern Europe, was suffering from a shortage of food in the late sixteenth and a great part of the seventeenth century. Besides providing an outlet for Dutch manufactures, these areas produced salt—essential for the curing of herring—and wine. The trade of the Atlantic ports of France was dominated by the Dutch, with Rotterdam merchants especially prominent in the commerce in French wine and salt. Similarly, until the passing of the Navigation Act of 1651, much of English exports to the Continent were carried in Dutch ships. Already by 1616 the Dutch were dominant in the export of British coal. In that year, of 686 cargoes of coal leaving Newcastle 537 were carried by the Dutch and French, and many of the nominally French were Dutch ships on hire.[6] Later in the century, despite large-scale evasion of the regulations, the Dutch share in the carriage of English goods fell, and the decline was steep towards the end of the century.

This trade hegemony allowed the growth of a number of industries which were directly dependent on it. These industries, called *trafieken* by the Dutch, used imported raw materials or half-finished manufactures and the greater part of their production was exported. Chief among these were sugar-refining, the working of tobacco, and the making of earthenware goods (especially at Delft), and they all employed considerable numbers of people. They could never have developed into important branches of industry if Dutch trade had not been so powerful and ubiquitous. Similarly, a merchant fleet as large as that of Holland gave rise to many industries serving its needs. First in importance, of course, was ship-building, which was concentrated particularly around Zaandam, a little north of Amsterdam. This area was the largest centre for the building of ships in Europe in the seventeenth century, though other towns, such as Amsterdam itself and Rotterdam, also had important branches of the industry. Besides ship-building the merchant fleet gave employment to large numbers of rope- and sail-makers and others in similar service trades. In such ways the expansion of Dutch trade stimulated the growth of industry and helped to provide an increasing number of jobs.

The most important industrial centres, however, were the textile towns, Leiden and Haarlem, both of which profited immensely from the influx of immigrants from the Southern Netherlands in the last decades of the sixteenth century. Flemish textile workers, especially from the area around Hondschoote, continued to be attracted by the Leiden woollen industry almost throughout the seventeenth century. These immigrants were important for the new techniques which they brought with them, in particular for the manufacture of the new light cloths. These new products not only opened up fresh markets for the Leiden industry, but they also diversified its production making it much less vulnerable to variations in demand which were liable to affect any of the various branches of the industry.[7] Leiden's production was already improving by 1584 with 27,000 pieces a year, and reached a peak in 1664 of 144,000 pieces. Foreign competition and protectionism—notably in France—caused a slow decline to set in towards the end of the century, and this became disastrous in the eighteenth century. The linen industry of Haarlem, where the bleaching of imported cloths was very important, followed a similar development, reaching its peak around 1650.[8]

Dutch capital was as ubiquitous as Dutch trade. In 1659 Jean Deutz, an Amsterdam merchant (and brother-in-law of De Witt), secured the monopoly of Austrian quicksilver in northern Europe. Scandinavian industrial development, particularly in iron and munitions, was largely financed and organised by Dutch merchants; and land reclamation and drainage schemes in England and France were the result of Dutch initiative and capital. The first Danish East India Company, set up in 1616, was the work of two Dutch financiers; and Amsterdam merchants were prominent in the farming of the Russian tsar's export monopolies.[9] Dutch commercial success provided the capital which made such wide-ranging enterprise possible, but investment abroad soon became in itself a major source of profit and capital for further investment, either at home or abroad.

In all these branches of trade and industry the province of Holland was predominant. Indeed, it was not so much the Republic which exercised hegemony over European trade as Holland alone. It was only to be expected that the economic success of this one province would stir up jealousy in the less favoured members of the Union. Not only was Holland very much more wealthy than the other provinces, the sources of its wealth were distinctly different and thus the policies it supported, particularly with regard to foreign relations, also tended to differ from those pushed by the lesser provinces. For Holland the interests of international trade were of paramount importance, but only Zeeland and Friesland shared in this trade to any significant extent. Statistics for the trade of the Republic are difficult to arrive at, but it has been calculated[10] that in the third quarter of the seventeenth century Amsterdam's trade was five times greater than that of Rotterdam—which emphasises the overriding importance of this one town in the economy of the Republic—and that Zeeland, Holland's chief trading rival, could hardly match even the performance of Rotterdam. The two chief ports of Zeeland were Middelburg and Vlissingen (Flushing) and the trade of the first was in terms of value less than a seventh of that of Amsterdam, while Vlissingen's trade was only a tenth of Amsterdam's.[11] Friesland's shipping was not unimportant, and even increased in size in the second half of the seventeenth century. It was able to increase its share in Baltic trade when Amsterdam's grip on cargoes began to loosen. The Friesland shippers were still only carriers, however, and the trade remained in the hands of Amsterdam merchants.

As far as industry is concerned, Holland was even more dominant. Apart from some textile manufactures in Twente (in the east of Overijsel) and in Tilburg (in the Generality Lands), Leiden and Haarlem, together with the larger Holland towns practically monopolised the production of, and the trade in, wool-, linen- and silk-textiles.[12] The trafieken were almost totally confined to Holland, dependent as they were on the flourishing overseas trade of this province. The towns of Friesland, Overijsel, Gelderland and even Zeeland remained throughout the seventeenth century very much what they had been at its beginning. Indeed, the once-great towns of the land provinces—Zwolle, Kampen, Deventer, Zutphen—with their memories of prosperity as members of the Hansa took almost no part in the economic expansion of the Republic in the seventeenth century. Their populations remained very much what they had been in the later middle ages and they showed no sign of emulating the rapid growth of the Holland towns. Much of the political differences between Holland and the land provinces can be traced to the limited influence of the towns in the political systems of the latter; and this weakness of the towns can be directly related to the inability of these provinces to share in the prosperity which was the strength of the Holland towns. The towns had become dominant in the political system of Holland only at a very late date—in the course of the first decade after the Revolt, in fact—when the number of towns represented in the States of Holland was increased from six to eighteen. The towns of the eastern provinces were in no position to take advantage of the disturbed times in this way.

It is clear that Holland's prosperity was not confined to one section of society alone. Although its merchants and manufacturers undoubtedly benefited most, and most spectacularly, from Holland's economic development, large sections of the middle and lower-middle classes in the towns shared in this prosperity to an extent remarkable in the seventeenth century. Many men of small means were able to take part in trade and shipping activities through the *rederij* system, which enabled them to join associations to, for example, fit out a herring-boat or buy cargoes for trade. The eventual profits were distributed among the associates according to the size of their share in the venture. Also the competition for manpower in Holland meant that artisans and labourers here were among the best paid in Europe.

Some idea of the income structure of the towns of Holland is given by the registers drawn up for the abortive income-tax (*Familie-geld*) of 1674.[13] This impost was to have been levied on incomes of about f.182-p.a. and over, thus the registers included artisans and the lower-middle sections of society. In Rotterdam this covered nearly 4,300 heads of households (from a total population of approaching 50,000), thus probably nearly half the population. The great majority of these, 3,639, were assessed at incomes between f.182- and f.1,000-p.a., but such incomes represented at least a modest level of prosperity—and

658 were assessed at over f.1,000-p.a. Evidence of this nature cannot be expected to be too reliable, but it does suggest that a large proportion of the population of the towns of Holland was well above subsistence level, and thus constituted a market with considerable total spending power. This fact helps to explain why the Dutch art-market, as will appear later, was not dominated by the very rich.

In contrast, the eastern provinces as a whole, including Utrecht, had changed little since the sixteenth century or even the later middle ages. Their chief activity was still agriculture, often subsistence agriculture. Until well into the seventeenth century most of these provinces were still suffering heavily from the consequences of the Eighty Years War. It was as late as 1627 before Gelderland was brought fully under Dutch control with the successful siege of Grolle (Groenlo), and only after the taking of 's-Hertogenbosch in 1629 was it properly shielded against invasion from the south. Similarly, Overijsel was only finally cleared of Spanish troops in 1626. Subsequently the action of the war moved further south and these provinces were undisturbed until the 1660s and the first disastrous years of the war with France which began in 1672.

Some developments did take place in these economically backward areas: the draining of the peat bogs and the bringing under culture of the heath in Friesland, Groningen and Drente were particularly important. Even here, however, the scale of the changes was small compared to the large-scale reclamations which took place at about the same time in North Holland, making this region a homogeneous land mass for the first time in its history. Also it is significant that the greater part of the capital required for these reclamation projects, even in the eastern provinces, was provided by Amsterdam merchants and regents.

The extent of the contrast between Holland and the less prosperous provinces is evident even where agriculture is concerned. While the peasants of the eastern provinces lived very much in the way they had lived a century before, agriculture in Holland had received a considerable stimulus from the expansion of the towns. The widescale land reclamations provided the space required to allow dairy farming to start on the considerable expansion made possible by the growing demand from the expanding towns. The market for dairy produce grew not only because of the requirements of the growing town populations; butter, milk and cheese were also important in certain branches of Dutch trade, in particular that with England. In response to similar pressures market-gardening also began to develop rapidly, especially in the region between Leiden and Amsterdam, and such specialised branches of agriculture as cultivation under glass and the growing of bulbs were started. In other words Holland's agriculture began to take on important commercial aspects, and production for the market brought an end to the days of closed subsistence farming.

The great differences between the provinces, or more precisely between Holland and much of the rest of the Republic, are brought out with especial clarity by what is known about the demographic development of the Northern Netherlands.[14] Holland was, of course, by far the most populous province: in 1622 it accounted for around 670,000 of a total population of about 1,400,000 in the Republic; at the end of the eighteenth century Holland had 780,000 inhabitants from a total in the region of 2,000,000. Under the Republic the population of Holland seems to have reached its peak around 1680 at c. 883,000 of a total of c. 1,900,000. Not only was Holland more densely populated than the other provinces, but its pattern of demographic development was also substantially different.

For the province of Holland the population explosion came in the sixteenth century and the first decades of the seventeenth. Between 1514 and 1622 the population of this area rose by about 145 per cent—from c. 275,000 to c. 672,000—the town population rising much more rapidly than that of the country areas (185 per cent as against 110 per cent). It is significant that while in the countryside the rate of growth was greater in the period 1514–69 than it was in 1569–1622, in the big towns—Amsterdam, Leiden, Haarlem, Rotterdam, Delft—the great expansion came only after 1580.

The course of demographic development is rather difficult to trace for the seventeenth century, but it would seem that the rise in population continued, though much more slowly than in the preceding period, until about 1680. This growth was particularly marked in the towns—Leiden grew from c. 45,000 in 1622 to c. 60,000 in 1685; Rotterdam from 19,532 in 1622 to about 51,000 around 1690;[15] Amsterdam, c. 104,900 in 1622, probably passed 200,000 by the end of the century. Delft followed a similar course to the other big towns and the population of Haarlem, 39,500 in 1622, was most likely greater than this in the period 1650–70.

After the peak in the late seventeenth century, the Holland population began to fall. The first area to be hit was the countryside of North Holland, which began to lose inhabitants after 1650 and suffered badly in the early eighteenth century: from 1650 to 1795 the population of this region fell from around 200,000 to c. 130,000. The towns were hit a little later: only four—Amsterdam, Rotterdam, The Hague and Schiedam—were bigger in 1795 then they had been in 1622, and in most towns the population fell. This decline took place chiefly in the late seventeenth and early eighteenth centuries. The textile towns were especially hard hit: Leiden fell to c. 35,000 in 1750 and 31,000 in 1795; Haarlem to 32,500 in 1707 and 21,227 in 1795. Even in the more favoured towns, the eighteenth century saw stagnation rather than growth. Rotterdam, for example, reached its peak at about 1690 then lost population, and the 1690 figure was not touched again until the end of the eighteenth century.

Overall the population of Holland grew rapidly in the sixteenth and early seventeenth centuries, continued to expand, though more slowly until around 1680, and then fell rapidly until the middle of the eighteenth century:

1514	275,000	
1622	672,000	+144 per cent
c. 1680	887,000	+31 per cent
c. 1750	783,000	−11 per cent
1795	783,000	

During the period of decline most of the losses came in the countryside of North Holland and in the towns. Even the most successful towns only held their late seventeenth-century peak during the following century. They were unable to make up for the losses occurring elsewhere.

In contrast, the other provinces (with the exception of Zeeland, which probably followed the Holland pattern fairly closely) showed neither the early dynamism nor the later decline. In Friesland there was a notable population rise in the sixteenth and early seventeenth centuries—75–80,000 in 1511, at least 129,000 in 1689—though this was well below the rate of the expansion in Holland. Stagnation followed in the late seventeenth and early eighteenth century, but there was considerable growth after about 1750—in 1744 the population was about 135,000, in 1815 173,000. This development is a weak reflection of the Holland pattern except for the growth in the later eighteenth century. Overijsel, on the other hand, experienced a slow but steady growth throughout the early modern period:

1475	53,000
1675	71,000
1723	97,000

1748	122,000
1764	132,000
1795	134,000

From these statistics it is clear that for this province the late seventeenth and early eighteenth century was a period of population growth, and not decline on the Holland model. Similarly in the Veluwe, part of Gelderland, there was a steady rise in the sixteenth and seventeenth centuries, while in the 100 years after 1650 this growth accelerated, especially in the rural areas. After 1750 the towns also began to take part in this modest expansion. The figures are:

1526	36,000
1650	40,000
1749	54,200
1795	65,800

The small total populations of the lesser provinces contrast sharply with that of Holland, and the small size of their towns in comparison with the boom towns of Holland is a reminder that a town was a very different phenomenon in Overijsel, for example, than in Holland. The *total* population of the three chief towns of Overijsel (Zwolle, Deventer and Kampen) was only 19,700 in 1675 and 26,720 in 1795. Also the only areas to share Holland's eighteenth-century decline were some towns and rural districts which were engaged in shipping, trade, industry or livestock farming. The economically backward areas of the land provinces did not share in Holland's expansion, but began to increase their populations in the eighteenth century when Holland was in great difficulties.

As Holland dominated the Republic economically, so Amsterdam dominated Holland's economic life. Similarly, as the greater prosperity of Holland gave rise to jealousy in the other provinces, so the wealth and power of Amsterdam exacerbated and confused political matters at issue within Holland. Rivalry between the towns, and particularly between Amsterdam and the other towns, was one of the most important constant elements in the internal political life of the province. Normally the attitude adopted by the government of Amsterdam in crucial questions was decisive in the long term. Oldenbarnevelt's fall in 1618 was as much a consequence of Amsterdam's opposition to his policies as to the decision of Prince Maurice to support the Contra-remonstrants; and the Orangist triumph in 1672 was to a great extent prepared by the Amsterdam government, which began to undermine De Witt's position in the late 1660s. On both these occasions Amsterdam's move into the opposition was motivated at least in part by jealousy of the influence which other towns were exerting on the government of Holland. During the Truce, the increasing bitterness of the political and religious disputes forced Oldenbarnevelt to rely more and more on the support of a number of towns with extremely Republican and Remonstrant governments: the 'eight towns', Haarlem, Leiden, Gouda, Rotterdam, Schoonhoven, Brielle, Alkmaar and Hoorn.[16] The feeling that Amsterdam's interests were not receiving proper consideration from the government of the province was especially strong among those regents who were interested in the foundation of a West Indies Company, as Oldenbarnevelt had prevented this projected company from receiving a charter from the States General in order to facilitate the signing and the maintenance of the Truce. The importance of such dissatisfaction should not be overestimated, but it does help to explain why the town departed in these years from its normal policy of opposing any increase in the power of the stadhouder or of the Reformed Church.

Similarly, from around 1667 the most determined supporters of the States-party and of the policies of De Witt—when these did not include too many concessions to the Orangists—were a group of towns in South Holland: Rotterdam, Delft, Dordrecht. These towns had also formed an informal league, together with the Orangist town Leiden, against the influence of Amsterdam, and had—at least in the opinion of the Amsterdam regents—gained too great a say in the government of Holland. Amsterdam's feeling that its voice was not being accorded its proper weight in the affairs of state helped to turn the town against De Witt, and to weaken the cohesion of the States-party in Holland.[17] When the crisis of 1672 occurred the Republicans, lacking the support of Amsterdam, no longer had sufficient strength or self-confidence to make even a show of opposing the Orangist offensive.

Normally, however, Amsterdam was the bulwark of Republican strength in Holland. During the stadhoudership of Frederick Henry it was Amsterdam which put itself at the head of the peace party, and was finally able to compel the reluctant stadhouder to start serious peace negotiations and was able to ensure that these led to a successful conclusion. Again, as we have seen,[18] Amsterdam was the centre of the opposition to the policies of William II and bore the brunt of his resentment in 1650. The town was thoroughly committed to the

States-party through the 1650s and most of the 1660s, and De Witt owed much of his influence to his alliance with the government of this very powerful town. After the aberration of the late 1660s and early 1670s, Amsterdam soon appeared in its more usual rôle of opponent of the power and policies of the stadhouder, agitating in favour of peace and advocating the primacy of the interests of trade.

As a general comment on the rôle of Amsterdam in the political conflicts of the seventeenth century, it would be very near the truth to say that when it stood at the head of the Republicans (or the States-party), this political grouping was the strongest force in the Republic. Only when this great town broke with its natural tradition, usually in a great measure for economic reasons, to side with the stadhouder and the orthodox Reformed could these hope to control the government of Holland—and, by extension almost, of the Republic—for long. These defections by Amsterdam from the Republican cause were always short-lived, but they had their roots in long-standing rivalries between the Holland towns, and these rivalries in their turn chiefly turned on conflicts of economic interest.

A further aspect of the economic power of Holland in the seventeenth century was the supremacy of Amsterdam as a money market. European trade in capital was in the hands of the Dutch perhaps even more completely than the carrying trade, and the merchants and financiers of Amsterdam left little room for those of other towns as far as this specialised business was concerned. The foundation of the Exchange Bank at Amsterdam in 1609 helped to raise the town's capital market to its position of European dominance, and to keep it there.[19] When the Dutch lead in trade, fishing and textiles had begun to fade away in the early eighteenth century, Amsterdam's financial predominance was maintained almost unimpaired.[20]

Any discussion of the remarkable economic expansion of the Republic in the seventeenth century must include some mention of that branch of Dutch endeavour which very possibly impressed contemporaries most of all, i.e. the establishment of the Dutch empire in the East Indies, together with their remarkable, if short-lived, successes in the Americas. There is no space here to describe the establishment of the Dutch trading monopoly and then of an empire in the South-East Asian archipelago, nor for a discussion of the reasons why they failed to maintain their position in either Brazil or North America.[21] On the other hand, given the spectacular nature of these activities outside Europe, it might be as well to point out that they were only a minor part of the Dutch economy as a whole, and the impact of both successes and failures on Dutch society was surprisingly limited. For example, although the v.o.c.,[22] through its monopoly over the supply to Europe of many East Indian spices, was able to bring its shareholders enormous profits during the course of the seventeenth century, the importance of the company for the general prosperity of the Republic remained small. In terms of tonnage the cargoes carried by the ships of the v.o.c. were insignificant compared with the total tonnage passing through the ports of the Republic; and, even though it was concerned with very valuable items, the trade of the company before the eighteenth century never accounted for more than about 9 or 10 per cent of the total value of the trade of the Republic.[23]

Certainly, a number of individuals waxed fat on their profits from the v.o.c., but the company employed relatively few ships, accounted for only a small fraction of the total value of Dutch trade, and most of the goods it brought into the country did not encourage *trafieken*. Similarly, contact with the exotic cultures of the East Indies and Asia (including that of Japan where from 1641 the Dutch were the only Europeans allowed to trade) seems to have made remarkably little impact on Holland. Apart from the Brazilian paintings of Frans Post and a number of engravings, chiefly mediocre, the Dutch genius for the realistic reproduction of land- and town-scapes was hardly applied to the Dutch possessions in the East or West. Despite the hopes of a number of active men at the beginning of Dutch imperial expansion, no serious and continued attempt was made to establish colonies even at the Cape of Good Hope or in North America where the conditions were most suitable for European colonisation; nor is there much evidence to suggest that many Dutchmen were in any case willing to emigrate. The Republic in the seventeenth century attracted immigrants from other European countries; it does not seem to have had the problem of endemic underemployment. Industry, fishing, the merchant fleet, all these could soak up more labour than even the demographic expansion of Holland could provide. There was certainly little in the way of a surplus which could be diverted to colonies. Moreover, the pressures of religious intolerance were minimal in the Republic, and so one of the major spurs to emigration was very largely lacking.

The Dutch imagination may have been stirred by the possibilities of profit offered by the empire; it does not seem to have been fired to any marked extent by the new worlds with which its sailors and merchants came into contact. Service in the v.o.c. was ill-paid—though

8 Jan Vermeer,
Street in Delft, *c.* 1660
(Rijksmuseum,
Amsterdam)

9 Jacob van Ruisdael,
The Damrak, *Amster-
dam* (Mauritshuis,
The Hague)

10 Adriaen van Salm, *View of Leuvehaven, Rotterdam* (grisaille)
(Ferens Art Gallery, Kingston-upon-Hull)

11 Johannes Dircksz. Oudenrogge, *Weaver's Work-place* (Rijksmuseum, Amsterdam)

12 Jan Steen, *Skittle Players outside an Inn, c.* 1660–63 (National Gallery, London)

13 Jacob van Ruisdael, *Wheatfields, c.* 1670
(Altman Bequest, Metropolitan Museum of Art, New York)

14 (opposite)   Meindert Hobbema, *The
Water Mill, c.* 1665 (Wallace Collection,
London)

15   Jan Vermeer, *View of Delft*, c. 1662 (Mauritshuis, The Hague)

corruption allowed fortunes to be made—and it attracted neither the most able nor the most imaginative. Consequently there was, in the first century of Dutch power in the East at least, little attempt to investigate the complexities of the cultures which were being conquered and slowly destroyed. At the most a few curiosities from the Indies might be found in the cabinets of wealthy collectors. Dutch cultural life remained largely untouched by the imperial experience until a much later date.

★   ★   ★

The great economic expansion of the seventeenth century was the achievement of the towns, and this meant to an overwhelming extent the towns of Holland. In short, and with some exaggeration, prosperity was an urban phenomenon. It is true that there was a certain development of commercial farming in Holland to supply the rapidly-growing towns, but the prosperity this brought was very modest compared with the wealth that accumulated in the more successful of the Holland towns. Indeed, to a considerable extent the countryside was being bought up by the towns: rich merchants and *rentiers* looking for safe investments or for pleasant country estates forced up the price of land, so that it was difficult for even the more prosperous farmer to compete. Big farms or estates could only be built up by using the sort of capital which was only to be found in the towns.

The concentration of economic activity within the established urban centres was furthered by the conscious policy of those towns represented in the States of Holland. They used their political power to inhibit the development of industries in the villages or in the countryside to save their own manufacturers from competition. The political domination of Holland by the towns was not only caused by their economic power, it also helped to advance and preserve it.

As the towns of Holland dominated the political and economic life of the province—and by extension of the Republic—so they dominated its cultural life also. Indeed it is possible that there was a mounting progression here: the voting towns of Holland were a vital element in politics, but the federal system and the influence of the stadhouder meant that there were always considerable limitations to their power; in the economy of the Republic the Holland towns were the force behind the great expansion, but the growth of trade and industry had to be shared to some extent with the towns of Zeeland, and Utrecht,

Friesland and Groningen; but as regards the cultural achievements of the seventeenth century what did not begin in Holland was drawn to it, and it was drawn to the towns. The only major exceptions to this rule are the school of Italianate painters in Utrecht, and the universities outside Holland. The Holland towns were more dominant culturally than economically, economically than politically, their prosperity allowing them to develop their vital and varied culture. It was the social and political structure which allowed so much freedom of thought and expression. Both these elements were necessary to provide the atmosphere which made Dutch society so conducive to the flourishing of the arts, literature and thought.

Notes

[1] See C. Wilson, *Profit and Power. A Study of England and the Dutch Wars* (Cambridge 1957)

[2] The best general account of the economic history of the Dutch Republic is now J. G. van Dillen, *Van rijkdom en regenten. Handboek tot de economische en sociale geschiedenis van Nederland tijdens de Republiek* (The Hague 1970)

[3] J. E. Elias, *Het voorspel van den eersten engelschen oorlog*, vol. I (The Hague 1920), pp. 60–62

[4] J. A. Faber, 'The decline of the Baltic grain-trade in the second half of the seventeenth century', *Acta Historiae Neerlandica*, vol. I (1966)

[5] The activities of De Geer and his business associates are well brought out in P. W. Klein, *De Trippen in de 17e eeuw. Een studie over het ondernemersgedrag op de Hollandse stapelmarkt* (Assen 1965)

[6] J. U. Nef, *The Rise of the British Coal Industry*, vol. II (London 1932), p. 24

[7] Th. van Thijn, 'Pieter de la Court. Zijn leven en zijn economische denkbeelden', *Tijdschrift voor geschiedenis*, 69e jaargang (1956), pp. 305–7; J. A. van Houtte, *Economische en sociale geschiedenis van de Lage Landen* (Zeist/Antwerp 1964), pp. 183–4

[8] J. A. van Houtte, *op. cit.*, pp. 184–5, 189

[9] V. Barbour, *Capitalism in Amsterdam in the 17th century* (Baltimore 1950), chap. VI

[10] Calculated on the basis of the revenue brought in by the *convooien en licenten*—the export and import duties at each port. These figures are, naturally, made unreliable by the great amount of evasion which took place, but they do have a certain comparative worth as there is no reason to believe that the incidence of evasion was not roughly the same at each port (although it was almost certainly much higher in Zeeland)

[11] J. A. van Houtte, *op. cit.*, p. 161

[12] There was a silk industry in Utrecht, but it was overshadowed by the production of Holland as a whole

[13] See W. F. M. Oldewelt, 'De beroepsstructuur van de bevolking der Hollandse stemhebbende steden volgens de kohieren van familiegelden van 1674, 1715 en 1742', *Economisch-Historisch Jaarboek*, xxiv, pp. 90–91

[14] For this section, see J. A. Faber *et al.*, 'Population changes and economic developments in the Netherlands: a historical survey', *Afdeling Agrarische Geschiedenis*: Bijdragen 12 (Wageningen 1965), pp. 47*ff*

[15] G. J. Mentink and A. M. van der Woude, *De demografische ontwikkeling te Rotterdam en Cool in de 17e en 18e eeuw* (Rotterdam 1965), p. 39

[16] J. den Tex, *Oldenbarnevelt*, vol. III (Haarlem 1966), p. 471

[17] M. A. M. Franken, *Coenraad van Beuningen's politieke en diplomatieke aktiviteiten in de jaren 1667–1684* (Groningen 1966), pp. 76–7

[18] See above, pp. 25–7

[19] V. Barbour, *op. cit.*, chap. II

[20] J. de Vries, *De economische achteruitgang der Republiek in de achttiende eeuw* (Amsterdam 1959), pp. 58*ff*

[21] An excellent general study is C. R. Boxer, *The Dutch Seaborne Empire* (London 1965)

[22] I.e. *Vereenigde Oostindische Compagnie* or United East India Company

[23] J. A. van Houtte, *op. cit.*, pp. 153–4

four

Holland as Town

The most important political institution in the province of Holland was its states. This body exercised sovereign power within the province, and all important political decisions were made or had to be ratified by it. The States of Holland were dominated by the towns which were represented there—the *stemhebbende* or voting towns. Before the Revolt only six of the Holland towns had been regularly called to take part in the meetings of the States—Dordrecht, Haarlem, Leiden, Delft, Amsterdam and Gouda. They each had one vote in the States, and the seventh vote was that of the nobility. Although they were thus heavily outnumbered by the towns, the nobles were nevertheless able to exercise considerable influence as they were held to represent the countryside and the towns not otherwise represented in the States. In other words they spoke for a large part of the county, and this part was probably wealthier than the six towns combined. As the States were chiefly concerned with financial matters, particularly the voting of new taxes, the attitude of the nobles was very important—if they withheld their support from a tax it could not be expected to bring in very much revenue. As individuals the nobles were also influential: besides the lordships (used in the sense of the French *seigneuries*) which they held,[1] they also occupied the most important official posts from the stadhoudership—governorship of the province—down to the office of *schout* in the towns and *baljuw* in the countryside. The stadhouder was appointed by the sovereign's representative in the Netherlands, the governor or governess, and he appointed—on the instructions of the governess—the *schouten* and *baljuwen*. These latter posts had important police and judicial powers attached to them, and they exercised the sovereign's right to appoint local magistrates and lesser officials. Further, a number of the greater Holland nobles were large landowners outside the county as well as within its borders, and owed much of their political importance to their contacts with the court of the governess of the Netherlands. Through this connection they gained their most important and lucrative appointments—membership of the Council of State, colonelcies of *bandes d'ordonnance* (the élite cavalry units), and governorships of provinces. William of Orange, the wealthiest and most powerful noble in the whole of the Habsburg Netherlands in the years immediately preceding the Revolt, had great estates in Brabant and Franche Comté as well as in Holland, was prince of Orange in France, a member of the Council of State, and stadhouder of Holland, Zeeland and Utrecht. His was an unusual case, however, and it is probable that the lesser nobles, with chiefly local ties and power, played a more important rôle in the affairs of the province on most occasions. The importance of these local nobles in the early years of the Revolt has been stressed in recent studies.[2]

Despite the part the nobles played in bringing Holland into revolt against Spain, it was the Revolt and its consequences which broke the power of the nobles in this province, and established the dominance of the towns. How and why the nobles lost power is still far from clear, though some suggestions can be made. Firstly, most of the more important of the Holland nobles probably held more land in provinces which eventually reverted to Spanish rule, and many of these preferred to return to the Spanish obedience rather than have their property in the South confiscated. Next, many of the nobles who had at first supported the insurgents were more concerned with the preservation of their own privileges than with the establishment of protestantism. Such men were alienated by what seemed to them the socially disruptive effects of the success of militant Calvinism in Holland and elsewhere—the happenings in Ghent in the late 1570s appeared a serious threat to social order.[3] Consequently they turned to Parma and to Spain as the guardians of the old order, in which the nobility had an assured place, and lost their positions in Holland. Again, in some areas of Holland, particularly the Northern Quarter (which included most of the county above Amsterdam and Haarlem), the nobles had never been very firmly established. Finally, the economic importance of the towns became clear during the Revolt, and many more of them were able to win representation in the rebel States, but why the deputies of the towns were able so quickly and easily to push the nobles out of the most important political positions is a matter which needs further investigation.

In Holland the fluid situation created by the Revolt allowed previously unrepresented towns to gain entry to the States in the 1570s. By the end of this decade the constitutional position had settled down,

with 12 new towns added to the six 'great' towns. Of the new towns—
Rotterdam, Schiedam, Den Briel, Gorinchem, Schoonhoven, Alkmaar,
Hoorn, Enkhuizen, Medemblik, Purmerend, Monnikendam and
Edam—the most important was Rotterdam which was soon recognised
as the seventh of the great towns rather than as first of the lesser.[4] Most
of the other newcomers were of very minor importance, with the
exception of Hoorn and Enkhuizen, but they all had the same formal
power in the States as the bigger towns, i.e. one vote each. So against
the 18 votes of the towns the nobles had only one, although they were
still held to represent the countryside and the towns without a place in
the States. However, as all the towns of any note were now in the
States, the importance of the nobles' 'constituency' had fallen considerably. From this time on the nobles could only play a very subordinate rôle in the political life of the province. Indeed, they became
very much dependent on the dominant power within the province—
under Oldenbarnevelt and De Witt they were steady supporters of the
policies of the grand pensionary, and when the princes of Orange were
predominant in the state they appeared as firm Orangists. The surviving Holland nobility was on the whole far from wealthy and had
little or no contact with the new and expanding sources of economic
power. They were to a great extent dependent on favours and offices in
the hands of the state—commands in the army or navy,[5] lucrative
administrative posts, or the position of *schout* in the towns or *baljuw* in
the country areas.[6]

During the Republic, the native nobility of Holland had very little
influence in politics or even in the States of Holland. In the meetings of
this body they spoke first, but as their spokesman was the grand pensionary—who was also the pensionary of the nobles[7]—their freedom of
expression was normally severely limited. They could often help to
bring about a compromise between two opposed views, but they
could not hope to oppose with any success the policies supported by
the majority of the towns in the States. Only under Frederick Henry,
when a somewhat artificial court was built up around the stadhouder,
and later under William III, could the nobles have any notable political
influence—and then only through the favour of the prince, and through
the influence they might be able to exercise over him. Even here, however, they acted normally as tools of the stadhouder and were never able
to build up any independent basis of power.

The nobles in the other provinces of the Republic, with the exception of Zeeland, exercised considerable power in their provincial

states, but they tended equally to be drawn to the stadhouder in a system of clientage, as they were also in the main poor. They could exercise little influence as independent patrons on the cultural life of Holland. In any case, the great majority of them resided in their provinces, or held posts in the army which were likely to keep them outside Holland for much of the time. There were no great provincial nobles, large landowners who could be attracted by the social and cultural possibilities of Amsterdam and The Hague, and there materially affect the social structure of the most wealthy and vital province.

In short, the nobility played an insignificant rôle not only in the political life of Holland, but also in its economic, social and cultural activities. The situation was very different in, for example, Gelderland and Overijsel where this was the dominant social class. It would be misleading to relate directly the cultural sterility of these provinces to the continuing dominance of this group. Rather, it was the relative economic backwardness of the land provinces which allowed the nobles to retain their power and position almost undisturbed, and that it was this lack of economic vitality which inhibited artistic and intellectual development. In these areas there was no growth of a prosperous and influential urban middle class which could provide a stimulus to cultural activity; nor could the impoverished nobility of these provinces play the rôle of the patron of art and literature which the aristocracy of many countries of western and southern Europe were performing with success at this time. Social stagnation and cultural sterility were the results of the failure of the land provinces to emulate Holland's economic growth.

If the nobility, which had normally been decisive in determining the nature of the culture of a country in the past, as in most European countries in the seventeenth century, had lost most of its influence in Holland, another element in society which had also been of the first importance in the past disappeared almost entirely as a consequence of the Revolt and the triumph of protestantism. The Roman Catholic Church ceased to be an important factor in Dutch cultural life. Although Dutch catholics were excluded, in law if not always in practice, from all political posts and public office, they were still numerous; but as a cultural influence the Catholic Church could play only a very modest rôle—it could act as a spiritual stimulus to religious poets, and encourage writers and theologians to defend the church from the attacks of its enemies and to maintain the morale of the faithful. Much of the writings aimed at the Dutch catholics, however, were of a pious or homiletic nature, and intended for a fairly unsophisticated audience. Such circumstances need not have depressed the literary standards of catholic writing, but in the event such works only very rarely rose above a low literary and intellectual level. This weakness was, however, not peculiar to the repressed church; very little of the pious or inspirational writings produced by the Dutch in the seventeenth century had much merit as literature, but one cannot help admiring the painstaking effort which must have gone into the production, and consumption, of the mountains of such gritty works published in the Republic. Only in the field of theological controversy, particularly in pamphlets and libels, was much vitality introduced into such works.

Institutionalised religion failed to play a major part in the cultural life of the community, despite the undoubted political influence which the Reformed Church could exercise. The Catholic Church had been reduced to a defensive rôle and served a largely ill-educated and culturally deprived section of the Dutch population. The gap thus left in the life of the community could not be filled by the Reformed Church. The latter did not and could not replace the old church as a patron of painters and musicians; on the contrary its influence tended more or less consistently to be inimical to art and music, as they appealed to the senses rather than expressing moral or religious ideals. As Van Es said of the protestant literature of the early seventeenth century in the Republic, 'It is more ideal than visual, more ethical and intellectual than sensual: it is concerned more with the expression of ideas than with the picturing of reality.'[8] As with literature, the Reformed Church demanded that art be morally and religiously didactic to justify its existence. The visual and musical arts were neither—or were so in such subtle and intangible ways as to escape the appreciation of the ministers of the Reformed Church who, as a group, seem to have possessed very little cultural vision. At best austere, they were more commonly philistine. In any case, the Reformed Church lacked the financial resources to act as a patron on a large scale—it never had sufficient money even to support its charitable functions, and the deacons were continually having to ask for help from their town governments.

The influence of the Reformed Church was strongest in music. The churches of the Netherlands had long been the leading centres of musical life, and in the sixteenth century nearly all the major composers were church organists. After the protestant take-over of the churches, the Reformed Church's suspicion of music was a major obstacle to its further development in the Republic. The town governments were able to counteract this unfortunate attitude to some extent by insisting that the church organists (whom after all they paid) give public performances outside the hours of the church services.[9] In the event, however, the stimulus thus provided does not appear to have been sufficient to prevent the decline of Dutch creativity in music, and after the death of Sweelinck[10] in 1621 almost nothing of note was produced by Dutch composers—an interesting negative aspect of the cultural vitality of the Republic in the seventeenth century.

Religion had, of course, a very great effect on all aspects of Dutch life in the seventeenth century. The Christian attitude was fundamental to all intellectual and emotional activity; in a very real sense it determined what questions were asked, what lines of thought were pursued, and what ways the individual would react to his life. It is very difficult to evaluate how far this religious base was a Reformed base.[11] The effect of Reformed ways of thought and feeling on Dutch life was very marked, though it must be added that a notable proportion of the leading artists and writers were not members of the Reformed Church: the protestant nonconformists were a particularly productive section of society, outstanding both in quantity and quality. However important the Reformed Church may have been as a source of ideas and inspiration, as an institution it could not hope to fulfil the function in society which the Catholic Church had done in the past, and was still doing in other parts of contemporary Europe. The contrast with the Southern Netherlands is most revealing in this respect. In the sixteenth century the Netherlands had been an artistic unity, particularly where painting was concerned. After the political division between North and South, the art of the two areas developed in very different ways, and the extent of this divergence became increasingly apparent throughout the first half of the seventeenth century. Rembrandt and Rubens were both painters of religious inspiration, but the contrast between their different approaches emphasises the fundamental divergence of the two schools of painting: both artists have been termed baroque, but this usage only illustrates the vagueness of the term. Even more striking is the contrast between the overall artistic production of the two schools. While the great difference in the nature of the two societies must be taken into account in explaining this divergence, the existence in the South of a vital, resurgent Catholic Church as a patron of Flemish art was an element of very great significance.[12] In the South the visual arts were seen as an important aspect of the religious renaissance by a church which was ready to emphasise the emotional side of religious life and had very considerable financial resources. In the North the didactic and moralistic elements were stressed by the Reformed Church, which saw these as the most important aspects of the religious re-education of the country. The difference in the attitudes of the two churches was accompanied by an even greater difference in the direct influence each could exercise over cultural developments—the Catholic Church was a great patron, commissioning numerous and large-scale works for its churches, but no such possibility was open to the Reformed Church.

With the great patrons of the past absent—the nobility and the church—the cultural life of the Republic was dominated by the middle and upper classes in the towns of Holland. The painters found their market partly among the regent élite but more largely in a wide section of the town population—not only the rich, but those sections of the population with money to spend, or rather invest, in works of art in the same way as they spent it on plate, fine furnishings and curiosities. Similarly, Dutch writers had in mind a public which was essentially drawn from the same sections of society, although here the emphasis fell on a certain level of education and a certain conception of the importance of literature rather than on the possession of surplus money. In both cases, the audience was urban—the absence of a significant aristocracy or gentry robbed the countryside of its importance as far as culture was concerned. Money was moving into the countryside in so far as wealthy townsmen were beginning to buy country houses and estates as places of rest and recreation, particularly for the summer months, but these men remained essentially town dwellers—they did not so much leave the towns as colonise the countryside. The famous *Muiderkring* (i.e. the circle at Muiden), although it met at the castle at Muiden (on the border between Holland and Utrecht) where P. C. Hooft was *drost*,[13] was composed of people from the urban oligarchy or middle classes. It was an offshoot of the literary culture of the Holland towns, particularly of Amsterdam.

The political and economic power of the Holland towns has already been made clear. It was in these powerful and wealthy urban centres that the cultural life of the Republic centred. Dutch civilisation was an urban civilisation: its writers, painters, theologians, philosophers, scientists all lived in the towns and sprang in the main from urban upper- and middle-classes. They also found their public and their inspiration in the towns and in the life of the towns. They took their style and their approach inevitably from the society in which they lived and to which they referred; and in Holland this society was largely urban and middle-class (in the broadest sense of the term). In the peculiarity of Dutch society, more specifically the society of the Holland towns, lay the origins of the freshness and individuality of Dutch culture.

For it must be remembered that the remarkable development of Dutch civilisation which took place in the seventeenth century was almost entirely a phenomenon of the province of Holland. The cultural life of the provinces outside Holland lacked vigour, and it is difficult to point to any independent artistic or literary tradition in any of them. Notable artists and writers were indeed born outside the narrow boundaries of Holland, but it was only here that they could develop their art and find an audience or a market for their work. The works of such men had little or no provincial characteristics; they worked within and were inspired by the cultural atmosphere of the Holland towns. In fact some of the men who are now taken to be typical of the art and literature produced by Holland were born elsewhere, but were drawn early—often very early—into the cultural life of this province and played their parts in building and developing its traditions. Jacob Cats,[14] for example, was born in Zeeland, but spent the greater part of his mature years in Holland. His best work is a reflection, in its diction, subjects and morality, of the life, interests and aspirations of the Holland middle-classes. Town life was also important in Zeeland, but in Holland this life was more lively and it was in response to his experience here that he wrote his best and most characteristic work.

Similarly, Jacob van Ruisdael, though born in Overijsel, spent his working life in Holland and his pictures represent the peak of the achievement of the Holland school of landscape painting. He did not bring anything with him from Overijsel except his talent—his works sprang from and developed the established Holland style. His originality and individuality came from his personality; they were not the product of provincial inspiration. Something similar can be said of the many painters who came to learn, and later work, in Holland from the other provinces or even further afield; they were completely assimilated into the Dutch school, which is as much as to say into the Holland school.

With regard to the institutions of higher learning the situation is a little more complicated. The universities outside Holland—at Utrecht, Franeker (in Friesland), Groningen and Harderwijk (in Gelderland)—lacked the prestige and international reputation of Leiden and never achieved the intellectual vigour and independence of the Illustrious School at Amsterdam,[15] but they were nevertheless important centres of learning. (Harderwijk was the least important of them.) These provincial universities were especially important as centres for training in theology, and were the bulwarks of orthodoxy in the Reformed Church. In this relative rigidity they can be seen as reflecting the attitude of the provinces in which they were situated— Reformed orthodoxy had a much stronger hold in the lesser provinces than in Holland—and this circumstance may help to explain why these areas were less vigorous culturally than the more liberal Holland. The university of Utrecht is an interesting exception—a stronghold of orthodoxy, particularly in those years when Voetius[16] was the dominant influence there, in a society which had much in common with that of Holland, at least as far as the attitudes of the regents were concerned. On the whole these provincial universities were training colleges for future ministers of the Reformed Church rather than centres for intellectual inquiry; given a free rein the latter would necessarily have involved a more critical treatment of orthodoxy than the church felt itself able to allow.

As has already been suggested, apart from the relative poverty of the lesser provinces, the influence of the Reformed Church in these regions must be seen as an important factor in explaining the very limited part which they played in the development of Dutch culture in the seventeenth century. A much greater proportion of the population in Zeeland, Groningen and Friesland were members of the Reformed Church than was the case in Holland, and its influence on the life of these provinces was consequently stronger. Overijsel and Gelderland present a rather different picture for, while in both provinces protestantism was preponderant, they each contained whole regions which were overwhelmingly catholic—resembling extensions of the predominantly catholic Generality Lands rather than anywhere else in the seven provinces. The catholics, however, were largely confined to these areas and were able to play very little part in the life of either province. Their situation was probably worse than that of the catholics in Holland, and they were certainly unable to challenge the protestant dominance of political, social and cultural life. The Republic outside Holland then was much more in the grip of the Reformed Church than that province. Moreover, the conquest of the land provinces for protestantism came relatively late, taking place chiefly in the first few decades of the seventeenth century if not later in some areas, and so here the ministers still retained much of their militant missionary zeal. This first-generation protestantism was much more rigid and less prepared for compromise than the church in Holland, which was having to come to terms with a complex society. In these regions the attitude of the Reformed Church was less favourable to artistic developments even than in Holland, and it worked on a society where the development of art and letters was still in a primitive stage. Again, however, it was the social and economic backwardness of these provinces that laid them open to the rule of rigid orthodoxy: a more wealthy, complex and fluid society would have offered much greater resistance.

Zeeland and Utrecht possessed something approaching a flourishing town life, but in the rest of the lesser provinces the towns were small and often in decline, the nobility was poor and not noted for cultivated tastes, and the mass of the population was poverty-stricken peasants. In these circumstances there was little stimulus towards the growth of a lively culture outside Holland, and any consideration of Dutch civilisation in the seventeenth century must concentrate on this latter province.

Regent and society in the towns of Holland

The 18 towns represented in the States of Holland were controlled politically by closed corporations. The members of this political élite were known as regents. The political systems of the towns varied considerably, but each town government was composed of three basic elements: the burgomasters, who formed the executive and dealt normally with local affairs; the council or *vroedschap*, which advised on and usually determined matters concerned with provincial and state policy; and the *schepenen*, who formed the urban court of law with very wide powers.[17] The balance between these various elements of the magistracy differed greatly from town to town—in Amsterdam, for example, the burgomasters were very powerful and in most important matters decisions were taken by the college of burgomasters and ex-burgomasters, leaving for the *vroedschap* only a subordinate rôle; in Rotterdam real power lay with the *vroedschap* of 24 men, the burgomasters being subject to its direction in important matters. One constant factor was that in all the voting towns the magistracy was co-optative in practice (though some towns retained a formal rôle for the citizens in the choice of their rulers). The members of the oligarchy usually remained for life and vacancies were filled by co-option. The burgomasters and *schepenen* were changed every year or every two years, but they were appointed by the sitting members of the oligarchy and usually came from their ranks.

Thus there was a political élite in the towns which held all offices of importance and there was very little check on its exercise of power. It controlled the affairs of the town, including the collection of both ordinary and extra-ordinary taxes. This practice was, of course, tied up with the financial independence of the towns. No town could be forced to levy any tax to which it had not agreed, and the town governments ensured that this freedom was maintained by keeping tax-collection in their own hands. The magistracy was also in control of the administration of justice, the regulation of local economic activity, and the relations of the town with the government of the province—which the town governments largely directed through their deputies in the States of Holland. This relatively small number of regents from the 18 voting towns dominated the States, and there was very little in the way of limitations to their power, or balances against their influence. The town regents were especially independent when there was no stadhouder in Holland (1650–72) who could use his rights and influence to oppose their policies or rival their power.

It would be misleading, however, to see the regent group as a closed oligarchy sharply divided from the rest of the population, and exercising its power exclusively in its own selfish interests.

The urban oligarchies were far less closed than they might appear at first sight. The regents were clearly distinct in political power and privileges from the rest of society, but at least for the greater part of the seventeenth century, and in most Dutch towns, they formed an élite in political terms only—they were neither a social nor an economic élite. As we shall see,[18] the regents produced some of the most important Dutch literary figures and they shared a common literary culture with the educated and literate in Holland; they possessed no distinct, élite culture of their own. There was also no clear social division between the regents and other wealthy groups in the Holland towns. One of the more important reasons for this integration of the regents in society was the fluidity of the composition of the regent group itself. Almost throughout the century it remained possible for new men and families to gain places within these apparently closed oligarchies, and this process led to a continuous renewal of the political élite as old families faded out into private obscurity and new men took their places.

As the nature of the dominant political group within a society is of major importance for the culture of that society, and as the view of the Dutch regent group here presented is far from generally accepted, it seems necessary to examine this question more closely. Two factors in the history of Holland in the seventeenth century can be singled out as helping to keep up this constant renewal of the regent oligarchy, thus preventing the growth of a social as well as a political élite: the economic expansion of the towns, and the recurring political crises.

The population of most of the towns of Holland continued to grow until the third quarter of the century at least, and although it is dangerous to make such a sweeping statement it would seem true that the most prosperous and rapidly growing towns also saw the most frequent changes in the composition of their regent élite. As the towns expanded, new men and families were attracted from elsewhere and new wealth was won by native families. The wealth of the old regent families was often overshadowed by that of families which had been obscure in the sixteenth century, and the rise in the number of prosperous families increased competition for places in the regent group. Much of the liveliness of the political life of the towns of Holland may have been a consequence of the fact that too many families were competing for too few places. Entry into the oligarchy of a town could be gained by the power of wealth demanding recognition, but the process was very rarely as simple as this. More often a complex intermingling of political, family and religious affiliations would be involved. One of the simpler and most common ways to gain a place in the government of a town was to marry the daughter of a sitting regent, preferably one with more than average influence within the oligarchy. Most towns had strictly enforced regulations forbidding brothers, or fathers and sons, from sitting in the *vroedschap* or holding important office at the same time, thus finding a seat in the *vroedschap* or a post for a son-in-law was one of the best ways left open for the regent to extend the influence of his family in the town government. Once the new man was in the oligarchy, it was open to him—if he had the ability, wealth and connections—to consolidate his own position and to try to bring in his own relatives and friends, usually in alliance with his original benefactor and his connections.

Considerable social mobility was to be expected in towns which were expanding as quickly as were the towns of Holland. The change of scale as far as town life was concerned was considerable in the transition between the sixteenth and the seventeenth centuries, for the towns of Holland on the eve of the Revolt were small compared to their size in the following century. The fortunes of even the richest families in the middle of the sixteenth century could not compare with those that were being made in the years of Holland's economic greatness. So the members of the old oligarchy often failed to maintain their positions and were replaced by new families which had kept pace with the expansion of the economy. This mobility was exaggerated, or rather its progress accelerated, by the frequent political upheavals which made changes in the regent oligarchy more easy and rapid. Whatever tendency there may have been for the regent élites to become closed and to cut themselves off from the rest of society—and there is evidence to suggest that such a process began as soon as the regents were free from outside pressures—was checked by the effect of the crises of 1618, 1650 and 1672.

By the time the Truce was signed in 1609, the generation which had come to power during the Revolt and the first decades of the Eighty Years War had established itself or its younger relatives firmly in office; the *vroedschappen* and the other governing institutions of the Holland towns were largely controlled by families which had either been able to ride the storm of the Revolt or had broken through to political power in these disturbed years. However, a substantial proportion of this oligarchy in nearly every town was attached to the person and policies of Oldenbarnevelt: these regents found themselves in danger at the time of Maurice's *coup* in 1618. The 'purges' of the town governments carried out by the prince involved large numbers of regents—in Amsterdam only seven out of 36 councillors,[19] but in Rotterdam 15 out of 23[20]—and in nearly every town this change allowed many new families to enter the political élite.[21] Indeed, there can be little doubt that the sharpness of these local power struggles arose as much out of the presence of a rich and influential section of the population which was excluded from power, but was capable of allying itself with a minority group within the oligarchy, as from religious or political clashes. These outsiders were determined to break the power of the existing oligarchy, but they had no intention of changing the political system, only the membership of the ruling group.

In this way the oligarchies of most of the towns of Holland were broken up in 1618, and a large number of new men with their own family connections and clients entered the system. By 1650 the regent oligarchy had begun to stabilise itself again in nearly all the voting towns. Most of the men who had come to power in 1618 and immediately after had died, and it had become clear which families had been able to establish themselves firmly as members of the political élite and which had failed to do so. A number of the newcomers had been unable to retain their positions either through inability to form sufficiently powerful allies or for other reasons. The appointments had been made in haste in 1618 and some very unsuitable men had been chosen. Some turned out to be unsound financially, and the families of these men were unable to keep their hold on power. One of the new regents in Rotterdam went bankrupt and had to be expelled from the *vroedschap*.[22] Rotterdam was, however, an extreme case: the regents here had been very strongly in favour of the Remonstrants, and this attitude had been shared by a good part of the richer merchants of the town. Consequently, it was not too easy to find socially suitable yet religiously orthodox replacements for the dismissed regents—with less than 20,000 inhabitants in 1622 Rotterdam was still quite a small town —and some of the new regents were too modestly placed financially to be able to establish their families in the oligarchy.

The political crisis of 1650 and its aftermath disturbed the stability built up within the urban oligarchies in 30 years of manoeuvring. The blow to the prestige of the Orangist regents was great, and they were moreover deprived after the death of William II of the support of the stadhouder. Also the increased freedom of action the town governments enjoyed under the stadhouderless régime allowed them to ignore in practice certain laws and regulations which they found inconvenient. Notably, a number of towns opened up their governments to men who had formerly been excluded on the grounds of religious unorthodoxy. In particular, Remonstrants began to appear among the Holland regents again, though they usually maintained a certain discretion about their religious views and practices.

Certainly the membership of the regent élite in many of the voting towns changed decisively, if slowly, in the decade or so following 1650. The oligarchy which had seemed established by the 1640s was forced to submit to its partial replacement by new men, more clearly marked by the dual stamp of adherence to the politics of the 'True Freedom' and suspicion of the influence of the Reformed Church in affairs of state. Perhaps 'new men' is a misleading term, for many of the newcomers in the 1650s were members of families which had been thrust out of the oligarchy of their towns in 1618. With them they brought members of families with whom they had established connections, especially through marriage, during their years in the wilderness. On this occasion the process of renewal was necessarily a slow one as, in a system where the regents held office for life, the speed of change depended on the frequency of deaths among the sitting oligarchs. It would seem, however, that by the middle of the 1660s considerable changes had occurred and that in many towns a new oligarchy was in the process of being formed which differed greatly but not completely from the old. Although the period between 1650 and the next upheaval in 1672 was too short for the lines of development to be clear, there are strong indications that the oligarchies were already beginning to close up again by the early 1670s, and that the leaders of these élites were the recent arrivals politically. Political power was once more becoming confined in practice to a smaller number of families than in recent years.

In consequence, a group of outsiders formed again, composed of rich and ambitious men who were being kept out of the oligarchy, and they found ready allies in the families which had been squeezed out of the regent group in the previous decades. These malcontents found in 1672 that they could rely on the co-operation of minority groups within the town government who felt their positions threatened by the dominant party or who resented their lack of power.

The large-scale changes in the composition of the regent oligarchy caused by the military and political crisis of 1672 were probably even more disruptive of the existing political élite than the purges of 1618. Moreover, they were accompanied and forced through by prolonged and violent popular disturbances. The purges in 1618 had been carried out by Prince Maurice in an orderly manner, imposed on the town governments from above and with a semblance at least of legality. In 1672 the pressure came from below: it was mob violence which first caused the regents of Holland to appoint William III as stadhouder, and it was further violence which forced the unpopular regents to resign. After the reality of the threat had been demonstrated by the murder of Johan de Witt and his brother Cornelis in The Hague, such men were happy to retain at least their property and their lives.[23]

There can be little doubt that these popular disturbances of 1672 were far from wholly spontaneous in character. They were encouraged, directed and organised by men of considerable standing in society, rich merchants and manufacturers who hoped to force their way into the oligarchies. They were helped by discontented regents who supplied information and worked from within to undermine the will of the town governments to resist. These intriguers could not cause the popular discontent, but they could channel it in directions suitable to their ambitions, particularly in the conditions of the summer of 1672 when the Republic was swept by an epidemic of fear and suspicion and the mass of the population in the towns of Holland became even more volatile than usual.

It is remarkable how many of the regents who were forced out of the oligarchy in 1672 came from families which had suffered similarly in 1618, but had painstakingly fought their way back to political power since then. We have suggested that many of the new regents of 1618 were unable to maintain their places in the political élite because of their lack of wealth. After the changes of 1672 the charge was made that the new men of this year were also much poorer than the men they replaced—and this charge had the force of: thus less respectable, less trustworthy, and less qualified for leading positions in the state. Pieter de Groot wrote of the changes in Rotterdam:

> Premièrement il est bien penible pour les gens d'honneur et de bien de voir la canaille, qui n'a rien à perdre, posseder leur charges et disposer de leur bien, car, pour vous parler seulement de Rotterdam, il est certain, que de ceux, qui y sont entrez dans le gouvernement, il n'y a que deux personnes qui ont quelque bien, la ou ceux, qui en sont sorti, ont ensemble plus de trois millions de vaillant.[24]

There seems to have been very little truth in such statements. A few men gained office on the tide of Orangism who for lack of wealth or social position would not have been considered eligible before, but on the whole the new regents were men of considerable wealth. They may perhaps have been less rich than the men they replaced, but the difference was minimal. The new regents came from the same social and economic class as the old, and indeed many of them came from families which had formed part of the regent élite in the past.

For the first three quarters of the seventeenth century the nascent patriciates of the Holland towns had been prevented from forming fully because of the frequency of changes in their composition. The oligarchies had remained fluid through the social mobility of an expanding and volatile society, and this tendency had been supported periodically by the effects of the recurrent political crises, each of which brought an immediate change in the personnel of the town governments or speeded up the process of renewal of the political élite. The situation began to change in the last quarter of the century. There was no further general political upheaval in Holland—though there were local troubles leading to changes in the personnel of the oligarchy—and the oligarchies seem to have taken advantage of these new conditions to establish themselves firmly and to prevent many new families from making their way into the town governments. It was in this period also that the 'Contracts of Correspondence', designed to distribute posts of profit and honour among all the members of the correspondence, became the rule in the Holland towns. The object of these agreements was to reserve these offices for a select group within the oligarchy itself, and by using a strict rota system to prevent disputes and rivalries which might weaken the coherence of the group in power. The eighteenth century brought no further threat to the power of the established oligarchies, as after the childless William III's death no successor was appointed, and this second stadhouderless period lasted for most of the first half of the century.

The lack of serious political upheavals to disturb the political élites in the towns of Holland was not the only factor helping the consolidation of these oligarchies. By the last quarter of the seventeenth century the economy of the province had, as we have noted, already passed its expansive stage and the populations of the towns had ceased to grow, or even started to fall. In consequence society ceased to be as fluid as it had been in the earlier part of the century, and this stabilisation weakened the pressures which had acted on the political élites in the past. The accent was increasingly on preservation, not on change or adaptation, in social as well as in economic terms.

The consequence seems to have been an increasing separation of the regents from the rest of the population, though this matter needs much more investigation.[25] The development of an urban aristocracy, which was a social as well as a political élite, seems to have taken place in the late seventeenth or early eighteenth century in most of the Holland towns, but in some it must probably be dated rather earlier. In the smaller and less prosperous towns, particularly those which like Enkhuizen were faced with economic stagnation and even contraction by the middle of the century, the social forces keeping society fluid and helping to ensure the continual renewal of the regent élite may have been weak or perhaps absent altogether. At the other extreme, Amsterdam, the biggest and most prosperous town in the Republic, seems to have experienced the closing-up of its oligarchy soon after the death of the first generation of regents following the Revolt. The families composing the Amsterdam oligarchy may not have remained always the same, but by the middle of the century the regents were already beginning to appear almost as remote from the mass of Dutch society as was the court of the stadhouder.

A striking illustration of the distance the Amsterdam regents had moved from the tastes and attitudes current in the rest of Dutch society is provided by the new town hall, finished in 1655. This outstanding building was designed in the full renaissance style, and its decoration, both in sculpture and in painting, was a very fine example of the types of art prevalent in the Southern Netherlands and in Italy. It was clearly felt that the native forms of art were not impressive or noble enough to express the greatness of Amsterdam and the power and position of its rulers. However impressive the building and its decoration may have been, they were imports from the south—imitating the styles suitable to aristocratic and monarchical societies, and not that of the Republic. The complex and careful imagery—renaissance-classical in its allusions —although pleasing to the historians of art seems very much an alien element in the Dutch Republic, and it was a sign that the regents in architecture and the other visual arts as well as in literature were beginning to take their models from abroad, and develop a separate and distinct élite culture very different from that of their fellow citizens. It is a little paradoxical that this building which should have been the symbol of the greatness of Amsterdam, and by extension of the Republic, in fact shows almost nothing of the strength and individuality of Dutch culture.[26]

Apart from this matter of taste in art—the growing tendency to accept the general European criteria of worth rather than those implicit in the art of the Dutch School—one of the most obvious and important aspects of the transformation of the oligarchies into true urban aristocracies was the tendency of the regents to move away from active involvement in trade or industry. In Holland towards the end of the seventeenth century the regents began to move from an active economic rôle towards investment in land, stocks and government funds, particularly English. This movement away from trade can be seen throughout the seventeenth century. As soon as a family was established in the oligarchy it would send its young men to study law at Leiden as a preparation for a public career. They would then practice as advocates at The Hague or in their home town until places in the town government came open for them. When a regent family had reached this stage, it began to cut its connections with the trade or industry from which it had originally obtained its wealth. The regents in this way became *rentiers* and also increasingly interested in the profits of office.

An example of the history of a powerful regent family is given by the Vroesen family of Rotterdam. Cornelis Pietersz. Vroesen entered the *vroedschap* at the time Rotterdam went over to the side of the Revolt in 1572, and subsequently became one of the most powerful men in the government of the town. His son studied law at Leiden and became *schepen*, but the family lost office in 1618. After the death of William II the family was able to make its way back to power: in 1658 Adriaen Vroesen, the grandson of Cornelis, entered the *vroedschap* and became burgomaster within three years. Both his sons studied law, the eldest, Adriaen, being appointed town secretary in 1664 (at the age of 23) before replacing his father in the *vroedschap* on his death in 1669. Adriaen's place as secretary was taken over by his younger brother Willebord. Unfortunately for them, as their great-grandfather Cornelis had lost office because of his close association with the party of Olden-barnevelt, so Adriaen and Willebord lost their positions and power in 1672 through their similarly close association with the party of De Witt.

As this example would suggest, for most of the century this process of closing-up and professionalising the oligarchy was not able to go too far; the constant renewals of the regent élite meant that new men and families with intimate contacts with trade and industry were more or less regularly finding their way into the town governments. So at any given moment only a limited number of regents would have lost contact with active trade, and even of these few would have come from families which had been *rentiers* for more than one generation. As the oligarchy began to close up against outsiders, however, in the last decades of the seventeenth century, the way of life of the regents became increasingly distinct from that of the merchants, their former social peers. They started to form an aristocracy, politically, socially and economically distinct from the rest of Dutch society.

At this point it might be useful to look more closely at the regents before this change took place—when they had not yet become a separate class or caste, but only a political élite still integrated socially and economically with Dutch urban society.

In considering the republican system of the seventeenth century, the points that must be emphasised are that it was not only remarkably free of intolerance, by the standards of the time, but that it was more efficient than other contemporary states, even those with political systems which now seem more rational and more conducive to efficient administration. The absolute monarchies have been praised for their efficiency, and this may have been their *raison d'être*, but the Dutch Republic, on paper so hampered by its federal structure and far-reaching decentralisation, made better use of its resources. Although the

Republic may have been a much-governed country, it was certainly, by seventeenth-century standards, well-governed. Public credit was very high, tax revenue was adequate for the ordinary requirements of government, and even under the pressure of constant warfare state bankruptcy was never in sight. No class was exempt from taxation, and after the middle of the century direct taxes on property were introduced in time of war from which no section of society was exempt. The regents had control over the assessments for these extraordinary taxes, and they may have underestimated their own wealth, but such estimates for members of the oligarchy in the surviving records are certainly not scandalously low—and individual assessments increased over the years.[27]

The system was, of course, far from perfect. The greater part of tax revenue came from indirect imposts, especially on foodstuffs, which not only pressed most heavily on the poorer sections of society but forced up wages, thus helping to undermine the competitiveness of Dutch manufactures in the European market.[28] The regents accepted the direct taxes on wealth but rejected the proposals for a graduated tax on incomes, the so-called *Familie-geld*. (An assessment was made for this tax in 1674, but it was never levied.) Only the necessities of war could bring the regents to accept even a moderate amount of direct taxation—but accept it they did at such times.

It is difficult, and perhaps deceptive, to try to characterise a social group as large and diverse as the regent oligarchy of the towns of Holland. Both extremes are present: the corrupt politician or political boss, intent on his own advantage and a master of intrigue; the conscientious and hard-working regent, inspired by a concept of duty very close to that of service to the state. To the corruption of those regents of Amsterdam who used their inside information to make big profits out of the extension of the city's boundaries during the Truce, can be set such men as C. P. Hooft who opposed them, albeit unsuccessfully, and had a very high ideal of the duty of a regent.[29] Moreover, the very word corruption is a term which must be used with extreme caution in discussing seventeenth-century government—much that appears corrupt can better be understood as socially-accepted augmentation of inadequate official salaries.

More clearly against the public interest than financial corruption was the concentration of all offices of power and profit into the hands of a very limited group of families. Though a family had usually gained a place in the regent élite in the first place through the enterprise and

financial success of one of its members, there was of course no guarantee
that succeeding generations would produce men of ability or even
competence. As long as the oligarchies were kept in a fluid state, the
influx of new men—marked by business sense, strength of character,
or professional expertise (particularly in law)—ensured a remarkably
high level of administrative competence. Even in the case of established
families, the lack of any criteria of choice other than birth for entry into
the town government was compensated for to some degree by the
professional training for government which the scions of these established families had undergone. This training was rudimentary—a
degree in law at the university of Leiden, some years as a practising
advocate before the Court of Holland, employment in some more or
less important post in the town administration—but it was more than
was enjoyed by any but professional civil servants in other countries.

The 'True Freedom' of the regents was in part at least negative—
defined only in opposition to the power of the stadhouder. The regents
believed—or those represented by the propagandists and theorists of
the States-party believed—that the Revolt had been fought to protect
urban and provincial liberties, and that religious persecution of the
protestants was only one form taken by the Spanish attack on Dutch
liberties. 'Freedom' in this sense was the preservation of local and
provincial rights and privileges from arbitrary interference. In practical
terms it meant provincial sovereignty and a high degree of autonomy
for the towns. This traditionalism and particularism was not a very high
political ideal, but it was preferable to that represented by the princes
of Orange at the time of Frederick Henry, William II and William III.
These had a very limited conception of the good of the state. At best
it was a concern for foreign affairs with little interest for or understanding of the needs of the economy or of society as a whole.

The policies of the regents were of course chiefly designed to further
sectional rather than national interests—or rather they interpreted
national interest to mean the good of the merchant and industrial
classes from which they had sprung, and to which they often still
belonged. However, the furtherance of the interests of these classes did
at least lead directly or indirectly to the prosperity of the community
as a whole in normal circumstances, and thus came much nearer to
answering the needs of the state than the policies of the princes of
Orange. Dedicated to profit and the good of trade, the regents chose
peace when it could be seen as leading to prosperity or the retention of
prosperity; this motivation was at the very least an improvement on the

concept of *gloire* which animated contemporary monarchs and even the princes of Orange all too often. It was also an improvement on the strict protestants' notion of the state as the tool of god.

Of course, the 'Freedom' professed by the regents with so much passion excluded any participation in political life by any but themselves. The oligarchy had very great freedom of action at any time, and during the stadhouderless period there was no power in the Republic which could check any arbitrary exercise of their authority against their subjects. Yet on the whole conditions forced the regents to act with considerable circumspection. The members of the oligarchy were closely integrated into the society in which they lived. In consequence they could not disregard the beliefs and attitudes of their fellow citizens, even in the political field where their separation from the rest of society was greatest. In their administration of day-to-day affairs they were inevitably influenced by the interests and opinions of the wealthier classes in the towns, among which their social life was passed. The regents were a very small group, and socially they were but a part of the Dutch urban upper classes. There were very few regents who were not closely related to families who, although wealthy, were not part of the restricted regent group. So just as the economic policies pursued by the Holland oligarchy reflected the interests of the merchants and industrialists of the towns of the province, so their actions in other respects were determined largely by the views current in those sections of society in which they were rooted.

Moreover, the regents were not only firmly placed within their towns socially, physically also they were in the midst of their fellow citizens. That is, they lived in the towns, surrounded by a usually over-crowded urban population. These closely concentrated masses of people were very volatile and riots of varying seriousness were frequent. Such violence was very disturbing to the propertied classes as a whole, but the threat to the regents was often more direct and dangerous, as they were the obvious targets for the resentment of rioters. The problem of the maintenance of public order was always very present in the seventeenth century, and the Holland regents had only very limited means at their disposal to meet the threat of such disturbances. The police system was rudimentary and was ineffective against serious outbreaks of popular violence; military help from the provincial government could take days to arrive. Thus, in practice the town magistracies were forced to rely on the civic guards, the town militias, to put down riots and to protect life and property. Service in the militia (the *schutterij*) was a duty imposed on all citizens with sufficient money to pay for their equipment—in consequence it was chiefly composed of men from the lower middle classes: artisans, shopkeepers and traders. Such men were very susceptible to influence and pressure from their peers, and so the attitudes displayed by the *schutterij* normally reflected those of wide sections of the town population. In ordinary circumstances they would obey their officers, who were in most towns regents, but at times of crisis they were perfectly capable of taking an independent line. Indeed, in a political system where the mass of the population had no part in government and no institutions to represent its point of view, it is easy to understand that the *schutterij* often set itself up as the spokesman of the ordinary citizens of the town. In general, if the militia was willing to act against a mob then even serious disturbances could be dealt with quite quickly and efficiently; but if, on the other hand, the *schutterij* was disaffected, the magistracy could find itself helpless. The militia did not frequently refuse obedience, but the possibility was always present in the minds of the regents, who consequently were very reluctant to take any action which might disturb the populace so much that they would find the *schutterij* unwilling to act against rioters. The events of the summer of 1672 demonstrate how helpless the regents were when faced with popular violence and the *schutterij* refused to act. In fact, in that year the militia was frequently the centre of Orangist activity and opposition to the regents in power.

Thus the regents were far from being an isolated class in society: their wealth was equalled by many of their fellow citizens, and certain limits were placed on their freedom of action by their need, in the end, of the support and at least tacit consent of a broad section of the propertied classes. The working of these restraints is not easily observed, but their effect is seen in the circumspection in action of the town governments of Holland.

However, if the regents normally conducted the affairs of their towns in accordance with the views and prejudices of the propertied classes, when their interests as individuals were challenged they could, and often did, act in an oppressive and tyrannous manner—particularly if their opponent was of modest means and lacking in powerful friends. They could influence the dispensation of justice in the local court, and could in practice prevent a case from going to appeal. A simple decision of the town government could banish an individual from town and province for life, without the possibility of appeal (or at least of a successful appeal). Redress of grievances was almost impossible against a determined town government.

Such arbitrary actions were not, however, the most distinctive feature of regent rule. The oligarchy of the towns of Holland was most clearly marked by its concern for the economic welfare of the province and the towns it controlled: the town governments can be seen encouraging trade, protecting existing industries and attempting to induce new ones to establish themselves in their towns. Such aims, together with the maintenance of order, were more readily achieved by a reasonable and compromising approach than by too frequent a use of arbitrary powers.

It was, indeed, in a large measure the attitude of the Holland regents which gave the province its deserved reputation of being the most open and tolerant society in Europe. The reasons for their generally tolerant attitude to religion have already been discussed,[30] and similar considerations were at work more generally with regard to ideas and their expression: Holland became a refuge for those who could not easily find tolerance elsewhere, and also became the great centre for book production in Europe—the place where books banned in other countries could be published with impunity. The regents, it is true, were sensitive about contemporary politics, and attempted (not always successfully) to bring their power to bear on those who offended them. The line between politics and religion was particularly difficult to draw, and the ministers of the Reformed Church were frequently in trouble with the town governments over the content of their sermons, exhortations and public prayers. If a minister seriously displeased his magistracy, he could find himself deprived of his salary and even threatened with prosecution. The influence of these ministers over their congregations was felt to be too great for them to be allowed to express their views clearly on political issues—such matters were not considered to be the concern of the general public and popular disturbances were always to be feared.

The publication of pamphlets on political affairs was looked upon with almost equal disfavour, though here the powers of the regents were not as great. There was no effective censorship and authors and publishers could only be prosecuted after the event. Even when books, pamphlets or libels were regarded as seditious it was usually very difficult to trace either the author or the printer. Throughout the seventeenth century every important development in Dutch politics was accompanied by a spate of pamphlets, some of which reached the extreme in crude and vicious polemic—though others included some of the liveliest prose written in Holland during this period—yet few people were successfully prosecuted for seditious publication. It was simply too difficult to track down those responsible, in particular because of the lack of a central or even provincial police organisation in the Republic. Through their jealous guardianship of provincial and urban privileges, and especially jurisdictional autonomy, the regents were in practice effectively ensuring the freedom of the press.

In practice thus, even more than in theory, the Holland of the seventeenth century was an open and tolerant society, which left a remarkable degree of freedom to religious dissenters and to intellectual, religious and political non-conformists. To foreign observers this freedom was so great that it often appeared to them as licence and the consequent diversity as anarchy. Such a freedom of thought and expression, and the lack of serious social sanctions against dissenters, encouraged the growth of a culture of great diversity and vitality. Particularly impressive was the extent of religious toleration, and the liveliness of ecumenical and irenic religious movements. The variety and achievements of the Dutch on the intellectual level will be discussed in more detail later.[31] At the moment it is enough to point out that they were possible because of the peculiarly open nature of Dutch society. The Dutch found that they had to pay a high price in the following century for the decentralisation of political power in the Republic, but the benefits which this system helped to bring about in the seventeenth century should make us consider it with considerable sympathy.

Moreover, the unique nature of Dutch society—considerably decentralised and dominated by merchant groups and commercial interests—when compared to its contemporaries among the European states, was reflected by a unique cultural, and especially artistic, development. This difference and originality was most apparent in painting, because of the social status of its practitioners and the nature of the market for its products. These circumstances meant that art in general was farther removed from the European influences so apparent in literature, where the tone was given by sections of society in much closer contact with the fashions of the rest of Europe. The nature of Dutch literary culture in the seventeenth century and its close connection with the more wealthy and highly educated sections of society will be discussed in the next chapter.

Notes

[1] These lordships included important judicial and police powers, and the revenues they brought their owners were often substantial

[2] See especially H. A. Enno van Gelder, 'De Nederlandsche adel en de opstand tegen Spanje, 1565–1572', *Tijdschrift voor geschiedenis*, jaargang xliii (1928), pp. 1–20, 138–59; 'De Hollandsche adel in den tijd van den opstand', *ibid.*, (1930), pp. 113–50

[3] Cf. T. Wittman, *Les gueux dans les 'bonnes villes' de Flandre, 1577–1584* (Budapest 1969)

[4] The 'great' towns had the privilege that all edicts issued by the States had to have the seals of these towns affixed to them

[5] Most naval officers were professional seamen, but the position of admiral was occasionally given to a noble, e.g. to Jacob van Wassenaer van Obdam in the middle years of the seventeenth century

[6] These latter posts were much sought after, as the holders received a proportion of all the fines they imposed. Also the system of 'composition', whereby an accused could choose to pay a fine to avoid prosecution and the consequent scandal, gave an unscrupulous man considerable opportunities for profit and the honest man a welcome addition to his income. The privilege of appointing to such posts had in many instances been bought by the town governments of the province after the Revolt

[7] The *landsadvokaat*, in fact, grew out of the office of pensionary—the legal adviser and spokesman—of the nobles

[8] In G. A. van Es and G. S. Overdiep, *De Letterkunde der Renaissance en Barok in de zeventiende eeuw* ('s-Hertogenbosch/Brussels 1948) part 1, p. 7 (vol. iv of *Geschiedenis van de Letterkunde der Nederlanden*, ed. F. Baur *et al.*)

[9] This policy was justified in part by the consideration that it would help to keep people away from more suspect places of entertainment—inns and pot-houses

[10] See below, pp. 182–3

[11] A short discussion of this problem can be found in J. Huizinga, *Nederland's beschaving in de 17de eeuw* (Haarlem 1963³), ch. 3; now available in English translation, *Dutch Civilisation in the 17th Century* (London 1968)

[12] The Dutch and Flemish schools approach each other most nearly in low-life paintings, particularly of peasants, by Brouwer and his northern contemporaries

[13] The equivalent of *baljuw*

[14] For Cats, see below, pp. 92–4

[15] Illustrious Schools were founded in a number of Dutch towns. They provided a similar education to that given by the universities, but they could not award degrees

[16] Gijsbert Voet (latinised as Voetius) was born in 1589 and became one of the greatest champions of religious orthodoxy in the Reformed Church, particularly after his appointment to the chair of theology at Utrecht in 1634

[17] Appeal from the decisions of the local courts to the provincial court of appeal was

84 HOLLAND AS TOWN

possible in most civil cases, but normally not in criminal, see S. J. Fockema Andreae, *De Nederlandse staat onder de Republiek* (Verhandeling der Koninklijke Nederlandse Akademie van Wetenschappen, afd. letterkunde, nieuwe reeks—deel lxviii, no. 3) (Amsterdam 1969³), p. 135

[18] See below, pp. 89–97

[19] J. E. Elias, *De vroedschap van Amsterdam* (Haarlem 1903–5), vol. I, p. lxx

[20] J. H. W. Unger, *De regeering van Rotterdam 1328–1892* (Rotterdam 1892), p. 87 (*Bronnen voor de geschiedenis van Rotterdam*, ed. J. H. W. Unger and W. Bezemer, vol. i). There were twenty-four places on the Rotterdam *vroedschap*, but one was vacant at the time of the change

[21] One exception was Dordrecht, where it was argued that the regents were too closely interrelated to enable any to be expelled without alienating the others. Also a Remonstrant majority was left at Gouda, as there were apparently too few sufficiently qualified outsiders to replace the sitting regents; Gouda had not taken much part in Holland's economic boom

[22] 20 years later he petitioned the town government for some small post to provide him with a living; he was placed in the Old Men's Home

[23] For the course of this crisis, see D. J. Roorda, *Partij en factie. De oproeren van 1672 in de steden van Holland en Zeeland, een krachtmeting tussen partijen en facties* (Groningen 1961)

[24] F. J. L. Krämer, *Lettres de Pierre de Groot à Abraham de Wiquefort* (Werken Historisch Genootschap, nr 5, The Hague 1894), pp. 92–3. Pieter de Groot had been a close associate of De Witt and pensionary of Amsterdam, ambassador to Sweden, then pensionary of Rotterdam and ambassador to France. In 1672 on his return from France he was brought into the Rotterdam *vroedschap*, only to become a particular target of popular hate. He lost his office and fled in fear, justifiable, of his life. His comment is thus far from unbiased

[25] A recent article on this subject is H. van Dijk and D. J. Roorda, 'Sociale mobiliteit onder regenten van de Republiek', *Tijdschrift voor geschiedenis*, 84e jaargang (1971), afl. 2, pp. 306–28

[26] For a study of this building and its decoration, see K. Fremantle, *The Baroque Town Hall of Amsterdam* (Utrecht 1959)

[27] In Rotterdam the 'cohiers' for this period show the regents as belonging to the wealthiest group of the town's population though not as a group wealthier than the richest non-regents. The estimates of nearly all regent fortunes rose considerably between 1656 and 1672 in these tax assessments. See also P. W. Klein, 'De heffing van de 100e en 200e penning van het vermogen te Gouda, 1599–1722', *Economisch-Historisch Jaarboek*, 31 (1967), pp. 41–62

[28] C. Wilson, 'Taxation and the decline of Empires, an unfashionable theme', *Bijdragen en Mededelingen van het Historisch Genootschap Utrecht*, vol. 77 (1963), pp. 10–26

[29] For Hooft's views on politics and society, see H. A. Enno van Gelder, *De levensbeschouwing van Cornelis Pietersz. Hooft* (Amsterdam 1918)

[30] See above, p. 33

[31] See below, chapter seven

five

The Poet as Artist

It has been argued in the previous chapter that the Holland regents in the seventeenth century did not form a separate social élite. Similarly, neither were they a cultural élite: particularly in literature they shared the tastes and prejudices of the wealthy and educated in general and the university humanists. Together these groups determined the nature of Dutch literature in the seventeenth century. They produced the theorists who defined the canons of correct taste in literature, and also a large proportion of the poets who were most admired and imitated. In this context the rôle of the regents was very important as their social prestige and influence helped to impose these, in some respect alien, standards on the whole of Dutch literate society.

Dutch literature was unable to match the achievement of Dutch art, nor was it able to produce works as distinct in style and content as those of the craftsman-painters. It is the major task of this chapter to try to explain why this was the case. Two general and related points must first be made: Dutch literary culture was a unity, and the lower-middle and artisan classes accepted the literary standards set by their social superiors. Writers from a wide range of social backgrounds, from the regent Hooft to the tile-maker Oudaan, employed similar styles and concentrated on similar subjects. We shall see in the case of painting that Dutch artists were able to develop an indigenous tradition, in response to the demands of a large popular market, and produce a school of painting which in style and subject clashed with the tastes of the most sophisticated and highly educated sections of Dutch society. No similar development occurred in Dutch literature.

This relative failure of Dutch literature can be explained partly by the lack of a strong indigenous literary tradition, and partly by the social origins of the most influential writers and the nature of the audience for works of literature. In poetry and drama the most powerful examples were set by writers who were chiefly from the highest ranks of society, and these men had all—and this is probably a crucial point—enjoyed the best education which their age could provide. In Holland as in most of Western Europe in the seventeenth century this meant an education firmly centred on the study of the classics, indeed for many theorists this was the only education worthy of the name.[1] In the Latin Schools of the Dutch towns the Latin language was the medium of instruction, and the Latin classical authors the chief object of study. Whether a child was educated by a tutor at home or went to one of these Latin Schools, the Latin language would be the language of his education, and much of the child's time would be spent reading, writing or declaiming Latin. Greek was only a very subordinate part of the curriculum in the Latin Schools of Holland, and was treated in general as an aid to the understanding of classical Latin literature. Certain concessions were made to the demands of religion, and some religious instruction was given in these schools, but even the catechism was taught and explained in Latin.[2]

Writers who had passed through this educational system were inevitably influenced powerfully by classical literature, and in the Republic the inhibiting effect was stronger than the inspiration. There was no formal instruction under this system even in the writing of Dutch, and certainly no attempt to study Dutch literature. The Dutch had no considerable body of vernacular literature on which they could build, or at least they found it difficult to appreciate its positive qualities. Chambers of rhetoric, local literary associations employing the vernacular, had flourished in the Netherlands, especially in Brabant, in the fifteenth and sixteenth centuries. They had put on plays and held literary competitions, but their function seems to have been very largely festive or ceremonial. By the end of the sixteenth century they were very much in decline, but in any case their contribution to verse was to stress technical virtuosity at the expense of the other elements in poetry. From about the middle of the sixteenth century there was a self-conscious movement among Dutch-speaking writers and intellectuals aimed at the improvement of the Dutch language to make it a better vehicle for literary expression,[3] but they took as their models works in Latin and the more developed vernaculars, French and Italian, of their time. So this lack of any strong indigenous literary tradition, combined with the bias instilled by their education, forced writers back to the classics and to the renaissance-classical literature of France and Italy for their inspiration. By the early seventeenth century, the more talented and sensitive a writer was, the more likely he was to be drawn from his roots in Dutch society by the attraction of the renaissance, whose achievements in literature were so great, particularly in comparison with the poverty of the Dutch tradition. For such talented and well-educated men there already existed a set of aesthetic standards which had been accepted on an international level, especially through the influence of humanism, and it was felt that these had to be imposed on Dutch literature for it to be able to stand comparison with works in French or Italian. Where the vernacular was already well-developed as a literary language, as in France or England, the influence of the classics which spread with the rise of humanism could be absorbed and become fruitful—though even here excessive reliance on classical forms and subjects could very easily stultify the vitality and originality of a literature, as some Italian poetry of the sixteenth century perhaps shows—but in the Republic the lack of a native tradition which was felt worthy to be built upon hampered even the most gifted and individual of writers.

There was no effective challenge to the influence of the renaissance-classical tradition because the rewards available to the successful writer were in terms of prestige rather than money. Dutch painters could and did live on the proceeds from the sale of their paintings, but no writer was able to earn a living from his poetry or plays. All Dutch writers had to compose their works in the time they could spare from the more pressing task of earning a living; even the enormously successful popular playwright Jan Vos confessed that he earned more as a glass-maker than as a writer.[4] In many countries of Europe at this period, writers seem to have been able to live directly or indirectly from their literary talents; such appears at least to have been the case for a small minority, particularly playwrights. Moreover, an aristocratic patron could solve the financial problems for some writers, especially when this patronage opened the way to a lucrative sinecure, or minor public office. Such forms of outdoor relief did not exist in the Republic for writers as such. Vondel, it is true, was given a post in the Amsterdam Loan Bank, but while there he had to work as hard as any other clerk—and one can assume that the town government received full value for the money it paid him. Certainly what sinecures there were were not for writers, unless they came from powerful regent families, and then they would have been given in response to family influence and not as a reward for literary talent. In brief, only the rich could afford to give themselves to writing full-time.

On the other hand, considerable prestige was attached to the writing of poetry and plays in the styles accepted by the cultured élite. If composition of poems was a rich man's hobby, it was also one of the few ways by which those lower in the social scale could bring themselves to the notice of their superiors, and thereby gain markedly in status. Joachim Oudaen, a modest tile-maker, could be on almost familiar terms with a number of regents of his town, Rotterdam, through his poetry and his activities as a zealous Collegiant. His poem on the death of the wife of a burgomaster, Gerard Gael, is an example of the delicate services which could win such social success. Vondel, of course, is another who was able to become a much more important figure within his society through his writings than he could otherwise have hoped to be. In all such cases, however, recognition was achieved by conforming to the artistic and cultural norms of the wealthier and more powerful groups in Dutch society, and these norms were largely determined by the standards of the international aristocratic culture.

Although the playwright might be seen as necessarily aiming at a much broader public than the poet and thus constrained to develop a dramatic form with much greater popular appeal and less strictly tied to classical rules, even here the opportunities and achievements were limited. Bredero, it is true, did write plays reflecting the society in which he lived rather than the classical ideal, and he does seem to have been aware to some extent of the clash between what he wished to say and the classical form in which he felt constrained to say it. He did not, however, carry his rebellion very far, nor was his example followed by later writers. The most popular playwrights conquered large audiences not by freshness of approach or originality of form, but by vulgarising and sensationalising the accepted forms and subjects, as in the case of Jan Vos. Moreover, the total audience for plays in the Republic was small, though its social composition was broad. There could be no mass audience for Dutch plays while there were so few theatres. Until 1658, when a theatre was opened in The Hague, the *Schouwburg* of Amsterdam was the only permanent theatre in the whole of the Republic, and the position hardly improved before the end of the century. The public demand for drama was satisfied by occasional performances by travelling troupes, largely foreign, in temporary accommodation. Even in Amsterdam the *Schouwburg* performances were not very frequent—a couple of times a week for a few months of the year.

In such a situation a healthy native school of drama could hardly be expected to develop. Also, the writer could expect no substantial return for his effort—at least not in financial terms. Usually he would receive no payment at all. Even in this field the writer could only be an amateur, working with a very limited set of possible outlets. The temptation was great to write plays to be read rather than performed. A serious writer would hardly relish the thought of his play being performed once or twice and then, because of the very small numbers of theatres and possible performances, being forgotten. It was much more satisfying to write dramas which were suitable for reading alone or in groups, and to aim them at the cultivated few who could be expected to spend their time in this way, rather than at a mass audience. Here again economic and physical circumstances turned the writer towards the few rather than the many, and encouraged him to turn out imitations of the admired foreign products rather than to develop a form of drama which would appeal to large sections of the Dutch public.

In practice the foreign literature most frequently taken as an example was the French. Italian writers first and the French later had faced the problem of the imitation, or rather emulation, of classical authors and literary forms, and they served as the great exemplars for the rest of Europe in the sixteenth and seventeenth centuries. France was of crucial importance for the Netherlands as the mediator between the Italian literary renaissance and Holland. (Similarly, Dutch literature in the seventeenth century was the medium through which Germany and Scandinavia received the renaissance.[5]) P. C. Hooft was unusual because of the direct influence which Italian poetry had on his work, partly at least through his visit to Italy in his impressionable youth. In general, however, it would be difficult to overestimate the influence which such French writers as Du Bellay, Ronsard and Du Bartas had on Dutch literature. Du Bartas was especially important: not only was he a protestant, but his contemplative verse dealt in a serious manner with religious and moral problems which were to exercise the protestant poets of the Republic.[6]

The influence of the politically and socially dominant minority on Dutch literature was reinforced in the first half of the seventeenth century by the practical example of writers from this very restricted section of Dutch society. Hooft, Vondel, Huygens, Cats and Bredero can, with little fear of dissent, be taken as the outstanding poets of the century, both for the high quality of their works and for their popularity and influence on later writers, and they include three men from regent families. These regent poets can be taken as exemplifying different directions in Dutch writing, and also as illustrating three very distinct types of social and political success.

Pieter Cornelisz. Hooft (1581–1647) was the son of a burgomaster of Amsterdam, C. P. Hooft. The elder Hooft had played an important part in the politics of his day, being one of the leading figures of the generation of regents who had come to power after Amsterdam had gone over to the side of the rebels in 1578. He had kept up the merchant activities on which he had built up his fortune, and was a prominent supporter of broad religious toleration and an enemy of the claims of the Reformed Church to a significant rôle in the political life of the Republic. He was a firm supporter of Oldenbarnevelt and of the 'maxims' on which his policies were based.[7] In his later years he lived to see the triumph of the Contra-remonstrant group in the Amsterdam town government and the *coup* by Prince Maurice in 1618, both of which seemed to signal the defeat of the ideas he held. His son, while sharing his social and political attitudes to a certain extent, was to come to a very different view of the rôle of the stadhouder in the Dutch political system.

The younger Hooft can be taken as an extreme example of a development far from rare among established regent families in that he adopted in his life and work much of the style and the attitudes of the European aristocrat of his day. Not only did he refuse to take up the career of a merchant, he also declined to take part in the political life of Amsterdam, where his father's influence could certainly have ensured him a successful career. Hooft enjoyed a very thorough education, with the stress on the classics, which was completed by a tour of France and Italy. After his return, he declared himself unsuited to the life of a merchant and, in 1606 at a relatively late age for his time, went to the university of Leiden to study law. In 1609 he was appointed *drost*[8] of Muiden, near the border of Holland with Utrecht, being the first non-noble to gain this prestigious post. For the rest of his life he divided his time between the castle at Muiden and Amsterdam. Although the office was important, especially when Holland was threatened with invasion, he seems to have had ample time to devote himself to literature.

Building on the achievements of the writers of the late sixteenth century—in particular Spieghel and Coornhert—and strongly under the impression of his stay in Italy while still a young man, where he had been struck by the self-conscious cultivation of Italian as a language capable of equalling the literary possibilities of Latin and Greek, he dedicated himself to the task of trying to make Dutch as expressive a literary language as the more developed vernaculars of his time, Italian and French. While his greatest contribution to this task must be seen as lying in his historical works in prose which will be discussed later,[9] his plays and lyric poetry alone make him one of the most important and influential figures in Dutch literature.[10] He is the most complete renaissance writer produced by the Dutch, and the difficulties he experienced in attempting to use the precepts and examples of the great writers of the French and Italian renaissance make very clear the problems which faced Dutch writers when they tried to imitate these models. Imitation so easily slipped into a sterile copying of ideas and forms which could only be made to fit the Dutch language and experience with difficulty.

Hooft was particularly susceptible to the lure of the classics because he was as much an intellectual as a poet. Despite the individuality and outstanding quality of his poetry, it was never his chief preoccupation. He admitted himself that his poetry could never become great as he was not prepared to give it sufficient attention. In one of his letters he wrote that he did not put all his efforts into poetry, as those who strove for perfection had to do.[11] One of his main interests seems to have been politics and political theory, though his approach was not that of a systematic thinker. Hooft's political preoccupations can be clearly seen, for example, in one of his most influential plays, *Geeraert van Velsen* (1611), where he is concerned to justify his own attitudes to contemporary politics, though the action of the play is set in the past. Although his plays display his great poetic talents, the combination in Hooft of outstanding literary ability with an overriding concern with the political problems facing Dutch society in the early seventeenth century was only to find a really suitable medium when he turned to the writing of history.

In *Baeto* (1616) Hooft's strengths and weaknesses as a dramatist are clear. This work is again set in the past, on this occasion the legendary past, and is concerned with Baeto, the prince who was thought to have been the founder of the Batavian state. Here again it is the author's political views which are expressed in this highly sophisticated drama of ideas. While the play shows Hooft's fundamental conservatism and rejection of force as a solution to political problems—a significant intellectual position for the son of a revolutionary—there is little conflict, even of ideas, and the characters are little more than vehicles to express the thoughts of their creator. After this point Hooft, deeply disturbed by the crisis of 1618, became yet more involved in the problems of authority and the rôle of force in society and turned to history to work these questions out for himself.

A man of much less poetic talent, but more able to free himself when necessary from the powerful influence of the classical and renaissance tradition and produce a series of poems reflecting the experience and attitudes of a broad section of the Dutch population, was the Zeelander Jacob Cats (1577–1660). He must also be placed in the category of the regent-poets, but his work is a clear illustration that members of the oligarchy, and even those who had reached the highest positions in political life, could still remain in contact with and retain sympathy for the spiritual and intellectual world of the middle ranges of Dutch society.

Cats was born into a Zeeland regent family and received the education that was standard for a child from such a background—first at the Latin School at Zierikzee, then literature and law at the university of Leiden, and finally a doctorate in Roman law from Orléans. He then began to practice law in The Hague, which again was a conventional way for a well-educated son of a regent family to begin his career. In 1603 he became town advocate (pensionary) to the important town of Middelburg in Zeeland, but gave this post up in 1611 to concentrate on reclaiming land in Zeeland–Flanders. At the end of the Truce military necessities required that this land be flooded again, and Cats picked up his public career once more. He was offered a chair in law at Leiden, but preferred to return to Middelburg as pensionary. His political career was to occupy much of the rest of his life: he moved to Dordrecht in Holland as pensionary in 1623, became acting grand pensionary of Holland in 1629–30, and finally grand pensionary from 1636 until his retirement in 1652. Thus he rose to the highest political post open to a citizen of the Dutch Republic, but this success was not due to any peculiar abilities or strength of purpose. He was recommended to the stadhouder Frederick Henry by the very mediocrity of his talents and by his readiness to follow the courses indicated to him by the prince of Orange. Unlike his predecessor, Adriaen Pauw, he was not the man to act as the leader and spokesman of the Holland opposition to the policies of the stadhouder.

Nevertheless, although not a powerful or influential figure, he occupied the highest political office in the Republic for 16 years, and in terms of his career had made a success of his life. Yet his nature, as revealed by his verse, remained rooted essentially in the attitudes and ideas of the Dutch middle classes. He was an essentially ordinary man in nearly all senses of the term, and there was certainly, in complete contrast to Hooft, no aristocratic style to him. Especially in his early years, he made some bows to the classical and renaissance literary tradition, but his lyric poetry is not the reason he is remembered. His early pastoral verse is clearly set in the Zeeland countryside, and the characters with the standard Greek names are Zeeland peasants, so these works reflect the least classical elements in contemporary Italian pastoral. The work most typical of Cats, however, is his didactic poetry and emblems.[12] These are also the most interesting of his production, not through their beauty of language or rhythm—Cats was little better than a composer of plodding verse—but for his conscious rejection of the normal poetic language of his time, and for his successful attempt to write in the ordinary language of the people at whom his 'improving' verse was aimed. The greater part of his work—and certainly that part on which his contemporary popularity was based—was heavily didactic, using homely terms and well-known proverbs to drive home simple religious and moral points. He seems to have had little ear for rhythm, and his alexandrines are wearisome in their dull regularity, but compensation is provided by a language which is more alive than that of most of his contemporaries. If the moral lessons seem simplistic and, indeed, shallow to the modern taste, they were certainly more than acceptable to the people from whom he drew his inspiration and to whom he spoke—the middling classes in the Republic, sufficiently educated to read his work and with enough money to buy it, but lacking the high sophistication of the regents or the wealthier groups in society.

Cats was neither a great writer nor a profound thinker, but his works show a certain vitality and even originality which escaped more subtle talents and more profound minds.[13] 'Father' Cats, for so he came to be known, must be seen as one of the most Dutch of all writers active in the Republic during the seventeenth century, and here we have perhaps another hint as to why Dutch literature in this period failed to reach the heights so clearly achieved by Dutch painters. Cats' very lack of feeling for great poetry limited the influence on his work of the renaissance-classical tradition. Moreover, he shared the tastes of the middling classes of the Republic to a remarkable extent, and was further protected from the international literary culture by a Calvinistic emphasis on the didactic function of literature which verged on philistinism. For him the creation of poetry with only aesthetic worth would have appeared a sinful waste of talent and energy—his writings were designed to inculcate moral and religious values in the minds and hearts of his readers, not to excite their aesthetic sense. This purpose led him to realise that the normal poetic language of his time was un-suitable for him, and this realisation set him on his very individual path, which marks him off from almost all the other leading writers of the seventeenth century in the Republic.

In contrast to the narrowly-Dutch Cats, Huygens can be seen as the almost perfect representative in Holland of the international, European literary culture, with all its advantages and disadvantages. As secretary to the stadhouder Frederick Henry he also occupied an office which brought him into contact with the most important affairs of state, and he retained this post under William II and returned to it under William III until his death. Particularly under Frederick Henry, the stadhouders' court at which Huygens spent so much of his life attempted to emulate the life and spirit of the monarchical courts of the age, and conse-quently he lived chiefly in a self-consciously aristocratic environment. Also he had had a thorough grounding in classical and renaissance literature, and this left a lasting impression on his intellectual and literary life. Nevertheless, he never became completely the aristocrat he wished and perhaps believed himself to be. He was also a product of Dutch society in its most vital phase and the effect of this background was never entirely erased by his later courtly surroundings. Beneath the courtier, the Dutch burgher remained lively, and can be seen most clearly in his poetry.

Constantijn Huygens (1596–1687) was the son of a jurist and civil servant rather than of a regent in the more precise sense. His father, Christiaan, had been born in Brabant, studied law at Douai, and had practised law in Brussels and served the chancellor of Brabant before becoming secretary to William of Orange in 1578. At his master's death he moved to the secretaryship of the Council of State in the rebel provinces. This post was an important one and meant that the young Huygens was born into a fairly wealthy family, but more important than wealth were the influential connections a man in Christiaan's position was able to maintain. The family lacked the local roots in the North and the urban base of political power which marked the regent group proper, and so Huygens' career would be dependent on his talents and on the strength of his father's connections, especially at the court of the stadhouder.

Huygens was educated at home by private tutors in an almost exaggeratedly renaissance manner. He was born and brought up in The Hague, the most cosmopolitan of all the towns of the Republic, and so his physical surroundings as well as his father's occupation prepared the European orientation of his mind which was to be so clear in his later life. The basis of his education was a very thorough study of Latin and, to a lesser extent, Greek literature, but he also learnt Italian and English—the latter being a somewhat unusual accomplishment which was to make him susceptible later to the influence of contemporary English poetry. In accordance with his family's position in society, Huygens finished his education by studying law at Leiden, and then he practised law for a while at Zierikzee in Zeeland. As was to be expected, considering the office held by his father, Huygens aimed at a public career. However, he could not enter the hard school of town politics, as here regent connections were essential if even a beginning was to be made. The only post in most towns which was open to outsiders was the office of pensionary, and this was usually reserved for professional lawyers. Moreover, this career had limited possibilities as in normal circumstances only two lines of advancement were open to town pensionaries: a very few could, if very able and with very good regent connections, aspire to the post of grand pensionary; otherwise they could hope to gain a seat in the Court of Holland or in the other high provincial court, the High Council. Both these latter bodies had legal rather than political functions, and so Huygens turned to diplomacy where his father's knowledge and influence was more than useful. He was able to travel to England in the entourage of Sir Dudley Carleton (the English ambassador to the Republic) in 1618, and to Venice with François van Aerssen, the Dutch ambassador to that ancient republic. In England his patrons were sufficiently influential to enable him to be presented at court, a shock from which his republican sentiments, such as they were, never entirely recovered.

In 1625 Huygens became secretary to Frederick Henry and subsequently his life centred on the court of the princes of Orange. Here he came into constant contact with what remained of the Dutch nobility, and with diplomats and aristocrats from the monarchical societies outside the Republic. In 1622 he was knighted by James I and ten years later was invested with the order of St Michel by Louis XIII, and these experiences affected both his general attitude to life and his poetry. From early youth he wrote fluently and by choice in French and Latin. His early autobiographical writings were in Latin, and in old age when he looked back on his life he expressed his thoughts in Latin verse (in De vita propria). His correspondence with humanists with European reputations was considerable, and his extraordinary command of languages, the breadth of his classical and renaissance learning, and his

skill in music, reflect his absorption in the European aristocratic culture
—and in this world he was admired particularly for his versatility.

Yet he did not lose contact with his Dutch audience. His poetry was
not easy of access, and he took pride in the fact. He was concerned to
express his ideas and emotions in unusual and striking ways (his interest
in the English metaphysical poets indicates clearly enough his approach
to literature), but there remains much of the seventeenth-century
Dutchman in Huygens. Despite his apparent absorption in the international world of courtiers, aristocrats and the literary culture which
they encouraged, Huygens produced a substantial body of poetry in
Dutch which fitted the tastes and needs of educated Dutchmen, not
least through its seriousness—its didactic and contemplative nature.[14]
He tried to deal with the problems facing Dutch culture and his Dutch
contemporaries in two very important areas: he was concerned to
improve the quality of Dutch as a literary language, and he tried to put
his learning and his poetic ability at the service of Reformed protestantism.

These three figures from the regent group—Hooft, Cats, Huygens—
were almost without question the most important poets writing in
Dutch in the seventeenth century—with the exception, of course, of
Vondel. Despite their elevated position in society, their works were not
simply aimed at their social peers, and much of the importance of their
writings came from their awareness of the general problems facing
Dutch literature and of the cultural requirements of the educated
Dutch. All three were far from typical regents, although they must be
included in the political élite. Hooft and Huygens took no part in town
politics, the importance of which was the distinctive feature of the
Dutch political structure, and they had only a limited involvement in
town life in general. Hooft came from a regent family, but avoided
involvement in Amsterdam politics and finally lived away from the
town for much of the time, retaining contact only with his circle of
intellectuals and literary figures. Huygens lived in The Hague, but this
town was very different in atmosphere from the voting towns, and his
contacts were chiefly among those frequenting the stadhouders' court.
Of the three, only Cats had an intimate experience of town politics
and close contacts with regent and other circles in the voting towns.
Even he was occupied for much of his life with the politics of The
Hague and with his country estate, rather than with the life of the
ordinary regents and the society of the major towns.

Thus all three were exceptional cases, and were further removed from the normal forms of Dutch social life than the mass of the regents. Yet even these peculiarly isolated figures show in their works that they shared many of the themes and preoccupations which can be found in the writings of men from very different social backgrounds: even the style and vocabulary of these patrician figures was the common currency of Dutch poetic expression. Hooft stands farther apart than the other two—he seems much more of a representative renaissance man of letters. In his lyrical poetry in particular, the purely aesthetic response is much more marked even than in Huygens. Both Cats and Huygens, in contrast, with their concern to make their verse a vehicle for Reformed ideas, and in their didactic and even dogmatic tone and purpose, express the problems which faced all the Dutch protestant writers in the seventeenth century.[15]

The impact of the Renaissance on Dutch literature was not only a consequence of the impression made by French and Italian writers and the influence of the regent poets, the renaissance interpretation of classical literature was also spread among intellectuals and the well-educated in general by the humanists, especially those in the universities. Remarkably soon after its foundation in 1574, the university of Leiden became one of the most important centres of humanist learning in Europe. Two of the greatest sixteenth-century humanists, Justus Lipsius and J. J. Scaliger, were drawn successively to Leiden and established there a tradition of classical studies which was to maintain its vitality until the eighteenth century. The prestige of the leading humanists was considerable. Wherever they happened to live and work they were recognised throughout Europe as the interpreters of the intellectual and literary heritage of the ancient world and consequently as the most reliable of literary critics. The influence which the Leiden classicists exercised over Dutch writers is perhaps most clearly illustrated by the career of Heinsius, a pupil of the great Scaliger.

Daniel Heinsius was born in Ghent in 1580, the son of Nicolas Heyns, clerk to the Council of Flanders. In 1583 his family emigrated to Zeeland, and Heinsius received his education at the Latin School in Vlissingen (Flushing), then at the university of Franeker in Friesland where he studied law, and finally he transferred to Leiden in 1598 where he was able to combine further law studies with attending lectures on Greek literature. His interest was soon drawn chiefly to the classics, and he was introduced into Scaliger's circle and began to devote himself to editing and translating classical texts. In 1600 (at the age of 20) he published an edition of Silius Italicus and during the next ten years he produced editions and translations of, among others, Seneca, Virgil, Theocritus, Aristotle and Horace. He became extraordinary professor of poetry in 1603, and in the following few years successively ordinary professor, professor of Greek, and university librarian. In 1613 he was appointed professor of politics and in the same year of history also. Although his academic work is not considered by modern scholars to have been of the highest quality, his contemporary reputation was second to none and his authority immense. His fame was international, and he was appointed Royal Historian by the Swedish crown in 1620. (He was also made Historiographer of Holland in 1627.) As an academic of high repute he was one of the lay commissioners at the Synod of Dordrecht, and in his later years worked on a textual commentary on the New Testament and was involved in the preparation of the official translation of the Bible, the States-Bible, where he was mainly concerned with the New Testament. The last decades of his life were disturbed by acrimonious academic disputes which severely damaged his reputation. One of the most important charges against him was that he was guilty of plagiarism, in particular from the unpublished papers of Scaliger. His fellow professor at Leiden, the Frenchman Claude Saumaise (Salmasius), was especially prominent in these attacks, which were also supported by such eminent scholars as Grotius, Meursius and Vossius. He died in 1655.

What is of more concern to us here, however, is his influence as a poet in the vernacular. The very fact that a member of the élite of humanist academics should have found it worthwhile to write, and indeed publish, poems in Dutch was an event of the first importance for Dutch literature. Earlier Dutch humanists had also written vernacular poetry—one thinks of Van Hout[16]—but the publication of Heinsius' *Emblemata amatoria* (of which only the title was in Latin) in 1605 was nevertheless a landmark, because of the success and immense influence of the work. By putting the weight of his prestige behind Dutch poetry, Heinsius gave it a respectability which it had formerly lacked, and forcefully made the point that the writing of poetry in Dutch was an activity worthy of the time and effort of educated and cultured men—even for those who were steeped in the classics and perfectly capable of writing Latin verse. Such an evaluation of the influence of an academic may seem a scholarly exaggeration, but there can be no doubt that the people who read and wrote poetry—at least until the second half of the seventeenth century—were profoundly influenced by the opinions and tastes of the humanist scholars who enjoyed such considerable prestige in Holland and throughout Europe. Men such as Heinsius who had specialised in the study of classical literature were seen as the representatives not only of the great heritage of Greek and Latin poetry, but also of the great flowering of literature which had taken place in Italy and France in the preceding centuries. At the time, no clear distinctions were made between the writer as literary artist and the writer as scholar: the humanist Baudius, for example, towards the end of the sixteenth century frequently expressed the opinion, as a commonplace, that poetry was nothing without the solidity of scholarship behind it to give it weight and profundity.[17]

Unfortunately, the influence of such men as Heinsius, great as it was, was not entirely beneficial as far as the development of Dutch literature was concerned. They encouraged both the dominance of the classics as models for imitation, and the articulation of rules, chiefly drawn from Latin poetry, to guide composition in the vernacular. In the case of Heinsius, while his example encouraged the acceptance of Dutch as a respectable literary language, it also strengthened the tendency to look for rules applicable to the writing of poetry and to write by rote. Heinsius himself was rather a rhetorician in verse than a true poet,[18] and the influence of his verse was especially unfortunate as far as rhythm was concerned. He contributed largely to the movement towards a stricter application of the rules regarding metre, which the humanists had drawn up on the basis of Latin precepts and examples, to Dutch verse which began to triumph by the 1630s, aided considerably by the enthusiasm of Huygens. This insistence on the strict iambic alexandrine and the strongly marked caesura was clear in Heinsius' practice as well as in his precept, and the controlled regularity of his verse was much easier to imitate than the subtleties which Hooft introduced into his rhythms. Moreover, Hooft's example could hardly be expected to triumph when he himself was so influenced by his literary friends that he felt it necessary to rewrite his poems in a stricter rhythm.

Heinsius, indeed, can be seen as exemplifying many of the fundamental weaknesses which inhibited the development of Dutch poetry in the early seventeenth century. His worship of the classics, which sprang from his education and his professional interests, led him to see Greek and Latin poetry as the only proper models for imitation. Again, his interpretation of the examples provided by antiquity was in terms of rules rather than of spirit. The effect of this somewhat insensitive and pedantic approach was to impose upon Dutch poetry a number of narrowly-defined forms, which were probably completely unsuited to the nature of the Dutch language, and at the very least inhibited experiment and individuality in form, diction and content.

Dutch was especially vulnerable to such influences as the Dutch literary tradition was weak, or at least the writers of the seventeenth century were not aware of any literary achievements in Dutch in the past which they could use as an alternative source of inspiration. In consequence, the forms and modes which had been worked out by poets in the romance languages were seen as the ideal ways of imitating classical literature in the vernacular. French, with its much stronger literary tradition, had the vitality to put up an effective resistance to the technical pedantry of the humanists and was able to develop forms suited to the nature of the language;[19] Dutch was in a much weaker position, and was contorted under the influence of the renaissance by the use of unsuitable models for imitation.

The linguistic reformers of the sixteenth century were followed in their objective of making Dutch a more expressive and flexible literary tool by the poets and scholars of the seventeenth century. In this period Huygens was an outstanding figure. He was especially interested in formulating rules to regulate the use of the language—in spelling as well as in grammar—and in using guidelines derived from classical and renaissance poetry to ensure that Dutch poetry developed in harmony with the rest of Europe, in content, style and metre. It must be admitted that he often went too far in his worship of ancient models, and that his applications of the rules he had helped to formulate lacked flexibility. More than any other it was Huygens who persuaded Hooft to abandon his metrical freedom for a more regular and duller rhythm. He was so persuasive that Hooft, when he prepared his earlier poems for a new edition in 1636, altered them to fit Huygens' rules.[20] Nevertheless, his positive achievement was considerable, based as it was on a wide knowledge of the Dutch language and the richness of the vocabulary hidden in its various dialects. The task of the Dutch language reformers was so great that it is the successes and not the failures which are surprising.

Hooft was also an important figure in this context. He too was aware of the weaknesses of the Dutch language and tried, especially in the last decades of his life, to create a flexible, dignified and expressive Dutch prose. This task involved more than developing a particular style; he felt that the language had to be purified and improved by the judicious expunging of a host of loan words and the invention of new words, based on Dutch roots, to take their place. In this way he tried to create a suitable medium for the noblest of subjects—such as the history of the revolt against Spanish tyranny. His failures, however, are perhaps even more significant than his successes. If even a poet with the talent and sensitivity of Hooft could find the situation of Dutch in the early seventeenth century too much for him, then for lesser writers these difficulties must have been almost crippling. Hooft's lyrical gift is best seen in his earlier work, as later his concern for the improvement of the language—and the influence on him of men with similar preoccupations—led him to adopt a stricter attitude to the imitation of classical verse forms and to lose much of the ease and spontaneity of his earlier poems. This tendency towards an imitation of the superficial aspects of the Latin poets in particular, rather than the emulation of their poetic achievement, led Dutch writers to use metrical forms unsuited to the language and to employ themes which were alien to Dutch society. While literature could not perhaps be expected to achieve that originality of form and content which Dutch painting reached, and while great poetry can come through the use of forms, themes and even images taken over from other authors and traditions, the general quality of Dutch writing remained low as the emphasis was too often put on careful imitation rather than on individual expression. Dutch poets could reproduce mechanically the metre and verse structure of their models; they were in the main unable to reproduce its spirit.

There was, naturally, some resistance to this exaggerated admiration of ancient and romance writers and forms, but this resistance usually came from those who had distinctly limited poetic gifts, or who lacked intellectual distinction. Cats, for example, freed himself to a considerable extent from the trammels of the accepted attitudes to poetry of his time, chiefly because of his desire to carry his moral teachings to as wide an audience as possible—certainly much wider than could have been reached through the medium of the highly-sophisticated renaissance poem. Unfortunately, Cats was unable to transmute his moralising content and popular idiom into poetry: he expressed commonplaces in dull verse. (One senses a reluctance among modern critics to allow Cats any real merit as a writer. The great popularity of his works and his attempt to employ the ordinary language of his time, however, give him great significance for the historian.) Of those writers with more obvious poetic merit, Vondel almost alone showed some awareness of the dangers of too close an imitation of foreign models. In 1650 he warned against too great an artificiality of style and praised the naturalness of Middle-Dutch lyrics—but he continued to regard Du Bartas as the poet most worthy of imitation.[21]

A particularly distinctive feature of Dutch literature in the seventeenth century was its strong religious emphasis. Cats and Huygens were clearly convinced of the necessity of using poetry to spread and reinforce the message of Reformed protestantism. Of the major writers from the regent group, only Hooft appears to have rejected the primacy of religion—his lyrics aim at beauty of form, sound and imagery and not at the edification of his readers, and his historical works are in the *politique* tradition, which regarded the good of the state as the proper object of political action not the propagation of the true religion. His early hero was Henry IV of France who, as a convert to catholicism for political reasons, could hardly be seen as an exemplary figure by ardent protestants.

Although with this exception the regent poets were fully involved in the religious preoccupations so typical of Dutch literature, writers from middle-class and artisan backgrounds were probably in general even more heavily involved in the consideration of moral and religious questions. Two of the more important poets of the first half of the century, Revius and Camphuysen illustrate well the importance of the religious inspiration. Jacobus Revius (1586–1658) was born in Deventer in Overijsel, brought up in Amsterdam, and studied theology at Leiden, then at Franeker, and spent two years at the centres of Huguenot learning in France. On his return he became a minister of the Reformed Church, sharing the religious orthodoxy of Cats and Huygens among the regent poets—he was a militant Contra-remonstrant. His poetry was very largely concerned with religious subjects, and probably helped him to gain the important post of regent of the States-College at Leiden in 1642.[22] Dirk Rafaelsz. Camphuysen (1586–1627) was very different both as a man and as a writer, but the religious impulse was as strong in him as in Revius. He was originally trained as a painter, but then studied theology at Leiden where he became a supporter of the ideas of Arminius. He accepted the post of secretary and tutor in the household of the governor of the castle of Loevestein, where he lived what he later considered a 'worldly' existence, but after he had married and become a teacher in Utrecht he experienced a conversion and became a minister in the Reformed Church of the town, and then at Vleuten nearby. After the triumph of the Contra-remonstrants, Camphuysen came into serious conflict with orthodoxy and was banned from the Republic in 1620. He remained illegally in the Republic at first, then spent some time in East Friesland, and finally spent his last years in Dokkum in Friesland trying to earn his living by trading in cloth. In these difficult years his friends were chiefly among religious radicals, particularly Mennonites and Socinians. His early, worldly, poetry has unfortunately not survived—Camphuysen destroyed it after his rejection of earthly things—but in his later work the religious spirit was dominant, and he saw it as a conscious opposition to the renaissance poets of his time, whom he regarded as worldly. He was particularly original in his rejection of mythological imagery drawn from classical literature, and not only for religious reasons. On linguistic and aesthetic grounds he felt that such importations were unsuited to the Dutch language.[23]

The centrality of religion in the concerns of Dutch writers of whatever background in the first half of the seventeenth century, and the strength of the moral impulse in them, is shown very clearly in the life and works of the man who was probably the greatest poet produced by the Republic in the days of its greatness—Vondel. With Vondel we are concerned with an unusual and perhaps even perverse man; in his change of religion and in his direct involvement in political controversy he differs from all the most important Dutch writers of this period. Nevertheless, despite these differences from his regent fellow poets—and despite a very different social background and way of life—his classical inspiration, worship of the renaissance, and style of poetic diction were essentially the same as those of Hooft or Huygens. The religious impulse is another common factor, and Vondel's work provides the most successful combination of renaissance-classical style and imagery with religious content, both emotional and intellectual, which Holland was able to produce. His work was admired and understood even by those for whom his later religious views were anathema. His style was theirs, and so was the high seriousness of his approach to his art and to his life.

Joost van den Vondel (1587–1679) was born in Cologne of Mennonite parents who had fled from Antwerp when that city was taken by the prince of Parma in 1585. The family moved to the Dutch Republic around 1596, settling first in Utrecht and, a little later, permanently in Amsterdam. Before his arrival in Holland the elder Vondel had been a hat-maker, but very soon after settling in Amsterdam he became a trader in silk and began to prosper. While not becoming rich, at his death in 1608 he owned property valued at about f.50,000—which at the very least suggests a comfortable financial situation.[24] Joost was born too early to benefit as a child from this improvement in the fortunes of his family, and his formal education was minimal—at least in the eyes of his literary contemporaries and his later self. It was only as an adult, and with his literary ambitions as the spur, that he began with much labour to learn Latin and Greek, and to read classical literature in the original, accepting as he did the received opinion of his time that a first-hand knowledge of the classics was the best possible training for the would-be poet. Although he was able to master these languages, and indeed later published translations from Latin, he could never be as fully at ease with them as Huygens and the other poets who had been compelled by the educational ideas of the day to study the classics intensively from a very early age. Vondel's brother, Willem, who was 15 years younger, was enabled by the later prosperity of the family to enjoy the standard formal education of the time. He finished his studies by reading law at Leiden and then taking a doctorate in law at Orléans—an achievement of which Vondel showed himself to be inordinately proud. Vondel himself had only had the education suitable to the son of a prospering but not yet prosperous trader, and his know-ledge was chiefly of the Bible and book-keeping—which one cannot help feeling is a very Dutch combination.

After the death of his father, Vondel helped his mother to carry on the family business, and he took over completely in 1613. During the life of his wife—he married in 1610—the business seems to have been reasonably successful, but after her death in 1635 Vondel appears to have encountered increasing financial difficulties (possibly through the failure of some speculations).[25] He finally gave up business in 1658, when he was given the position of clerk in the Amsterdam Loan Bank through the patronage of one of the burgomasters of the town. This post was no sinecure, as has been thought, but a full-time job which Vondel retained until he was 80, when he retired with full salary. Throughout his life, and particularly in its last phase, Vondel's social position presents a marked contrast to those of the regent poets. While he was never destitute, and may even have enjoyed a modest prosperity before the death of his wife, he was most certainly never wealthy and he spent a good part of his later life in simple, not to say straitened, circumstances. Nevertheless, the differences in social status between him and the more wealthy and influential of his fellow-poets did not prevent the maintenance of close literary contacts between Vondel and the other leading writers of the period. Moreover, his mature literary works show the same renaissance-classical inspiration as those of his social superiors.

Where the difference in social background did show was in his childhood education, and in the style of his early works. Lacking the thorough grounding in the classics enjoyed by such as Hooft or Huygens, his first poetic works were based on the rather uninspiring traditions of the Dutch chambers of rhetoric. Only after his late, conscious and laborious acquisition of a command of the classical languages, together with a knowledge of the literary theories which had grown up around the classical heritage in the preceding centuries, was he in a position to be able to adopt the style, diction and approach which brought him acceptance as a literary equal by his socially more elevated contemporaries. Vondel seems to have felt a certain inferiority because of these early disadvantages—his admiration for Hooft was expressed in rather exaggerated ways, and his pride in his brother's educational achievements (and his need to tell of them) suggests an acute awareness of his own lack of such a formal educational background. Vondel's acquisition of renaissance culture was the result of a conscious and sustained effort, and he did not wear his late-won learning with ease—this characteristic, rather than any difference in stylistic aims or literary ideals, distinguishes him from Hooft and Huygens.

The social gulf between Vondel and the regent poets was exaggerated by his religious convictions. In these he showed a steadfastness and a disregard for his material and social interests which would be wholly admirable, were not his lack of enlightened self-interest almost perverse, and the tactless pugnacity with which he tried to further the cause of his second religion a little unbalanced.

Vondel's parents were Mennonites, and he was brought up in this faith. The Mennonites, like the other protestant nonconformist sects, were viewed with suspicion by the Reformed Church and its champions, though they were not persecuted. The members of this sect could not, officially, hold any public office, though the tolerance of Dutch society was such that the Mennonite refusal to bear arms in the defence of the state was accepted. Similarly, their belief in the sinfulness of swearing oaths was respected and they were allowed to affirm instead, even when taxation was involved. When declarations of wealth for tax purposes were made an oath was usually exacted, but in the case of a Mennonite an affirmation 'on his man's word' was all that was required. Moreover, Vondel, who displayed a high seriousness in all that he did, was a serious Mennonite, becoming deacon of his congregation in 1616.

Thus he was to some extent at least an outsider in Dutch society, with certain social disabilities springing from his religious views and practices, and he had an approach to society and religious experience very specifically different from those of the orthodox members of the Reformed Church. It is an interesting speculation how far this early freedom from the original sin (in an aesthetic sense) of Reformed orthodoxy may have helped Vondel to develop in his work an emotional and religious depth foreign to the poetry of the orthodox didacts, Cats and Huygens, but on the other hand it is not clear that the atmosphere of a pious Mennonite household would be any more conducive to art or literature than that of an orthodox Calvinist.

Yet the difference from the norms of Dutch society which a Mennonite upbringing made almost inevitable was negligible in comparison to that which arose from the momentous change in late middle-age—his conversion to catholicism. Vondel had already started to move away from the beliefs of his youth by the 1620s. At the beginning of this decade he resigned his position as deacon and in the following years became involved in disputes within his community which resulted in his complete estrangement from both his own section of the Mennonites and from the sect as a whole. The chronology of his later religious development is obscure, despite persistent attempts to place his conversion at an early date, until he emerges in the 1640s as a militant Roman Catholic. As far as contemporary Holland was concerned this conversion made Vondel much more of an outsider than he had been as a Mennonite. If the protestant sects were looked upon with some suspicion—especially as areas susceptible to the infection of new and dangerous ideas, such as Socinianism—catholics were still to some extent at least regarded as enemies of the state. Although by the beginning of the 1640s the Eighty Years War was clearly approaching its end, and the fear that the catholics would act as a fifth column to undermine the Republic from within was consequently much less acute than it had been in the earlier years of the great struggle with catholic Spain, the catholics within the Dutch state were nevertheless still in a somewhat anomalous position. The principle of freedom of conscience was firmly established in the Republic—exception being made only for certain beliefs considered to be so horrible that no Christian state could tolerate them, for example Socinianism was equated with atheism and was, therefore, persecuted, though in the true Dutch manner with only sporadic efficiency—and freedom of worship was allowed for the protestant sects. The situation was very different for the catholics. While as a Mennonite Vondel had been able to worship in his own way without disturbance, after he turned catholic he encountered a situation where the exercise of his religion was forbidden by law.

However, the case of the Dutch catholics is one where the tolerant ideas of many of the regents worked together with the peculiar structure of Dutch society to create a greater practical freedom than the letter of the law allowed. In practice catholics were able to enjoy the public exercise of their religion through unofficial arrangements with local police officials: they paid a fine or a bribe and in return their services were not broken up by the authorities. This system worked to the benefit of both parties: the catholics found that the law was bent to allow them more or less undisturbed worship, and the *schouten* and *baljuwen* found these regular compositions a very welcome augmentation of their incomes.

A religious outsider and the social inferior of the regent poets, Vondel shared not only the renaissance-classical ideals of the regent group but also their political attitudes. To put the matter more precisely: Vondel was a fervent supporter of the Republicans in politics and in this loyalty he was in harmony with an important group of regents in his home town of Amsterdam. It is worth remarking, however, that although Vondel took his political ideas from such regents, he did not take them from the regent poets, Hooft, Cats and Huygens, all of whom were supporters of the house of Orange—though each in a distinctive manner. Vondel's position in society kept him, of course, from an active rôle in the political life of the Republic, but his interest in the problems facing Dutch society on the political plane was always lively and his influence as a polemicist was probably considerable.

His views were, naturally enough, not original, being in essence one-sided support for the republican idea and the tradition which had grown up around it, a tradition which stretched from the supporters of Oldenbarnevelt in the crisis of 1617–18 to the States-party of the days of Johan de Witt. During his own lifetime Vondel saw both of these men, Oldenbarnevelt and De Witt, pay with their lives for the republican idea they represented and he himself supported. Probably the most notable of Vondel's works directly inspired by the political conflicts of the century was the drama *Palamedes* which he published in 1625—after Prince Maurice was safely dead and the more tolerant and flexible Frederick Henry had become stadhouder. As the subtitle, *Murdered Innocence*, suggests this work was a full-blooded attack on the memory of Maurice. Under the transparent pretence of dealing with an episode from the Trojan War, in this play Vondel dealt with the conflicts which had arisen during the Truce and the execution of Olden-barnevelt. He placed all the blame for the tragedy on Prince Maurice, and on the machinations of the fanatically-orthodox ministers of the Reformed Church, who by their interference in affairs of state had dis-turbed the internal peace of the land and brought the great leader and benefactor of the Republic to the scaffold. This work maintained its political relevance and power to arouse strong emotions until well into the second half of the century, as the incident in 1665, when its per-formance provoked a minister to attack the government of De Witt in a sermon, illustrates.[26]

Vondel's admiration for the Holland regents, and especially those of Amsterdam, remained with him throughout his life, and his distrust of the princes of Orange was only interrupted by a decade of admira-tion for Frederick Henry—in whom he was for a time prepared, some-what unrealistically, to recognise the perfect prince, a ruler tolerant and impartial at home and successful in warfare against the country's enemies. The attacks on Maurice were matched by similar sallies against William II; and his lamentations over what he considered the judicial murder of Oldenbarnevelt were paralleled later by those over the actual murder of Johan de Witt and his brother.

Vondel conscientiously absorbed the culture of the humanists and the literary values spread by the patricians who set the tone in Holland, but he was able to use what he had learnt for his own ends. Like Hooft and Huygens, he was not a professional writer, in the sense that he earned practically nothing from his writing, but he differed from them strikingly in the overt seriousness with which he approached his poetry. Whereas both Hooft and Huygens accepted the conventions of an aristocratic culture which required that the poet should at least appear to be a *dilettante* and disclaim any serious intent in his work (which is not to say that neither of them in fact took their writing seriously), Vondel shared the culture but remained sufficiently himself to avoid this affectation. Perhaps in part as a consequence of his upbringing among industrious shopkeepers and small tradesmen, Vondel could not have contemplated spending much time or energy on anything he could not openly declare to be worthy of a serious man's attention. Certainly in every phase of his work from his plays on political themes and his political polemics, through his didactic verse—one thinks especially of that remarkable work *Bespiegeling van God en Godsdienst* (Contempla-tion of God and Religion) of 1662 in which he attacked Spinoza's concept of god—to his late religious plays, Vondel maintained an intense and almost humourless seriousness of purpose, which is perhaps less immediately attractive than the lofty playfulness of aristocrats such as Hooft, but which cannot fail to inspire admiration, mingled with not a little awe.

Vondel's *oeuvre* is indeed massively impressive, not least because of the sheer amount of his literary production. Also he is remarkable for his command of so many literary forms: lyric, didactic, pastoral and contemplative verse, plus verse drama. (Though it should be noted that Vondel's plays show a lack of stage sense. He was not a great dramatist, in the sense that his plays are better read than performed on the stage; their interest and value lie in the greatness of the poetry and its effect, even dramatic, on the reader.)

Indeed, despite the variety of his writings, his verse dramas must be seen as his greatest achievement. Excluding translations, he wrote over 20 plays, most of them with subjects drawn from the Bible and concerned with religious and moral problems. From *Het Pascha ofte de Verlossing Israels wt Egypten* (The Passover or the Delivery of Israel out of Egypt) of 1610 to *Noah of Ondergang der eerste wereld* (Noah or the Fall of the First World) of 1667, these religious dramas form the most important single element in his literary output. His concentration both on drama and on religious subjects increased after his conversion to catholicism, reaching an extraordinary peak in his old age after 1660. If it is necessary to pick out a single work as his greatest it would probably be *Lucifer* (1654) in which he dealt with similar problems to those faced by Milton in his *Paradise Lost*. Some of his plays had, of course, contemporary political significance, as has already been seen with *Palamedes*, though it has recently been questioned whether *Adonias* (1661), *Batavische Gebroeders* (Batavian Brothers) and *Faëton* of 1663 were chiefly concerned with the stadhoudership problem which was so real an issue in public debate at the time these plays were written.[27] In any event, Vondel's ability to present poetically so many profound political and religious problems with such notable success demands respect. No other Dutch author approaches his variety and solidity of achievement.

While this religious preoccupation was an outstanding characteristic of Dutch poetry, it must be emphasised that this is not evidence for the strength of any specifically Reformed influence on Dutch literary culture. The greatest expression of religious purpose came from Vondel in his later, militant catholic years and, as far as protestant writing is concerned, much of the best in both lyric and contemplative poetry came from writers who were not orthodox members of the Reformed Church—for example, Hooft, Camphuysen, Oudaen and Brandt. There were many religiously orthodox poets—Huygens, Cats, Revius, Dullaert—but they did not dominate Dutch writing, nor did they include many of the greatest writers.

The population of the Republic was small, compared with France, the Empire and even England, and so the audience available for writers employing Dutch was limited. On the other hand there is evidence to suggest that this relatively small population was unusually literate by the standards of the time. This can only be a suggestion as the evidence available is very limited, crude and of uncertain significance. One way of assessing the literacy of a given population is to discover the proportion who could sign their names rather than making a mark, the latter being clearly illiterate. Here again, however, there is little evidence, and in any case it remains uncertain how many of those who were able to sign their names were able to read and write with any facility. A study of the public betrothal acts in Amsterdam gave the following figures: in 1630 of members of the Reformed Church 43 per cent of the men and 68 per cent of the women were unable to sign their names; for the non-Reformed the figures were 25 per cent for the men and 53 per cent for the women. In 1660 39 per cent of the men and 66 per cent of the women from the Reformed Church made a mark, while in the non-Reformed group only 19 per cent of the men and 48 per cent of the women were unable to sign their names.[28] How typical these figures are for the Republic, or even Holland, as a whole it is impossible to say: there is evidence to suggest that the situation may have been very similar in the towns and the economically-diversified areas outside, while the purely agricultural areas had a higher level of illiteracy. The connection between types of employment and literacy may in part explain the high rate of illiteracy among women, while the surprisingly high literacy of the non-Reformed group as compared to the members of the Reformed Church may be a reflection of the social composition of the protestant sects, with a relatively small following from the lowest paid classes but attractive to such groups as artisans and skilled workers with some need for the basic skill of literacy.

Given such a relatively high rate of literacy, there must have been, potentially at least, a large reading public, but there is extremely little evidence as to who read what. With editions rarely exceeding 3,000 copies most books published could easily have been absorbed by a very small section of the population and so a study of titles published does not help much in finding out the extent and nature of popular reading. At times of tension, in 1618, 1650 and especially 1672, it is clear that there was a large market for political pamphlets; similarly, religious controversies could also produce a spate of publications aimed at, and presumably read by, a large audience. In the field of literature there seems to have been a ready market for didactic religious verse, indeed it has been said that most Dutch homes, if they possessed books at all, had only the Bible and the works of Cats. Whether or not this is literally true, it may well be far from misleading as to the general Dutch taste in books, though the demand for technical works, such as maps and charts, should not be underestimated in such a developed and diversified economy as the Dutch.

The existence of this public, however, did not lead to the development of a successful popular literature combining the general accessibility of Cats' verse with the higher literary qualities of such as Hooft and Vondel. The major writer who most nearly achieved the creation of a distinctive and popular Dutch literature was Gerbrant Adriaensz. Bredero (1585–1618). He was born in Amsterdam in a family whose origins were rather obscure, but which achieved a comfortable position in society. He was brought up in the expanding Amsterdam of the last decade of the sixteenth century and was trained as a painter. Perhaps surprisingly, he worked in the *atelier* of Francesco Badens, an Italianate painter and not one of the artists most in the Dutch tradition which was to achieve so much in the later years of the century. This training suggests that his family's position was not very elevated, and certainly Bredero's education was very different from that of most of the other leading Dutch writers of the period. In particular he had no command of the classical languages, and his only contact with the literature of antiquity seems to have been through translations. He did, however, have a reasonably good knowledge of French, and his general education does not appear to have been neglected. Nevertheless, the basis of his literary and intellectual experience was very different from that of Hooft or Huygens, steeped as they were in Latin and Greek from a very early age, or even of Vondel, who acquired his considerable classical learning as an adult. There is even a hint in Bredero's work of a certain antagonism to the continuous praise and imitation of classical models. In his preface to the *Spanish Brabander* (1618), one of his last works, he makes a point of proclaiming that this play does not 'smell of Greek thyme/Nor of Roman herbs' but of Dutch flowers.[29] (In fact, '. . . na 't gebloemt/Van Hollandt klein', a reminder that much that is considered specifically Dutch is rather specific to Holland—or even, as often with Bredero, to Amsterdam. A few lines later he refers to his work as *Amsterdams*.)

This emphasis on the Dutchness of his writing brings out the essence of Bredero's individuality as a poet and playwright, and gives the key to his freedom from many of the renaissance inhibitions which afflicted so many even of his gifted contemporaries. Bredero was brought up and lived his life in the middle of Amsterdam, and all of his literary work reveals the strength of the Amsterdammer in him. The everyday language of the people of this booming town is evident in his writings, particularly in the farces, and indeed it is clear that his intimate experience of the life of Amsterdam in its most vital period is the inspiration of his best work. Like Cats, Bredero drew on what was most typical, and most Dutch, in his society; and used as the raw material for his plays the lives, opinions and language of the middle and lower middle classes in Amsterdam. On the other hand his poetry and plays reach a much higher level of artistic achievement than the dull verse of Cats. Cats was able to make his contact with the people by using the lowest common denominator of response; Bredero incorporated the life of the Amsterdam he knew so well into works of a very high literary quality. Even his lyric poetry is remarkable for its simplicity and its native inspiration—as Knuvelder remarks, 'Bredero did not write the highly-cultivated renaissance poem, he wrote folk poetry.'[30] What is more, this 'folk poetry' must be counted among the greatest lyric achievements in the Dutch language in this or any other period. The popular element in Bredero's writing is even more evident in his comedies and farces on which his lasting reputation chiefly rests.

The realism of Bredero's plays, especially in the shorter farces (for example, the *Farce of the Cow* of 1612), is in marked contrast to the dramatic works of most of his contemporaries. Here we feel there is an immediacy of contact with the life of the Holland towns which is almost completely absent in the more sophisticated and carefully contrived creations of Hooft or Huygens. His freshness and individuality was perhaps possible because he had only a second-hand acquaintance with Latin and Greek literature. The authority of the ancients could not weigh as heavily on him as it did on those whose major experience in literature in their formative years had been the great works of classical antiquity. Moreover, he was also writing before the triumph of the poetic rule-makers in Holland: their period of greatest activity, particularly that of Huygens, came only in the 1620s and '30s, and they became dominant over Dutch poetry only after Bredero's death.

He could not, of course, escape entirely the influence of the classical tradition—the society in which he lived was, at least in its best educated layers, steeped in it—nor would he have wished to do so. Although he showed some signs of resentment at the tyranny of classical models, nevertheless even in his best play, the *Spanish Brabander*, he felt constrained to use the five-act formula, as this was the form a play was supposed to take. To follow this rule he had to pad out his material, and in doing so probably weakened the play in order to fit the theory.[31]

Thus it was possible for an authentic Dutch voice to be heard in the early seventeenth century when the influence of the renaissance on Dutch literature was at its strongest, but no major writer after Bredero was able to follow his example. Even one of the most popular of all Dutch playwrights in the seventeenth century, Jan Vos, although his only language was Dutch and he was a glass-maker by profession, was perfectly content to accept the rules derived from the ancients. His only real break with this great tradition was his bad taste—and even this was accepted, under another name, as a virtue by his contemporaries. Vos wrote extremely bloodthirsty Senecan tragedies which were enormously popular from the first performance of his *Aran and Titus* in 1641. This play caused a sensation, and not only among the uneducated and unsophisticated. It was praised by the great triad Hooft, Huygens and Vondel as well as by the classical scholar Barlaeus (Van Baerle). The reasons for its success, even among such eminent men, are clear—as its humanist admirers said, it was even more horrible than the most frightful of the plays of the Greeks or Romans. Sensationalism, not realism, made Vos popular with both the educated élite and the gallery.

The later part of the seventeenth century can show no writer to match the great figures of the first half of the century. One particularly interesting change is that, as the century progressed, the rôle of the regents in literature became qualitatively much less important. Whereas Dutch literary life had to a great extent been dominated by the patricians, Hooft, Huygens and Cats, in the first half of the century, after the deaths of these poets no major writer emerged from the regent group. The most prominent figures of the later period—De Decker, Brandt, Oudaen—were all from the middle or lower middle classes.

Jeremias de Decker (1609-66) came from a family which emigrated to the Northern Netherlands after the fall of Ostend in 1604. He was born in Dordrecht, but his father moved to Amsterdam soon after Jeremias' birth. There he earned his living as a trader in herbs and spices, and his son followed the same occupation. Neither father nor son were able to become particularly prosperous. Geeraerdt Brandt (1626-85) was born in Amsterdam, the son of a watchmaker, and was first trained to follow the same trade. However, the performance in Amsterdam in 1645 of a play by him in the style of Jan Vos, written the previous year, brought him to the attention of the Leiden professor, Barlaeus. He subsequently married Barlaeus' daughter, after he had studied theology at the Remonstrant seminary in Amsterdam and become a Remonstrant minister. Despite his contemporary reputation as a poet, his most interesting works were his histories, which will be discussed later.[32] Neither was a great poet but both had a depth of religious inspiration which made them typical for their period. In the middle years of the seventeenth century movements for religious renewal, particularly of a radical or ecumenical nature, flourished. Such movements were especially successful among the better-educated sections of the population, and had a surprising influence on young men from regent families. Joachim Oudaen (1628-92) is notable in this respect. He was born at Rijnsburg near Leiden, the son of a baker heavily involved in the Collegiant movement, received a good education at the Latin School at Leiden and in the home of the notable scholar Petrus Scriverius, but he later earned his living as a tile-maker in Rotterdam. Like his father he was a Collegiant, and was led by his religious convictions into lengthy polemics against catholicism, Spinozism and the followers of Hobbes in the Republic. He was a naturally pugnacious man, fervently attached to the cause of the 'True Freedom': he wrote a lament on the murder of the brothers De Witt, and had close contacts with Remonstrant and Republican regents in Rotterdam.

These writers—together with others such as Heiman Dullaert (1636-84) who shared their religious preoccupations and their admiration for Vondel and Huygens—can perhaps best be considered as belonging to a transitional phase in the development of Dutch literature: they were the heirs of the greater poets of the earlier years of the century, and they took these as their models, but even as they wrote new gods were being found. In the last decades of the century the dominant influence on Dutch literature ceased to be the poetry and plays of the renaissance and became the works of French classicism. If the dominance of the renaissance ideals of literature had made the development of a vital and unique Dutch style difficult, the influence of

THE POET AS ARTIST

French classicism was to make the Republic, as far as literature was concerned, a colony of French culture. French styles, and to some extent even the French language, became the only acceptable literary medium for the educated Dutch: the consequence was an even greater gulf between literature and the language and experience of the greater part of Dutch society than had existed in the earlier seventeenth century.

★   ★   ★

From what has already been said it should be clear that for most of the seventeenth century there was no marked cultural cleft in Dutch society, or at least that all those able to read and write shared a common literary culture. If Dutch literature was largely in the renaissance-classical tradition, then this tradition was shared to a greater or lesser extent by all literate people: it was not confined to those who had been able to enjoy the standard, but expensive, humanist education prescribed by the age. At one extreme the semi-aristocrat Hooft may be seen rather as a man of the renaissance than of Holland, yet he wrote by choice in Dutch and, indeed, devoted himself to the task of reforming Dutch prose. Heinsius, the Leiden professor and humanist of European fame, did not disdain to write in Dutch and thus to set the seal of his approval on literature in the vernacular. Huygens, with his European culture and courtly connections, nevertheless saw as his chief literary challenge the creation of a Dutch poetry which would be worthy of comparison with its classical models. The regent Cats was even more firmly committed to communication with his social inferiors, not only through Dutch but through *their* Dutch. Coming from a very different educational background, Vondel saw the conquest of humanist learning as the only way to prepare himself for the fulfilment of his literary vocation; and while Bredero showed some resentment at the dominance of classical models, he too accepted most of the renaissance tradition unquestioningly.

The predominance of the styles and approach characteristic of the late renaissance in literature was unchallenged; it was the only available or conceivable literary culture. Although Latin may have been the most important medium for the transmission of this cultural tradition, outside the academic world it was certainly not the medium for its expression. All sections of society—with the exception of the stadhouders' court with its large foreign element (especially in the 1640s and in the time of William III) and its French orientation—spoke and wrote

116 THE POET AS ARTIST

in Dutch. This literary culture was in the main an import, and in many ways an alien one, but it was given a typically Dutch stamp through the religious inspiration and moral seriousness of nearly all Dutch writers. This was a further element of unity in the Dutch response to literature in this period. Indeed, this religious emphasis has some claim to be the most distinctive Dutch contribution to a cultural tradition which had lost much of its original vitality by the time it reached the Dutch Republic. If the example of Du Bartas is sufficient to remind us that renaissance poetry with a strong religious stamp did not begin with the Dutch, in no literature was it as predominant as in that produced by Holland in the seventeenth century. Even Hooft and Bredero, who are to a certain extent the exceptions to this rule among the leading writers, were too Dutch not to be more than a little affected by the religious impulse, and for Vondel, Huygens and Cats (not to mention the large number of specifically religious poets, led by Camphuysen and Revius) service to their religion was one of their chief motives. If none of the protestant writers reached the greatness of those works which Vondel wrote in the service of catholic apologetics, it was not for lack of sustained and serious effort.

This relative homogeneity of literary culture was to be undermined later in the century, as the developing aristocracies of the Holland towns found the attraction of the French language and French culture too powerful to resist, but for the greater part of the seventeenth century Dutch society as a whole, and not a single section of it alone, accepted and adapted the literary influences coming from abroad. As the extent to which any individual could share in the literary heritage was largely dependent on education, which in turn was largely dependent on social position, this import was spread unevenly through Dutch society, but even those who could only read Dutch were able to play a part in making or enjoying this new literature. For better or worse the rich, but often inhibiting and irrelevant, culture of the renaissance was accepted by the Dutch, as far as literature was concerned, as a society—it was not the province of a small, wealthy and cultivated élite.

It is not surprising, on the other hand, that literature was on the whole dominated and had its nature determined by those classes which could afford the best education, and that, as these classes were also those most open and vulnerable to outside influence, Dutch found it very difficult to escape the trap of imitating foreign works which sprang from very different social systems. That the greatness, and especially the original-ity, of Dutch painting was in a very large measure a consequence of the lack of these powerful influences—dominance by the best educated and thus of foreign styles—will be shown in the following chapter.

Notes

[1] The nature of the education which became the rule after the renaissance is discussed in E. Garin, *L'éducation de l'homme moderne. La pédagogie de la Renaissance (1400–1600)* (Paris 1968), translated from the Italian

[2] See E. J. Kuiper, *De Hollandse 'Schoolordre' van 1625* (Groningen 1958)

[3] See L. van den Branden, *Het streven naar verheerlijking, zuivering en opbouw van het Nederlands in de 16e eeuw* (Ghent 1956)

[4] G. Knuvelder, *Handboek tot de geschiedenis der Nederlandse Letterkunde*, vol. 2 ('s-Hertogenbosch 1967⁴), p. 274

[5] T. Weevers, *Poetry of the Netherlands in its European Context 1170–1930* (London 1960), pp. 65–6

[6] For Du Bartas, cf. R. Morçay and A. Müller, *La Renaissance* (Paris 1960²), p. 381

[7] For the political ideas of Oldenbarnevelt and his supporters, see H. Gerlach, *Het proces tegen Oldenbarnevelt en de 'Maximen in den Staet'* (Haarlem 1965)

[8] A post similar to that of *baljuw*

[9] See below, pp. 191–3

[10] Besides those mentioned in the text, Hooft's chief dramatic and poetic works were: *Granida* (c. 1603–04); *Emblemata amatoria, afbeeldinghen van Minne, Emblemes d'Amour* (1611); *Warenar* (1616); *Gedichten* (1636)

[11] H. W. van Tricht, *P. C. Hooft* (Haarlem 1951), p. 43

[12] Emblems or *emblemata* were works combining both verse and pictorial images. They usually consisted of engraved pictures with a verse or verses illustrating their significance—in Cats' case they always had a very didactic and moralising nature

[13] Among Cats' chief works are: *Sinne- en Minnebeelden* (1618); *Houwelick* (1625); *Trouringh* (1637); and *Twee en tachtigh-jarigh leven* (1659)

[14] Some of Huygens' most notable works are: *Voorhout* (1621); *Zedeprinten* (1623–4); *Hofwijck* (1651); *Trijntje Cornelis* (1653); and *Cluyswerck* (1683)

[15] G. A. van Es and G. S. Overdiep, *De Letterkunde der Renaissance en Barok in de zeventiende eeuw* ('s-Hertogenbosch/Brussels 1948), vol. 1, pp. 7–10

[16] See J. A. van Dorsten, *Poets, Patrons and Professors* (Leiden/London 1962), pp. 36–8

[17] P. L. M. Grootens S. J., *Dominicus Baudius. Een levensschets uit het Leidse humanistenmilieu 1561–1613* (Nijmegen/Utrecht 1942), pp. 31, 38

[18] T. Weevers, *op. cit.*, p. 78

[19] R. Morçay and A. Müller, *op. cit.*, pp. 260–61

[20] G. Knuvelder, *op. cit.*, pp. 198–9; T. Weevers, *op. cit.*, p. 99

[21] G. Brom, *Schilderkunst en litteratuur in de 16e en 17e eeuw* (Utrecht/Antwerp 1957), p. 173

[22] Revius' collected poems were published in 1630 under the title *Over-ysselsche Sangen en Dichten*

[23] H. G. van der Doel, *Daar moet veel strijds gestreden zijn. Dirk Rafaelsz Camphuysen en de contraremonstranten* (Meppel 1967), pp. 74–5. His chief publications were *De Stichtelycke Rymen* (1624) and *Uytbreyding over de Psalmen* (1630)

[24] J. Melles, *Joost van den Vondel. De geschiedensi van zijn leven* (Utrecht 1957), p. 58

[25] Vondel himself blamed the business incompetence of his son, who went bankrupt, but the truth of this claim is more than questionable: J. Melles, *op. cit.*, pp. 141–6

[26] See above, p. 36

[27] A convenient short account of his life and dramatic works can be found in W. A. P. Smit and P. Brachin, *Vondel (1587–1679). Contribution à l'histoire de la tragédie au XVIIe siècle* (Paris 1964)

[28] J. G. van Dillen, *Van rijkdom en regenten. Handboek tot de economische en sociale geschiedenis van Nederland tijdens de Republiek* (The Hague 1970), p. 464

[29] G. Knuvelder, *op. cit.*, p. 159

[30] *Ibid.*, p. 148

[31] *Ibid.*, p. 159

[32] See below, p. 19

six

Painting—the artist as craftsman

Dutch literature was dominated by the example and tastes of a highly cultured élite, steeped in the literature and the values of the ancients and their renaissance emulators. Consequently it suffered from an acute sense of inferiority in face of its great models; the Dutch felt themselves to be a backward country as far as literature was concerned and they, therefore, lacked the self-confidence necessary for innovation. In contrast, the majority of Dutch painters and the greater part of their public were much less impressed, through education or foreign contacts, by the achievements of the rest of Europe in art and literature. They had not enjoyed the humanist education and were much less immediately aware of the classical and renaissance heritage, and were consequently hardly conscious of any inferiority. In part, their horizons were limited: they did not come into frequent contact with the more academic traditions of art which dominated southern Europe, nor were they trained to appreciate them. In part also, however, their independence was fed by the strength of the native tradition in painting. In contrast to literature, where the Dutch had no powerful and recent native achievement to draw on, Dutch painting was the heir of the great Netherlandish school and the Republic thus had no need to feel inferior to any European country in this field of the arts.

Clearly, the greatest cultural achievement—perhaps simply the greatest achievement—of Dutch society in the seventeenth century was the school of painting it produced: a school which was marked by a freshness and originality rarely experienced in the history of art. The works produced by its artists were clearly distinct both in content and style from the art of the rest of contemporary Europe. The argument of this chapter is that the roots of this originality and uniqueness lay in the nature of Dutch seventeenth century society which produced and maintained this school, and specifically in the social position of its artists and in the peculiar nature of the market for paintings. Dutch artists and the greater part of their market came from those areas of

society which possessed a sufficient surplus of money to provide a
group of considerable purchasing power, and yet were low enough
down the social scale to be relatively free from the renaissance-classicist
or French classicist views of art which were common among their
wealthier, better-educated and more highly-cultivated social superiors.
The style and content of Dutch painting in the seventeenth century was
not dictated or determined by the regents or even by the richer merchants, industrialists and *rentiers*, but by the middle levels of society,
including even artisans and the more prosperous peasants.

One of the most important distinctions between painting and
literature at this period in the Republic was that no one could earn a
living from his writing, whereas painters could, and did, live from the
proceeds of their art. As Gerard Brom has put it, '. . . painting was a
job, writing poetry a hobby'.[1] Similarly, the painter in Holland during
the seventeenth century was still regarded in the main as a craftsman,
an artisan, and lacked the prestige of the poet or the playwright. He
was looked upon as such by the rest of society and usually saw himself
in the same light. There was, it is true, a growing tendency among a
small number of painters, under the influence of Italian and French
developments, to regard themselves as artists. These men made demands
for prestige and status, and the styles of their painting reflected those of
their peers in the rest of Europe. These artists have to be considered in a
discussion of Dutch painting in this period, but what is important at
this point is that such self-conscious artists constituted only a very small
fraction of Dutch painters. In fact, most painters still were members of
their craft gild—the St Lucas Gild—and were subject to its regulations.
These varied from town to town, but they dealt in the main with such
matters as the permissible number of apprentices each master was
allowed to accept, and the production of test-pieces by the candidates
for admission as masters of the gild. These rules were framed with the
same intentions as those of the other craft gilds, namely to spread out
the profit available to the craft amongst all its practitioners. Limiting
the number of apprentices prevented a prominent painter from taking
more than his fair share of would-be painters, thus leaving some for his
less able or less well-known colleagues. The number of pupils or
apprentices a painter had was not an unimportant matter—besides the
payment he received from the parents or guardian of the apprentice, the
master was entitled to the proceeds from all work done by the learner
under his direction. Apprentices were particularly useful for the performance of menial tasks and for painting in backgrounds, though their

work might attain some independent value in the later years of their training. However, the strength of the gilds was waning in the seventeenth century, and the craft was losing some of its sense of solidarity. In Amsterdam at least the gild was unable to enforce its monopoly, and many painters worked outside the old system for many years without the gild being able to do anything effective about it. On the whole, however, most painters were gild members. Certainly this was true for the first half of the century, and the situation probably did not change much before the end of the century.

To say that the painter was primarily a craftsman is not to suggest that he saw no aesthetic value in his own work but to emphasise that his main object was to produce works that would sell and give him an income from which he could live. Moreover, he did not produce for a small, highly cultivated élite: his work was aimed at his social equals or immediate superiors—artisans, shopkeepers, small tradesmen, modest merchants. The Dutch painter's market was found in those sections of society where there was some spare money for investment in silverware, furniture or paintings, but which could not be expected to pay the prices current for the paintings of the Italian and Flemish masters. Thus the prices expected, and paid, for paintings were on the whole very modest. The prices we know fashionable artists could demand for their work—Rembrandt at the peak of his popularity, Gerrit Dou, Govert Flinck—are very misleading for the general level of prices for paintings. Such heights could be obtained only if the buyer came from the very wealthy sections of society. The prices paid for paintings in Holland were normally very low indeed, and reflect the craft nature of the occupation—they were determined by the cost of the material used as a base plus the cost of the paint, plus a little extra to give the painter his profit.

Towards the middle of the century the widow of a Rotterdam art dealer died, and the subsequent sale of her possessions gives some idea of the prices paintings fetched at that time. One lot of 180 paintings was sold for f.357 7st., another of 21 paintings for f.92–, and one picture fetched f.30–. Such low prices as these were not exceptional. In 1641 a certain Leendert Hendricksz ordered 13 paintings from Isaack van Ostade for which he was to pay f.27– in all. However small the paintings may have been, and however cheap the materials used, a little over f.2– a piece would hardly leave the artist with a great deal of profit for himself. Jan Steen was frequently in financial difficulties, and in 1660 he found it necessary to borrow f.450–. The interest to be paid on this loan in the first year was f.27-, and Steen arranged to pay this sum by painting three portraits for his creditor.[2] (The following wage-rates should give some idea of the contemporary value of money for comparison: in the middle of the seventeenth century a weaver in Leiden could expect to earn about f.7- a week, a fisherman on a herringboat f.5–6– a week, and in Amsterdam a skilled worker f.6–8– weekly and a shipscarpenter f.12– a week in summer towards the end of the century.[3])

A fine example of the commercial and quantitative attitude to painting is provided by a contract entered into by the painter of seascapes, Jan Porcellis, in 1615. Porcellis agreed to paint ships and seascapes on 40 boards supplied to him by an Antwerp cooper, Adriaan Delen. The latter was to provide him with the necessary paints, advance him f.30-, and pay him f.15- a week while he was working on the paintings. Porcellis agreed to provide two finished pictures each week which Delen would sell for their mutual profit, after subtracting f.40- for paints and f.160- for other materials and frames. Delen had also to provide a pupil for the 20 week period involved to aid Porcellis with the work.[4] Prices such as these, together with such business-like attitudes, left little room for an unreliable inspiration, and inhibited radical innovation. The painter was clearly seen as a skilled worker delivering a product for which there was a calculable market, and the works provided would have to answer the expectations of both the dealer and the public. Mass taste with regard to art is more conservative than that of a small, wealthy élite, at least given the limited advertising techniques available in the seventeenth century. Thus in the Republic, where painters were aiming at large sales at relatively low profit margins, changes in style or subject were likely to take place more gradually than in countries where the nature of the art produced was determined by an élite. Individual variations could only be made if they remained within the accepted form—the subject and its general treatment would have to conform to popular expectations. In this instance Porcellis could paint whatever ships and whatever seascapes he liked, but he would have to paint these subjects and paint them in the style that had come to be associated with his name.

The Dutch painter worked with both eyes firmly on the market, and the market he was chiefly concerned with consisted of the middle- and lower-middle classes, who had money to spare but not a great deal. In consequence both the subject matter and the treatment of the paintings were designed to appeal to the tastes of these classes and to answer their requirements. These tastes and expectations of what a painting should be were quite different from those of the cultivated élite, who had their gaze steadily directed towards the south as far as the standards by which they judged the arts were concerned. The clear differences within Dutch society as regards attitudes to the arts and taste in paintings are made particularly obvious by a consideration of the stadhouders and their court.

Few of the princes of Orange were notable for their interest in or knowledge of the arts, but where such interests are evident their tastes are aligned with those dominant in the international courtly culture of the period, with a marked French bias. If the language of the court was French, however, its taste in painting was for the greater part of the century directed towards the work of the great Flemish masters.

Prince Maurice showed little interest in the arts, although he did order a series of 23 portraits of notable captains of his army from Jan van Ravesteyn. Also Michiel van Mierevelt painted a number of portraits for him. If he was no great patron, Maurice at least showed that he had in common with the rest of his countrymen a particular liking for the portrait—that such paintings were the only ones he showed any interest for brings him even closer to the tastes of many other Dutchmen of his time. This situation changed almost completely when Frederick Henry became stadhouder. Not only did he systematically build up his power in the Republic until it approached that of many reigning princes, but he also tried to give his court some of the magnificence of those of contemporary monarchs. The French court was his chief model, but he was also influenced by the English court under the art-collector Charles I, especially in his choice of artists and styles in painting.

Moreover, Frederick Henry had the financial resources to set himself up as a patron of the arts on an almost royal scale. Maurice's death had brought the inheritance from William the Silent together into his hands, and he also derived a far-from-inconsiderable income from his various offices within the Republic, especially from his position as captain-general of the army. In practice, he probably had more money to spend on his artistic fancies than many ruling princes, although his resources could not compare with those of the French or English royal houses. What is perhaps more immediately important, he felt the need to use these financial resources to build up his prestige by giving his court a certain monarchical éclat, especially emulating his princely contemporaries in the buildings he commissioned and in the styles used in their decoration. With regard to painting Frederick Henry showed his colours early by commissioning Gerrit Honthorst to paint two pieces for his renovated castle at Honselaarsdijk. Honthorst was the leading figure in the Utrecht school of Italianate painters, had himself studied in Italy, and was thoroughly steeped in the international courtly style. He was admired by Rubens and received commissions from Charles I as well as from Frederick Henry. (It need hardly be added, given such patronage, that he made a considerable amount of money from his painting.) Honthorst's work was very different from that of most of his compatriots, not only in style but also in subject matter. His early works for the stadhouder were mythological pieces—'history' paintings were considered to be the highest and noblest form of art—and he continued to produce similar works for Frederick Henry, together with portraits of the prince's family and friends.[5]

Frederick Henry also gave commissions to Van Dyck, that master of the flattering princely portrait, and to another member of the Utrecht school, Cornelis van Poelenburgh. The latter had, like Honthorst, spent some time in Italy and was a specialist in arcadian landscapes with nymphs.[6] Rembrandt was also able to secure a number of commissions from the court chiefly through the influence with the prince of his secretary, Constantijn Huygens. Huygens regarded Rubens as the perfect painter, but he also had an eye for the merits of his fellow countrymen, especially Rembrandt in his early period and Jan Lievens. Neither of these painters, however, can be regarded as typical products of the Holland school. Certainly Rembrandt was very consciously the creative artist and at this stage in his career—the 1630s—was anxious to win for himself a European reputation. It is typical both of his desire for recognition and of his academic awareness of the accepted conventions of art that he took Rubens as his model for the first two commissioned pieces he painted for the court (a crucifixion and a deposition). He was well paid for this work, but was unable to make a lasting contact with the court—which was perhaps fortunate, for in his paintings for the stadhouder and for Huygens can be seen most clearly the effort Rembrandt was prepared to make to gain recognition by adopting the style of the masters of the international baroque.

Despite this flirtation with a Dutch painter of real individuality, the type of paintings required to enhance Frederick Henry's prestige were better provided by the great Flemings than by even the most Flemish in style of his compatriots. For the decoration of the great hall in the castle of Honselaarsdijk, the stadhouder used Dutch painters, but at a time when Dutch art was reaching the peak of its achievement the list of painters chosen by Frederick Henry is almost startling in its unfamiliarity. It is, almost wholly, a catalogue of artistic nonentities, distinguished only by their careful imitation of the Flemings. The architect Van Campen with Christiaen van Couwenburg, Paulus Bor, Moyses Uytenbroeck, Tyman Cracht and Pieter de Grebber produced for this hall Dianas and nymphs in Italianate landscapes.[7] This style was followed, often under the direction of Van Campen, in the other major projects undertaken by Frederick Henry before his death, and was adopted afterwards by his widow, Amalia von Solms, in the Huis ten Bosch. In this enterprise, Amalia aimed to create a fitting monument to her husband's greatness, and for the great allegorical pieces which were to decorate it she almost inevitably looked south. The direction was given to Jacob Jordaens and he was aided by no less than five painters from Brabant: Gerard Seghers, Thomas Willebroorts, De Crayer, Gonsales Coques and Van Thulden. The seven artists from the Republic who were also to take part in this great task present us, apart from Honthorst and Lievens, with the list of unfamiliar names which we have come to expect—Soutman, De Grebber, Cesar van Everdinghen, Bleeker and Claes Pietersz.[8] By this time the coming of peace between the Republic and Spain had made it more generally acceptable to commission Flemish painters, and this change allowed the 'southern' taste of the court full rein. Certainly the divergence between the art favoured by the stadhouder's court and the distinctive style of the Dutch school could hardly be more dramatically exemplified than by that monument to Frederick Henry, the Huis ten Bosch.

The court was, of course, not alone in the Republic in preferring the art of the international baroque. As the mention of Huygens might suggest, this taste for the Flemish and Italian styles and later for the academic classicism of the French was shared by the educated élite in the Republic. It is clear that those sections of society which accepted the literary culture sanctioned by classical tradition in its renaissance interpretation would also tend to favour those styles in art which were most closely in line with their literary tastes. Moreover, the experiences of these people in literature had accustomed them to look south for their cultural models. Thus they did not simply expect Dutch painting to suit the rules transmitted from the south in general terms; they were more specific and expected Dutch painters to adopt styles made fashionable by the Italian and Flemish masters.

The greater Dutch writers of the century were clearly out of touch with native developments in painting. They were, for one thing, chiefly of an earlier generation than the best painters. All the outstanding poets were born in the last decades of the sixteenth century—Vondel, Huygens, Hooft, Cats—and were already producing important work in the first three decades of the seventeenth. The great Dutch painters were, almost without exception, born after the turn of the century, and the great innovations of the Dutch School came in the middle decades of the seventeenth century. Thus, the poets were already established figures with fairly fixed opinions when Dutch painting was beginning to produce its first masterpieces. Vondel provides a telling example of the attitudes of these writers to painting. He was, after all, from a fairly humble background and had only acquired his humanist-classical learning as an adult. He had, however, taken in the academic prejudices of the late renaissance along with his literary ideas, and he maintained them with the firmness of the convert. As late as 1648 he was still able to regard Pieter Lastman as one of the more modern of Dutch painters—he was after all a history painter, and in Vondel's youth his opposition to the more egregious excesses of Mannerism could have been experienced as fresh and exciting. By the middle of the century, however, his work had been eclipsed by the real breakthrough of the Dutch School. The history painters were always most likely to win the praise of the poets, as it was for the latter an accepted dogma that the worth of a painting was, in the first instance, determined by the nobility of its subject. Landscapes, still-life, genre, might be well painted, but great art had to concern itself with great subjects. History and religious paintings were for the poets the peak of artistic achievement.

Thus it is hardly surprising that when Dutch writers expressed their preferences they did not choose painters who were typical of the Dutch School. Hooft favoured Sandrart, Cats Mytens, and Huygens Hanneman (what a catalogue of mediocrity!). All admired Miereveld.[9] Huygens saw Rubens as the greatest of all contemporary artists. He especially favoured his more sensational pieces, showing in a restrained manner a similar aberration of taste to that of those humanists who had admired the crude and exaggerated effects of Jan Vos.[10] It can hardly be coincidental that it is precisely in those pieces which he prepared for the stadhouder—through the mediation of Huygens—that Rembrandt shows himself at his most violent and least subtle. The undramatic nature of the paintings of the Dutch school can hardly have recommended them to men of such tastes, who seem to have looked always for powerful and immediate emotional effects or overt moral statements.

More particularly, the writers cannot be expected to have had much sympathy with or even understanding of the realism so characteristic of Dutch art. Even in the most romantic and imaginative of the painters of the Dutch School, Jacob van Ruisdael, the landscape though not a simple reproduction of an existing view looked as though it was; and the most composite of De Witte's churches appeared to be an actual building. Many Dutch painters, of course, were content to reproduce actual scenes and interiors. Such a conception of art could offer little to a poet such as Vondel who, as Brom remarks, could not mention a waterfall without first consulting Virgil to discover what a waterfall should look like.[11] The Dutch poets expected paintings, if they were to be considered true works of art, to express noble ideas or to preserve the memory of splendid deeds. This approach led naturally to a theoretical and practical preference for history and religious paintings, though Calvinist influences may have weakened the position of the latter.

There was a certain uneasiness in Reformed thought with regard to religious painting. Not that such works were formally banned by the Reformed Church, but it certainly made no use of them as propaganda as the Catholic Church did, and very few private individuals seem to have preferred such subjects. That there were so very few specialist painters of religious subjects in the Republic would suggest that there was no considerable market for such works. Rembrandt alone among Dutch artists of this century, in this an exception as in so many aspects of his art, devoted an important proportion of his output to paintings with religious subjects.

The subjects of paintings were very important to educated critics in the seventeenth century, representatives as they were of a literary culture. From this point of view Dutch painting was very deficient: it lacked nobility. The sheer insignificance of the subject matter chosen by Dutch painters surprised many foreign contemporaries, and this attitude was shared by those groups in Dutch society who were most in contact with the general European ideals of culture. Even Rembrandt was attacked towards the end of the century for the lowness of many of his subjects. Sandrart (in his *Teutsche Academie der Edelen Bau-, Bild- und Mahlerey-Künste* of 1675) praised Rembrandt's *chiaroscuro* and glowing colour, but complained not only of his failure to comply with the rules of art, but also because he painted so few subjects from classical poetry, allegories and histories.[12] Similarly, Samuel van Hoogstraten (in his *Inleyding tot de Hooge School der Schilder-Konst anders de Zicht-baere Welt* of 1678), while finding much to praise in Rembrandt's works, criticised him for his lack of taste, shown in the subjects he chose, and for his inclusion of elements which were clearly vulgar and unworthy of the serious painter.[13] Rembrandt's *The Rape of Ganymede* (Dresden Museum) painted as early as 1635 is an example of the aberrations in taste which seem to have upset Hoogstraten. Here the beautiful youth is transformed by Rembrandt into a baby urinating with fear as he is carried away by the eagle.

Such reactions are readily comprehensible when one considers the emphasis placed on the didactic function of all the arts at this time. Such an approach to poetry as well as painting was certainly not confined to the Republic, but it may very well be that the attitude to the arts which was dominant in the Reformed Church encouraged such ideas in Holland. Rigid protestants on the whole would only have felt easy in their consciences about writing poetry if they were able to persuade themselves of the moral utility of such an activity. Similarly, others in the Republic would find it easier to justify both reading and writing poetry against Reformed disapproval if they were able to use a moral line of argument. Given this emphasis on content, and on moral content at that, and this insistence on the utility of art, it is clear that most of the paintings produced by the Dutch School could be regarded by educated contemporaries as, at best, pleasant entertainments which ignored the higher purposes of art. At worst they could be seen as frivolous, and as such detrimental to the general moral standards of society.

There was a certain didactic element in Dutch art of the seventeenth century—one thinks especially of the number of apparently straightforward still-lives which on closer inspection reveal themselves to be *memento mori*—but it was a very formalised and conventional didacticism, and cannot be said to have been essential to the nature of many paintings. The real subject matter of the paintings of the Dutch School was the physical world surrounding both the painter and his public. There was little concern with overt commentary on life or allegorical representations of abstract ideas, whether moral or religious. This move towards an immediate reaction to the physical world is seen in its perhaps most extreme form in landscapes and interiors, particularly those where the human element is least important. While much of Dutch art was primarily concerned with man in relation to his environment—in genre, in peasant-pieces, in figures in a landscape—or with individuals in groups or by themselves (in portraits and group-portraits), there was a marked tendency, notably in some of the greatest artists, towards making the landscape or the interior itself more important than any figures which might be included. In the landscapes of Jacob van Ruisdael or Hobbema people are often either totally absent or quite insignificant, and the same could be said for many townscapes or church interiors. The interiors of Dutch houses painted by Pieter de Hoogh always include figures, but it is usually clear that the room and its furnishings are the chief subjects. It could similarly be argued that in many of Cuyp's pictures the real subject is cows in a landscape, with the shepherd or other human figures reduced to mere *staffage*.

Whether the chief subject of Dutch paintings was people, animals or their physical surroundings, the simple, everyday nature of the content prevented them from being properly appreciated by men whose approach to the arts was determined by a humanist education or the tradition of the renaissance. Much more to the taste of such people were the powerful, large-scale works of Rubens, whose subjects were always properly serious and noble. That they also seem to have preferred the Italianate landscapes produced by painters of the Utrecht school to the Dutch scenes provided by such artists as De Koninck, Van Goyen, Salomon van Ruysdael, or the more imaginative but still northern scenes of Jacob van Ruisdael, can perhaps be at least partly explained by a cultural nostalgia for the south. Their reading had given them a prejudice in favour of the southern landscape: the arcadian landscape was the natural background for the adventures of the heroes of the pastoral, and it was such scenes as those described by their favourite poets that they wished to see depicted.

The question arises how strong was the influence of such modes of thinking outside the court of the stadhouders? An inability to appreciate the worth of the paintings of the Dutch School was clearly very closely associated with the renaissance literary culture which has already been described. The leading Dutch poets were so affected by this conventional taste that they had almost no eye for the originality and worth of the native products and looked rather to the south for their models in art as in literature. Moreover, it has been seen that the literary culture which was largely shaped and propagated by these men, but also by the educated élite in general, had found a broad response and wide acceptance in Dutch society in the seventeenth century. The consequence of this success of an aristocratic literary culture seems to have been that the wealthier and better-educated people were the less they were able to appreciate the art of the Dutch School. There are many examples of the rich and the powerful, including those from the regent group, favouring native artists and their products, particularly in the earlier part of the century, but patronage in such cases should not be taken as implying that the regents and the wealthier social groups were unaffected by the criteria of judgement of art evolved by European cultural circles. The situation seems to be that this influence became dominant in the upper regions of society only slowly, and that many regents still shared the artistic taste of the lower regions of Dutch society until well into the second half of the century.

For there were no clear and sharp divisions within Dutch society which coincided with those of artistic taste. There were wide differences of opinion on cultural matters, but the transitions were gradual and, moreover, only in very general terms can they be said to have coincided with the gradual transitions of social status. Just as the enjoyment of a humanist education did not necessarily imply wealth or elevated position in society, so wealth or membership of the regent group did not necessarily imply adherence to the artistic criteria of renaissance classicism. What does, however, seem tolerably clear is that the taste of the wealthier and politically more powerful sections of Dutch society was moving steadily during the seventeenth century towards acceptance of those views on art dominant in educated and cultivated circles in the rest of Europe—at first towards the renaissance-classicist attitude, and then towards the standards set by French classicism. The movement was continuous, if irregular, and it varied notably from town to town.

It is of considerable importance for the nature and development of Dutch painting that this move away from acceptance of the Dutch style affected first and most clearly the commissions given by public bodies. We have seen already that the court of the stadhouders looked to the Utrecht school for its artists or, when given the opportunity, to the painters of the Flemish baroque. The town governments and other public bodies, at least in the first half of the century, showed more interest in the Dutch School—or rather, the Dutch painters could easily answer the demand created by the desire for group portraits of various types: civic guard pieces, and groups of regents. (It should be noted here that the 'regents' of so many Dutch group portraits were not regents at all in the strict sense. The regents proper were the members of the ruling oligarchies in the towns; the regents of the orphanage, of the cloth-hall and so on were the holders of minor, if prestigious posts. They were not usually members of regent families, but came from wealthy and respectable sections of society just outside the regent circle.) The group portrait with its emphasis on the individual and on realistic representation was one of the most typically Dutch of all the specialised types of painting developed during the seventeenth century in the Republic, reflecting as it does the importance of the collegiate method of government and administration in the Dutch system.

By the middle of the century, however, this type of official commission was becoming much less frequent, and the changed attitude of the regents in the demands they made on art was exemplified by the design of the new town hall for Amsterdam and the paintings chosen to decorate it. The building itself was a considerable architectural success: an impressive combination of the Flemish baroque with seventeenth-century Italian classicism, but it had very little contact with any indigenous artistic tradition. When Fremantle remarks, '. . . the Rubensian Baroque of Quellien's sculptural style matched that of Van Campen's decorative scheme, and where his Duquesnoyesque classicism, which seems to have come to the fore at this point in his career, matched the studied classicism of Van Campen's architecture . . .',[14] she is doing more than categorising the dominant styles in the architecture and decoration of the building: whether aware of it or not, she is making it abundantly clear that these styles were imported from abroad and had no roots in any Dutch artistic tradition. Apparently the rulers of Amsterdam by this time, the 1650s, had come to feel a need for a type of propagandist art which could not be provided by the painters of the Dutch School. The Amsterdam regent oligarchy seems to have developed into something approaching an urban aristocracy by the middle of the century—that is, considerably earlier than appears to have been the case in the other important towns of Holland—and it is hardly surprising that this change should have shown itself in official taste in art. The development from the simplicity of the group portrait to the complexity of reference and allegory manifested in the new town hall of Amsterdam is the most striking example of this change in public taste.

In very general terms, the effects of this alienation of the most wealthy and powerful sections of Dutch society from the work of the Dutch School meant that these painters had to look elsewhere for their market. They found the public for their paintings in the middle and lower-middle classes which had not been affected very strongly, if at all, by the criteria of worth in art propagated by the international aristocratic culture of the time, and yet could dispose as a group of a considerable amount of capital. It is true that a number of painters found an answer to this problem by adapting their art to the taste of their wealthiest potential customers. Such a development can be seen in the painters of the Utrecht school and, more generally, in all those Dutch painters who chose to follow Flemish, Italian or French modes in order to conform to the fashions in art prevailing in Europe in their time. This response was not, however, open to many Dutch painters.

In the first place, the baroque or classicist styles required of a painter a wider horizon than most Dutch artists possessed. Most of these painted as they did because this was how they had learnt to paint—they were, it must again be emphasised, craftsmen carrying on the trade they had learnt as apprentices. They were ready to modify their basic approach in response to changes in popular taste, but they were not well equipped for rapid and radical changes of style. They were only imperfectly aware of a wide variety of possible styles and academic traditions and the theories of art behind them. Secondly, to paint in the complex and allegorical style demanded by educated taste required a knowledge, particularly of classical mythology, which they neither possessed nor could easily obtain. Such an art was very much an art for the educated, and learning, particularly if it was to include a knowledge of Latin, was an expensive and time-consuming business, and thus out of the question for more than a small minority of Dutch painters. Moreover, while it was not absolutely necessary to travel outside the Republic in order to study the work of the great painters, past or present, it was certainly a great help to the career of an artist if he had studied or spent some time in Italy. Amsterdam was one of the great markets for art in the seventeenth century, and Rembrandt for one was able to study the works of the great painters of the preceding centuries, chiefly by means of engravings after the masters, without leaving the territory of the Republic. Yet as far as the buyer was concerned, a period in Italy was the stamp of quality for an artist. Throughout the century the painter who had been in Italy could ask, and receive, more for his work than his less-travelled competitors.[15] Such an Italian journey was beyond the resources of most Dutch painters, and this made any move into the world of academic painting an even more difficult and problematical matter.

Again, a move into the cultural world of Flemish and Italian painting would have involved not only a radical change of artistic and intellectual attitudes, it would also have required from the Dutch painter a complete readjustment in his approach to the activity of painting and his ideas about the position of the artist in society. The Dutch painter was a skilled craftsman, like a cabinet-maker; it would not have been easy for him to see himself as an artist, with a similar social prestige to that of a poet. The responses of individuals to a given situation are obviously very different, and just as there were a number of Dutch artists who set themselves to imitating the learned painting of the Flemings and Italians, so there were some who picked up from French and Italian theorists the idea of the exalted rôle and status of the artist and tried to make their lives fit the theory. One of the most notable of these, both for his initial success and later financial failure, is Rembrandt. One of his difficulties was his inability to see himself as a craftsman; another was his refusal to suit his style to the market in his later years. But perhaps even more important in explaining his failure was the unrealistic view he seems to have held as to the position of the artist in society. His chief problem was not that he earned too little—he was from time to time one of the best paid Dutch painters of the century—but he spent too much and unwisely, particularly on his lavish collection of paintings, sculptures and engravings.

Finally, the refusal, conscious or unconscious, of the great majority of Dutch painters to adapt their style to the tastes of the educated élite was made financially possible by the existence of an alternative market, ready to accept the sort of works they were already producing. Moreover, this market had the financial strength to support a large number of painters—if they were prepared to live on a modest income. One of the most noticeable differences between Dutch society and that of the rest of Europe in the seventeenth century was the amount of capital available for all purposes, and the generally wide distribution of this capital through the middling regions of society. The great economic success of the Republic meant that it was a comparatively wealthy society with much spare money available for all types of investment—in trade, industry, land-reclamation, foreign funds. Particularly surprising to foreign observers was the Dutch practice of investing surplus money in plate, furniture and other items for use in, or decoration of, the home. This practice was common in all sections of Dutch society which had any surplus at all—and in Holland this meant a much larger proportion of the population than in any other country. Certainly, the lower-middle and artisan groups had capital to spare for such investments, and it was noted by travellers that even the better-off peasants were able to spend money on paintings.

Paintings were treated in a similar way to furniture or plate—they embellished the home, and they could be expected to keep their value or perhaps even increase it. They were considered a worthwhile investment, even if they were uncertain as a speculation. What surprised foreign observers was not only the fact that people of modest means were prepared to buy paintings, but that they bought so many. Bredius claims that it was not unusual to find 100 or even 200 pictures in a modest household.[16] This tendency to buy large numbers of paintings was encouraged, of course, by their cheapness.[17] Thus on the one hand there was a market for paintings which was large both in the number of potential purchasers and in terms of the number of items each might be expected to purchase. On the other hand, of course, the capital available to each individual buyer within this market was small, especially in comparison with the sort of sums commanded by the princes of Orange, or even to the town regents or the wealthier merchants. The result was a large demand for paintings, but for paintings at low prices.

So the majority of Dutch painters found their purchasers among the less wealthy and less educated sections of Dutch society—chiefly merchants of modest wealth, small traders, shopkeepers and artisans in the towns of Holland. These painters were thus not influenced by the tastes and attitudes towards art common among the wealthier merchants and more aristocratic regents, but were able to develop their traditional styles and approaches in the directions encouraged by the tastes of those at whom their pictures were aimed. Such a situation clearly affected profoundly both the position of the painter within society and the way in which Dutch painting developed.

If one thing is clear about the great majority of Dutch painters it is that they were far from wealthy. Here we must leave out of consideration those artists—a very small minority—who became untypical by adopting a style which accorded with the tastes of the educated élite, by becoming dissatisfied with the status of craftsmen, or by simply becoming fashionable and successful, though remaining broadly within the stylistic range of the Dutch School. The great majority of Dutch painters, although they present a rich variety, remain within a fairly limited range. At the bottom of the scale there was the craftsman producing pictures for the market at very low prices, who must have found it very difficult to make ends meet, particularly as old age approached. The idea of the artist dying in abject poverty may have been a myth of the romantics, but it was certainly not without some basis in fact.

The number of painters who found it expedient to diversify their interests and seek other sources of income besides their art is suggestive. As Dutch painters usually saw themselves as craftsmen rather than as artists—that is, they lacked an exalted idea of their own talents and mission—they were quite prepared to turn their hands to anything which might increase their income. One of the most obvious steps was to turn to art-dealing. In this move the painters were paralleling developments in other crafts. In the expansive phase of the Dutch economy a typical development was for the craftsman to raise himself to the status of merchant by dealing in the raw materials of his trade. Thus the carpenter would become a merchant in wood, the weaver in textiles. Many painters were prepared to follow a similar course, though art-dealing was perhaps less likely to lead to even moderate wealth than most other fields of trade. Examples of the painter/art-dealer are Hendrick Volmarijn and Hendrick du Bois. Floerke suggests that the greater part of the art-trade was in the hands of painters. Art-dealing was the obvious salvation of the painter whose powers were beginning to fade.[18] It would be hard, however, to find an example of a painter who gained even moderate wealth in this way.

Perhaps more typical of the attitude of the Dutch painter towards his art is the frequency with which painters turned to other crafts or occupations, usually to supplement their income from painting but also as a substitute for it. One of the outstanding examples of an artist who turned to another occupation which offered better rewards is Meindert Hobbema. Here we have one of the finest of all Dutch landscapists—outstanding even in this field where the Dutch achievement in the seventeenth century was so impressive—and yet he gave up painting almost completely in his later years after he gained, in 1668, through his marriage to the maidservant of a burgomaster of Amsterdam, the position of wine-gauger in this town. This post gave him a secure income and one which only the most fashionable of painters would have been able to better. An even more striking case is that of Ferdinand Bol who appears to have given up painting altogether after his marriage to a wealthy widow in 1669. It does not seem that he had any inner compulsion to paint, and yet Bol's achievement as an artist was far from negligible even in comparison with the works of his most gifted contemporaries.

More common were the cases of simple diversification, with the aim of obtaining a greater and more secure income than could have been gained by most artists from the sale of their pictures alone. Again these painters were not noticeably sensitive about the social *cachet* of the jobs they tried: Carel van der Pluym, for example, became municipal plumber of Leiden, and many painters tried their hands at running taverns. Even the greatest artists found this connection far from degrading: Jan Steen, himself the son of a brewer, apparently ran a brewery in Delft for a while before opening a tavern in Leiden in 1672. Vermeer's father was an innkeeper as well as a weaver, and the son took over the tavern on his father's death as well as acting as an art-dealer and -valuer. Aert van der Neer also opened a tavern—in Amsterdam in 1659—but this enterprise failed after a couple of years. More successful were Samuel van Hoogstraeten and Philips de Koninck. The former won for himself the enviable office of provost of the mint at Dordrecht, and could afford the time to write about Dutch painting.[19] De Koninck was one of the more financially successful of Dutch painters. His works certainly seem to have sold well and at good prices, but it seems likely that the hostel and the shipping business he owned contributed more to his prosperity.

Some rather untypical cases are worth mentioning, if only for the reflection they cast on more normal situations. The fine painter of seascapes, Jan van de Capelle, was an exception among Dutch painters in that he came from a relatively wealthy family. From an economic point of view he was an industrialist rather than a painter as he ran the dye-works which belonged to his family. At his death he left a sum approaching f.100,000-, a not insignificant fortune for the time. His love of art was expressed through his collection as well as through his own works, and by his death it was one of the finest of the century in the Republic. Lambert Jacobsz of Leeuwarden in Friesland is remarkable as he was a Mennonite preacher as well as a painter and an art-dealer. While it was not unusual for clergy or ministers of the dissenting sects to be involved in crafts or trade, such a combination as this must be almost unique.

In a decidedly eccentric way, Emmanuel de Witte showed how strongly Dutch painters could be attracted by the idea of a steady, assured income. In 1660 he indentured himself to an Amsterdam notary. The terms of the contract were that, in return for an annual income of f.800-, De Witte would deliver all his production to the notary. The contract is a curiosity in itself, but the size of the income which De Witte asked is also significant—f.800- p.a. was a very modest demand on life, being perhaps the equivalent of the income of a reasonably prosperous craftsman/retailer. Such a position in society was probably the peak of most painters' ambitions.

This picture of the social position of the Dutch artist has been drawn largely from our knowledge of the leading painters, most of whom were recognised to be outstanding by contemporaries. If these men were on the whole unable to win very great material rewards from their painting, and had to be content with very little social recognition, the situation of the great majority of painters, with more modest talents, must have placed them yet more firmly in the craftsman *milieu* into which most of them were born.

For the social origins of Dutch painters are as significant as the status and prosperity they were later able to obtain. Two salient points emerge from a study of the social position and jobs of the parents of Dutch painters of the seventeenth century: they occupied, in general, very humble positions in society, and they were very often employed as painters or in closely allied crafts. The father of Gerrit Dou was a Leiden glassmaker and engraver; Saenredam was the son of an engraver and draftsman (and his art clearly shows the influence of this background); and Jacob van Ruisdael's father, Isaack, was a framemaker as well as a painter. More mundane crafts are represented by the father of Adriaen and Isaack van Ostade who was a weaver, and by Vermeer's father who was both a weaver and an innkeeper. The artisan background of these painters is further illustrated by Carel Fabritius who was a carpenter in his youth—indeed the occupation may have given him his surname—while Pieter de Hoogh began his career in an even more humble way: as late as 1653 he appears to have been the servant of a merchant.

The social backgrounds of the Dutch painters of the seventeenth century, and the limited education which they consequently received, meant that they were to a great extent isolated from the artistic fashions dominant in the rest of contemporary Europe. In this respect they present a marked contrast to Dutch writers, and to the leading poets in particular. One great advantage which the painters possessed and the writers did not was that they were able to build on the foundations of a vital indigenous tradition, and they had a well-developed artistic language through which they could articulate this tradition. The poets and playwrights were always conscious of the lack of any strong literary tradition in the Republic, and felt driven to take foreign works as their models. They even lacked confidence in the language which they had to use, and felt constrained to spend a considerable part of their energies in a conscious attempt to make Dutch a language flexible and subtle enough to support a great literature.

The Dutch painters faced no such problems. Firstly, they were the joint heirs—with the artists of the Southern Netherlands—of the great Netherlandish tradition in the visual arts, which was second only to that of Italy in vigour, originality, and sustained achievement. Many of the characteristics which seem at first sight peculiar to the Dutch School of the seventeenth century had their origins in Flemish painting of the previous century. For example, the great development of Dutch landscape painting, and particularly the growth of specialisation in this genre by a large number of painters, and the emergence of a 'pure' landscape without the classical or allegorical elements which marked contemporary French or Italian landscape, was based on the work of those, usually minor, Flemish artists of the sixteenth century who had specialised in producing landscapes in response to a specific demand, both in the Netherlands and in Italy.[20] In general, the contribution of the Netherlandish tradition to the art of the Dutch School, especially through its realism, is too clear to be ignored and helps to explain the confident development in the Republic of a form of art so different from that practised and appreciated in the culturally dominant areas of Europe. Such a confidence and independence would have been impossible without the strength of the great Netherlandish tradition. The art of the Dutch School was the development in a particular direction of one major aspect of the art of Flanders, this direction being decided by the peculiar nature of Dutch society in the seventeenth century. Dutch painters were probably not aware that they were producing anything original, but by working from the basis provided by the tradition they inherited they were able to produce and sustain an independent and essentially original style of artistic expression—in response to the particular demands made upon them by the society in which they lived.

Secondly, the painters had, by the nature of their art, no problem of language. The Dutch poets had to make heroic efforts to adapt fruitfully the experience of their Italian and French masters. Verse forms suited to the romance languages presented almost insuperable obstacles for a poet writing in Dutch. In contrast, Dutch painters, by the evidence of their work, seem to have experienced the very minimum of difficulty in learning from the examples of the Italian masters and in adapting the innovations of foreign contemporaries to their own needs. They were able to take what they could use fruitfully and reject the rest. A clear example of this process is the influence in the Republic of the works of

Adam Helsheimer. This highly original artist developed his style in Italy within the Italian tradition, but became an important influence on many Dutch painters, largely through the intermediary of engravings by Goudt. (At this time the rôle of graphic reproductions in transmitting the influence of painters throughout Europe was of profound importance—the work of most of the great Italian masters was known in the Republic chiefly through such reproductions.) Such stylistic and technical innovations were used to great effect by Dutch painters who remained completely within the Dutch tradition.

Of course, as has already been noted, a number of Dutch painters took a different path, either developing the Netherlandish tradition along the lines laid down by the painters of the Flemish baroque, or imitating the styles flourishing in Italy or France. At least in part they took such courses in response to the artistic requirements of specific social groups—the stadhouders and their courts, and those patricians who prided themselves on sharing the artistic taste of the European aristocratic culture. More important than these painters, few of whom achieved much of artistic note, were the painters within the Republic— indeed largely within the single province of Holland—who built up a style and an approach to art which, based on a strong inherited tradition and accepting selectively those outside influences which could be used with profit, was something specifically new in the history of art. There was, it is clear, a recognisable Dutch style of painting in the seventeenth century, very different in spirit and subject matter from the art of Italy, France or indeed anywhere-else in Europe at the time. Dutch painters were influenced by the work of foreign painters, and Dutch art was appreciated outside the borders of the Republic, but it remains true that such influence was largely limited to techniques, that Rembrandt was most appreciated by foreign contemporaries when he was least Dutch, and that the work of the Dutch School had to wait until the nineteenth century before its great qualities and the magnitude of its achievements began to be justly appreciated.

The essential difference of Dutch art is shown by the inability of art historians to fit it into any of the general categories normally used to describe European art in this period. This terminology simply does not seem to be applicable. The terms 'baroque' and 'classicism' which have been used to discriminate the two great traditions of European art in the Early Modern period (or even to describe the great antitheses in Art itself)[21] fail to include the works produced by the Dutch painters of the seventeenth century. Rembrandt has been claimed, with some justification, for the baroque, but he was untypical and the term can in any case only properly be applied to a part of his total production. Some of his work has also been claimed for classicism,[22] again with some justification. On the whole, however, the theorists of baroque and classicism have evaded the problem posed by Dutch art: it simply does not fit into the schema.

Huizinga when considering the applicability of the term baroque to the Republic found only one artist who fitted properly into this category, the writer Vondel. He continued, 'But for almost all the other expressions or figures our picture of Dutch culture in this time contrasts amazingly strongly with this schema of the Baroque. A landscape by Ruisdael or Van Goyen, a genrepiece by Jan Steen, a Civic Guard piece by Frans Hals or Van der Helst, and the most characteristic work of Rembrandt—all of them breathe a completely different spirit, sound an entirely different note. In its essentials, the Netherlands of the seventeenth century bore only a limited resemblance to contemporary France, Italy or Germany. Neither their rigid style and pretentious gestures nor their great pomp is characteristic of our country.'[23] One can only express one's agreement with these remarks, while adding that Dutch paintings fit in even less well with the norms of classicism, than with those of the baroque.

The reasons for the disparity between the art of the Republic and that dominant in the rest of Europe lie in the social position of the Dutch painter, his function in society, and the nature of the market for which he was working. The Dutch craft painters were to a great extent isolated from the rest of Europe in two ways: physically as they had neither the wish nor the financial resources to travel much outside their own land; and socially, as their origins and their place within Dutch society drastically limited their contact with the cosmopolitan atmosphere of court, intellectual and patrician circles. This isolation, coupled with the strength of the native tradition, helped first to preserve the peculiar virtues of the Netherlandish school and then allowed the growth within the Northern Netherlands of a new and recognisably distinct approach to the visual arts. During the great period of Dutch art—more or less the first three quarters of the seventeenth century—the influence on Dutch painters of the artistic fashions holding sway in southern Europe was minimal. Similarly, the low social status of Dutch painters preserved them from the influence of the cosmopolitan intellectuals with their theory of art, which was the product of a literary and classical culture and was not easily reconciled with the art produced in Holland in the seventeenth century. (The appreciative comment on Rembrandt and Jan Lievens by Constantijn Huygens stands in isolation, both among the leading writers and in Huygens' work. Moreover it does not in itself suggest that Huygens appreciated the great achievements of Dutch art. At the time he made the remark both Rembrandt and Lievens were still producing history paintings in the style of Lastman.)

Dutch writers did suffer from the strength of foreign influence, which notably inhibited the growth of an independent Dutch literature. It has been remarked, with reference to the failure of Bredero's work to lead to a flourishing independent Dutch literature, that the class from which he sprang and of which he was the spokesman had no social power and was consequently unable to produce new forms or spirit in cultural life.[24] The same writer adds, 'And the ruling class became too much an oligarchy alienated from the people, Holland had too little of an own cultural tradition for poets from another sphere to be able to take over from him (Bredero) the development of what was specifically Dutch (*het volkseigene*) and so continue his work.'[25] The history of Dutch painting in the seventeenth century suggests that this is an unsatisfactory explanation of the failure of Dutch literature to build on Bredero's achievement. The finest Dutch art was the work of precisely such a politically impotent section of society. Moreover, the oligarchies in the towns of Holland were for much of the century far from being alienated from the rest of the population. The stress must rather be placed on the strength of the native tradition in painting and its weakness in literature, and the existence of a large popular market for Dutch artists and its absence for writers.

Until late in the century a great part of the socially and politically dominant classes was prepared to accept the works of Dutch painters, even if not to regard them as great art. Only in the last decades of the century, when the regents began to turn away from the rest of Dutch society, and when French influence began to dominate the tastes of the educated, did a theory of art triumph which was inimical to the works of the Dutch School.

The second reason for the distinctive nature of Dutch painting in the seventeenth century is the character of the market for which painters were working. The Republic lacked a monarchy, a powerful and wealthy nobility, and a strong catholic church. While a small number of Dutch painters, by adopting Italian or Flemish modes, could win patronage from the court of the stadhouders, such a path was not open to the vast majority of artists. The princes of Orange were rich, but not so rich that their patronage could extend to more than a select few, and they were the only possible source of such patronage in the Republic. There was a nobility, but it was on the whole poor and dependent on the house of Orange for offices in the state or the army in order to maintain its position. Here were no great patrons comparable with the aristocracy in France, Spain or England—Dutch nobles lacked the necessary financial resources. Furthermore, the painters in the Republic lacked that other great patron, so important in France, Italy and Spain, the Catholic Church. This church may not have been totally suppressed in the Republic, but it certainly was in no position to act as a major patron of religious art. The Reformed Church while not necessarily inimical to art was certainly no patron of it, and may indeed, through its suspicion of idolatry and superstition, have inhibited the growth of a genre of painting with specifically religious themes and spirit.

The position of the Dutch painters in relation to their 'patrons' was very different from the common pattern in other European countries: they produced for the market rather than for individual patrons. Admittedly, many painters did produce works to order—especially portraits and group portraits—but this is specifically different from patronage in the precise sense. The generalisation is justified that Dutch painters produced works which they thought would be saleable, and for which they were prepared to accept very modest prices. Thus their art was designed to suit the tastes of a wide spectrum of Dutch society, not those of a small educated and highly cultivated élite. This situation determined some of the leading characteristics of the Dutch School. There is a great difference between a picture which is intended to be hung in a church or a large gallery in an aristocratic residence, and one which is destined for a private house and thus must be lived with, not visited. The demand in Holland was for paintings which would not be disturbing if hung in a living room. They had to satisfy a certain aesthetic sense, but one which was none too sophisticated, yet also be pleasant companions. It is this quality which is still striking in almost all the works of the Dutch School; both in size and subject matter they remain within the range of ordinary human experience. The landscape, the flower-piece, the genre picture, the interior scene—all were drawn from the experience of ordinary life and were intended to demonstrate and illustrate its quiet beauty. It was in this ability to see and express the beauty of everyday objects and scenes that the Dutch artists excelled, and it gives them their lasting attraction. Such an art was peculiarly suited both the decoration of the private house and to provide an aesthetic interpretation of ordinary experience.

Such commissions as were available differed from those of more aristocratic societies. Essentially—and with very few exceptions—they were limited to portraits, single or group. Commissioned portraits were more expensive than most paintings and were only within the means of the wealthier inhabitants of the Republic—though this was not a small group in Holland, and in Amsterdam particularly portrait painting could be a full-time occupation. This branch of painting certainly offered the richest rewards apart from official commissions. It is remarkable that the subjects of most of the Dutch portraits of the seventeenth century were contented with a much more simple and realistic style than might have been expected from a social group composed very largely of *nouveaux riches*. There was evidently little demand for the art of a Van Dyck with his ability to lend nobility and beauty to the most undistinguished of faces, but rather the work of Hals, Rembrandt, Van der Helst and others suggests that their patrons had the 'warts and all' attitude to portraiture. Thus the Dutch portrait-ists could build on the native realistic tradition and had little need to import foreign forms to express outer magnificence, nobility or pomp.

Even the official commissions were largely free from the demand for propagandist bombast or magnificence. They were chiefly group portraits designed to satisfy the people depicted rather than to impress a public; they were realistic records not pieces of propaganda. A change took place during the course of the century, heralded most clearly by the commissions for the new town hall of Amsterdam. As the regents became more conscious of their separateness and the oligarchies de-veloped into urban aristocracies, the demand for realism fell as the emphasis shifted in the direction of social propaganda and paintings designed to show the dignity rather than the personality of the sitter. This shift led directly to the decline of Dutch portraiture, as the Dutch painters could not perform such a task with the practised ease of French, Italian or even English artists.

The Dutch were also unable to produce much of any note in sculp-ture. The outstanding Dutch sculptor, Hendrick de Keyser (1565–1621), whose chief works were the tomb of William the Silent at Delft (1614) and the statue of Erasmus at Rotterdam (1618), had a style rooted firmly in the mannerism of the sixteenth century and, despite a certain psychological realism, he had little in common with the spirit of Dutch painting in the seventeenth century. There could be no such market for sculpture as existed for painting—its product was too expensive and too little suited to the private house. What demand there was for sculpture came from the court of the stadhouder during Frederick Henry's period of office and from public bodies, and their requirements were best met by the importation of sculptors from the Southern Netherlands. For example, the commissions for the sculptures to fill the new town hall in Amsterdam were given to a Southerner, Artus Quellien, and his assistants, who employed a style which was a full expression of Flemish baroque. The type of market which encouraged the independent Dutch approach in painting simply did not exist for sculpture, and moreover there were too few commissions available in the Republic to allow the growth of even a lively school imitating general European forms.

Similarly in architecture the major buildings produced in the seventeenth century followed the renaissance-classical mode predominant in the rest of Europe, though at a discreet distance. Here again it is high cost and the lack of a native tradition which prevented even Holland from taking an individual course. The chief commissions came, naturally enough considering the expense of major building projects, from the court of the stadhouder or from public bodies, and their needs were more than adequately met by the use of styles sanctified by the admiration of the rest of Western Europe. Only in private houses can the trace of an individual Dutch style be found, and even here it was limited chiefly to a continuance of the distinctive Dutch tradition in gable design. The middle and lower-middle classes lacked the resources to support a distinctive Dutch architectural style, the regents and the stadhouders had no wish to do so.

The fact that Dutch painters were craftsmen—or rather that they saw themselves and were treated as such—also helps to explain their pronounced specialisation. There had already been a tendency towards specialisation in the Netherlandish art of the previous century, and the large number of competing artists in Holland encouraged each to concentrate on what he could do best. Such specialisation could go to extremes, as with those landscapists who preferred not to paint figures and so left the *staffage* in their works to others. The Dutch public was clearly receptive to this specialisation of genre. The customer was not buying 'high art' or even the work of particular painters, but was buying landscapes, still-lives and so on. Painters did not feel the need to justify such subjects as proper matter for art. There was no theoretical discussion in the Republic on the question whether specialised landscapes, seascapes or interiors were viable subjects for painters. They were produced and accepted because they so clearly satisfied a need: the need for an art-form suitable for the private house. Because the painters saw themselves as craftsmen they had no theoretical inhibitions against adopting the radically new, if it could be shown that there was a demand for it. The painters of Flanders and Italy saw themselves as artists, and were developing an exalted conception of the task of the artist and of the function of art. They were impressed by theory and felt that their work had to be justifiable according to these theories; the Dutch craftsman-painters knew very little theory and produced what they expected would find a market.

Without this freedom from theory—in both the painters and in their public—the great innovations of Dutch art could never have taken place. As it is, the greatest of Dutch artists were—with the notable exception of Rembrandt—specialists, and some of them specialised very narrowly indeed. Ruisdael and Hobbema painted only landscapes; Cuyp almost exclusively landscapes with cows. Vermecr painted townscapes and the occasional mythological piece, but is remembered largely for his interiors, as is De Hoogh. Jan Steen's reputation rests on his genre pieces; that of Saenredam on his meticulous architectural paintings. One of the strangest of all the specialised genres developed by the Dutch was the church interior, which became the speciality of a number of very fine painters—De Witte, Houckgeest and Berckheyde, as well as Saenredam. The painters of seascapes were also highly specialised and with the younger Van de Velde reached a remarkably high standard.

One of the most notable gaps in Dutch painting can perhaps at least in part also be explained by the circumstance that Dutch paintings were intended to be hung in the home. This is the lack of works depicting contemporary events, particularly battles on land. Such paintings were perhaps not considered suitable for the home. During the later part of the Eighty Years War and for most of the rest of the seventeenth century—the great exception being of course the French invasion of 1672—the land-wars were kept remote from the Dutch population both physically and socially, for not only was the war carried on far from the central areas of the Republic, but the Dutch army was composed largely of foreign mercenaries. For most of the Dutch war was a matter of financial demands rather than personal involvement, and it may well be that they preferred not to be reminded of its physical reality. Many paintings of battles at sea, as a subdivision of marine painting, were produced, but a large proportion seems to have been aimed at the English market. Also a number of artists specialised in scenes of military life or battle scenes—Wouwerman, Codde, Terborch—but these constituted a minor 'military-life' genre and were not representations of actual events. So a certain distance could be maintained between the observer and any real, bloody battle—there is as great a difference between an imaginative scene of battle or pillage and a depiction of real warfare as there is between a war film and a newsreel film of an actual war.[26] It has been suggested that this interest in contemporary events of war through a general theme rather than pictures of particular events was '. . . un example caractéristique de la tendence du Baroque à s'éloigner du concret et à se complaire dans un symbolisme hérité du Moyen Age—même chez un peuple aussi foncièrement bourgeois et pénétré de rationalisme que le peuple hollandais.'[27] Such a line of argument seems dubious in the extreme—and unnecessary.

Throughout the seventeenth century, portraits and landscapes remained very popular, but other branches of painting had a more varied reception. One of the most striking developments was the rise to maturity and success of the civic-guard piece in the first half of the century and its rapid decline, and almost disappearance, in the second. Almost no paintings of this type were produced after the end of the Eighty Years War, though it seems unlikely that there was any causal connection between the signing of the Treaty of Münster and the loss of interest in civic-guard pieces. These bodies had played no immediate rôle in the war against Spain after the very early years of the Revolt, so they cannot be said to have suddenly lost their relevance to contemporary life in 1648. Moreover, they retained their importance for the preservation of order within the towns, and could occasionally play a decisive rôle in politics.

There was no parallel decline in the demand for the other chief branch of group portraiture, the 'regent' group. The 'regents' normally depicted were minor dignitaries, and there are no extant pictures of the town councils or even the colleges of burgomasters of any of the voting towns of Holland. It would seem that the regents proper felt no need to have themselves painted as corporations. When these wealthy and powerful men had themselves painted it was on their own or with their families—though some of the civic-guard pieces did include members of powerful regent families.

One notable evolution of taste was the rise in popularity of architectural paintings, especially of church interiors, beginning about the middle of the century. At roughly the same period townscapes also began to be popular. Both these genres were carried on by highly specialised painters and, in the main, failed to attract artists of the first rank. This circumstance may be more readily comprehensible in the case of church interiors, which might seem an unduly limiting subject, but the townscape did produce at least one unquestioned masterpiece— Vermeer's *View of Delft*.

The reason for the demand for such subjects must be sought in the increasingly urban nature of Dutch civilisation. Although the majority of the population of the Republic probably still lived and worked in the countryside and villages, the great majority of those who bought paintings, and the painters themselves almost without exception, lived in the rapidly growing towns. The population of most of the towns of Holland continued to grow until the last quarter of the century, and this process must have stimulated interest both in what was new and in the old that was disappearing or becoming overshadowed by new building. One thinks of Saenredam's painting of the old town hall of Amsterdam, which was based on drawings made in 1641, but only finished sixteen years later after the building had been burnt down and the new one built.

Just as Dutch landscapes stressed the countryside rather than any human figures in it, the paintings of towns, which include a number of views of a town taken from a distance, are not intended to show the life of a town but its physical aspect. The subjects are buildings, canals, and streets, not people.

Perhaps the aspect of Dutch painting in the seventeenth century which is most surprising is not that the Dutch School produced a number of great painters, but that there were so many really fine painters working in Holland at this time. The sheer quantity of production is amazing as is the astonishingly high general quality of these works. That Holland should have produced half a dozen great painters is worthy of note, but the fact that it produced a whole host of very fine and highly talented artists is an almost unique phenomenon, and one that is best explained by the peculiar nature of Dutch society in the seventeenth century.

A brief look at the lives, social position and work of a number of outstanding painters should help to elucidate the general argument through concrete illustrations. It is to be hoped that this use of specific examples will also in some measure serve to correct any oversimplifications which the generalising approach so far adopted in this chapter may have led to. First, four of the very greatest, and contrasting, of these Dutch artists of the seventeenth century will be dealt with in some detail: Rembrandt, Vermeer, Steen and Hals.

If there is one artist who stands out among the Dutch painters of the seventeenth century it is Rembrandt, and in some ways this fact is unfortunate for our present purpose. For, if the imagination of succeeding generations has been captured by both the power of his works and the story of his life, he is highly untypical in both. Dutch painters of the 'Golden Century' were not such as to inspire the imagination of the romantics: they neither lived the lives of artistic bohemians, nor were their works produced in despite of the tastes of their time. These men were true artists and the best of them achieved a very individual style and approach, but they sought to remain acceptable to the taste of their contemporaries for they had a living to earn. From this point of view it is unfortunate that Rembrandt's life lends itself so easily to a romantic interpretation and that he should commonly be seen as the ideal type of the Dutch painter.

Many great men, artists and others, do indeed seem to sum up or bring to perfection the most typical qualities of the civilisation in which they lived. Through them and their works we are able to reach a fuller and deeper understanding of their times. Rembrandt, however, is in many important respects very different from the majority of the artists of the Dutch School. Besides the interest which is naturally aroused by such a great artist and such a fascinating, if elusive, personality, he is worth considering in some detail precisely because of his lack of typicality. Through comparing and contrasting Rembrandt with the great majority of Dutch painters, the peculiar nature of these latter can be very clearly brought out.

The details of Rembrandt's life are well known, and this is the first clear instance of his atypicality, as the lives of most of the Dutch painters of the seventeenth century are known only in outline and with a general lack of detail, incident and clear evidence of character. Their work is the best witness we possess of them, and this is usually singularly uninformative as to character.

Rembrandt Harmensz van Rijn was born on 15 July 1606, the son of a miller in the important textile town of Leiden in the centre of the province of Holland. His mother was the daughter of a baker. These facts place pretty well the stratum of society into which Rembrandt was born. His brothers Adriaen and Willem stayed in the same, small tradesman's, *milieu*, one becoming a shoemaker, the other a baker. The family was not well off, but neither was it in difficult circumstances: at her death in 1640, Rembrandt's mother (his father having died ten years earlier) left property valued at f.10,000-,[28] which was a not inconsiderable sum, but one which a fairly prosperous small tradesman might be expected to accumulate in a lifetime. That there was money to spare, and also a certain modicum of social aspiration in the family, is shown by the fact that Rembrandt, unlike his brothers, was sent to Leiden's Latin School. He subsequently registered as a student at the university of Leiden, though possibly more to enjoy the privileges of a student than with any intention of embarking on a course of serious study.

In any event, Rembrandt was soon, in about 1621, apprenticed, like his brothers, to a trade. However, his aim was rather different, as he was apprenticed to the Leiden painter Jacob Isaacsz van Swanenburgh. His first master was perhaps as untypical as the pupil was to be. Swanenburgh came from a distinctly higher social class than most painters— his father had been a painter but also a burgomaster of Leiden—and he had spent some 17 years in Italy. Although Rembrandt spent a full three years with Swanenburgh, he does not seem to have been in- fluenced by him, and the short period—six months—he spent with Pieter Lastman in 1624-5 was much more important both for the formation of his early style and his attitude to art. Lastman had been influenced both by Dutch mannerism and by his stay, early in his career, in Italy. He was a history painter, taking his subjects largely from the Bible and from classical mythology and it may well be that the influence of Lastman was decisive for the development of Rembrandt's taste in subjects. Paintings on religious subjects were not very popular in seventeenth-century Holland, and apart from Rembrandt and his pupils, it would be difficult to find a painter who spent much of his time on them. Rembrandt, however, like Lastman, devoted a consider- able proportion of his *oeuvre* to Biblical subjects: in all about 160 paintings, 80 etchings, and 600 drawings.[29] While it can be argued that this preference was the act of a peculiarly strong religious nature, it is indisputable that in becoming a specialist in religious subjects Rem- brandt was following the example of the artist who was the most powerful influence during his formative years as a painter.

In his early years Rembrandt reflected very clearly the artistic *milieu* in which he worked, and the type of society in which he lived. After leaving Lastman he spent his first six years as an independent painter in

Leiden, and his work at this time, in its cool colouring and delicate
finish, fits in very well with the Leiden tradition of 'fine-painting'. One
of his pupils during this period was Gerrit Dou, who later became the
type of the Leiden painter, producing small genre pieces in a very
delicate and precise style. After his move to Amsterdam in late 1631 or
early 1632—a move which, like his period of training with Lastman,
suggests more than a little ambition on his part—Rembrandt responded
to the different atmosphere of this great cosmopolitan centre. Leiden
was a large town by contemporary standards, but remained somewhat
inturned and provincial; Amsterdam was a city, and more money was
available there for the purchase of luxuries such as paintings than
anywhere else in the Republic. Rembrandt quickly built up a reputation as a successful portraitist and, becoming fashionable, he prospered.
At the same time his style became bolder, and one suspects a bid for
European fame in many of his more striking history pieces of this
period, reminiscent as they are of the Flemish baroque. It was in this
period that he received his only commissions from the court of the
stadhouder, with its preference for the paintings of the Flemish masters.

The 1630s in Amsterdam were the years of Rembrandt's greatest
success, in terms of popularity and financial rewards. In these years he
was, one feels, consciously breaking out of the normal pattern of life
for a Dutch artist. He was aiming at the status of the Flemish painters.
He was not content to be seen as a craftsman whose work fetched high
prices; he needed to be recognised as an artist. Along with this search
for financial success and artistic recognition went a social ambition
closely related to these. It was thus perfectly consistent for the Rembrandt of this period that he should have married above himself, which
he proceeded to do. He married just as he was approaching the peak of
his popular success, and the wife he chose, Saskia van Uylenburgh, not
only brought a considerable dowry with her—she was also the daughter
of a former burgomaster of Leeuwarden (one of the most important
towns in the province of Friesland). A regent of Friesland could not
match the power, wealth and prestige of his compeers in Holland, but
he was certainly socially far above the Leiden miller's son.

Rembrandt also spent his money in an aristocratic fashion, particularly on *objets d'art*[30] and curiosities. In 1639 he bought a house in
Amsterdam for the large sum of f.14,000–, which was more than his
parents had accumulated in a lifetime of work. He was never able to pay
for this house and it finally played a major rôle in pulling him down into
bankruptcy. Perhaps his deliberate rejection of the ethic of the crafts-

16 Willem van de Velde the younger, *The River IJ at Amsterdam* (Rijksmuseum, Amsterdam)

17 Ludolf Backhuysen, *The Harbour, Amsterdam* (Kunsthistorische Museum, Vienna)

19 Rembrandt van Rijn, *Rembrandt and Saskia* (Pinakothek, Dresden)

18 (*opposite*) Jan van de Capelle, *The State Barge saluted by the Home Fleet* (Rijksmuseum, Amsterdam)

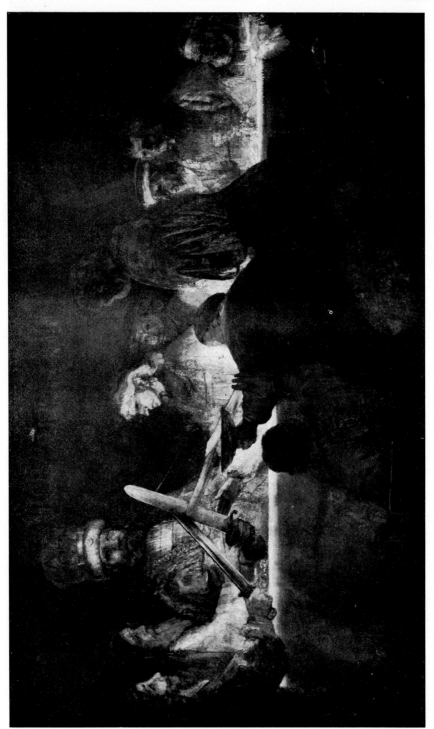

20 Rembrandt van Rijn, *The Conspiracy of Julius Civilis*, 1661/62

21   Jan Vermeer, *The Concert* (Gardner Museum, Boston, Mass.)

22 Emanuel de Witte, *Interior of a Church*, 1668
(Boymans—Van Beuningen Museum, Rotterdam)

23 Pieter Jansz. Saenredam, *The Old Town Hall, Amsterdam* (Rijksmuseum, Amsterdam)

man/painter, with his modest ambitions and necessary financial prudence, helped to lead him into these undoubted extravagances, for he does not seem to have been a man who was by nature drawn to the high life or rich living. The famous picture (in the Dresden Museum) of Rembrandt and Saskia in a carousal scene, with the painter himself as the gay drinker dressed in a rich fashion, was formerly interpreted as Rembrandt's affirmation of his own gay and extravagant style of living. It has, however, been persuasively argued that this picture is in fact a 'morality' set in a tavern (cf. the list of prices on the wall top-left) intended as a warning—perhaps particularly to himself.[31]

The height of his material success—if we need to point to a specific painting—may be taken as the *Company of Captain Frans Banning Cocq* (known as the *Night Watch*) painted in 1642. Not only is this work the consummation of his 'baroque' painting, solving the problems of group portraiture in a wholly original and lively way, but it was probably also Rembrandt's greatest financial success. It is usually stated that he received f.1,600– for the work, in itself a very considerable sum, but it has recently been suggested[32] that this amount was paid by the minor figures only (at f.100– a head), and that the two chief figures, Banning Cocq and his lieutenant, would have paid much more than f.100– each as their share. In any event, this painting fetched a higher price than the works of almost any other artist in Holland in this century, and it involved the patronage of some of the most important regent families in Amsterdam.

After this point, Rembrandt's work declined in popularity. Whereas in the 1630s he had been prepared to employ a variant of the international baroque style in order to gain commissions and win recognition, from the early 1640s he was no longer prepared to adapt his style and the treatment of his subjects to either the dictates of popular taste or in response to the restrictive canons of European art criticism. Popular taste in the 1640s began to favour a lighter, smoother style, and Rembrandt's heavy *chiaroscuro* and thick painting became less generally acceptable. Similarly, although he continued to produce history paintings, chiefly on religious and biblical themes, his concept of the subject was consistently in conflict with the received ideas of his time. One of the most shocking examples of this difference of vision— shocking to the people for whom it was painted—is his *Conspiracy of Julius Civilis*. Rembrandt's idea of the Batavian hero as a powerful barbarian chieftain must have been profoundly disturbing to the Amsterdam oligarchs who had commissioned the work. They drew the legitimation of their own power directly from the Batavians—such men as Civilis—and tended to picture them as respectable, dignified regents, very much like themselves, though perhaps, as a concession to history, in antique dress. Rembrandt was well aware of what he was doing, but was apparently no longer prepared to make too many concessions to the received ideas of his patrons. He was no longer ambitious for social success, and one suspects that his need for artistic recognition was already largely satisfied.

For although he went out of fashion, he was still considered one ot the leading painters in the Republic; and although he went bankrupf this was largely the consequence of his own former extravagance rather than of a lack of customers for his paintings. Patrons were still prepared to commission works from him at good prices and, apart from individual commissions for portraits, which continued to be given until his last years, Rembrandt as the acknowledged master of the group portrait was still employed for such works by official bodies: for example, the *Anatomy Lesson of Dr Joan Deijman* (1656) and the *Syndics* (1662). Also the *Julius Civilis* of 1661-2 had its origins in a commission from the burgomasters of Amsterdam, although this was given only after the death of Govert Flinck. That he was favoured with this commission is a better indication of his general standing as a painter in the eyes of his contemporaries than the fact that the painting was finally rejected. As S. Slive says, 'The picture we receive from a review of written references in the Netherlands to Rembrandt's work from the time he completed the *Night Watch* until his death is that he was respected by men of reputation and position in his community. His name came easily to the lips of his peers when they thought of painters; but none of them suggest he was an unparralleled (*sic*) genius or an uncompromising rebel.'[33]

The myth of the lonely, unrecognised, forgotten Rembrandt of his later years is precisely that—a myth. It is true that his work did not suit the most fashionable taste in Holland after the early 1640s, but it was still appreciated by many of his contemporaries and it remained in demand. During his life-time there was no condemnation of his painting;[34] the appreciation of contemporary critics was not as enthusiastic as modern opinion, but there was no negative criticism.

The last decades of Rembrandt's life illustrate the dilemma of the artist in a society which was not yet prepared to accord him any very eleveted status. Rembrandt attempted to break out of the craft tradition in painting, partly by accommodating to contemporary taste and becoming a fashionable portraitist, partly by adopting for a number of outstanding paintings that baroque manner which was the accepted European ideal in art. In order to maintain the position he had achieved, Rembrandt would either have had to follow closely the changing fashions favoured by the wealthier social groups, or to adopt more consistently the norms in art set by Italian, Flemish and French painters. He was not prepared to do either. By the ordinary standards of his time and society, his works continued to fetch high prices, but these were insufficient to maintain the inflated standard of living which he had already set for himself and he was forced into bankruptcy. He was never able to clear up completely the difficulties which arose from his financial collapse in 1656, and was still in straitened circumstances when he died.

In many ways Vermeer is a telling contrast to Rembrandt, in his life as in his art, and much more typical of the Dutch seventeenth century painter. Rembrandt is the obvious artistic giant with an enormous output covering nearly every possible subject. His life was dramatic enough to match his art, and we know enough about it to receive a strong impression of a very distinctive personality. He was recognised as an outstanding painter in his own time, and his reputation has increased steadily ever since (though there was a notable decline in appreciation for his work in the late seventeenth century). Vermeer, on the other hand, is and will probably remain a vague and shadowy figure. Very little is known of the circumstances of his life or of his character; only a very small number of his paintings has survived. His contemporaries do not seem to have considered him an outstanding painter, and after his death his name was practically forgotten for 200 years. Only in the course of the last hundred years has he come to be regarded generally as one of the truly great artists, and even now there are dissenters.

One can hardly be surprised either at this former neglect or at the difficulty experienced by many in appreciating his greatness, for it must be admitted that his art is extremely specialised, not to say limited. Here again Vermeer makes a quite startling contrast with Rembrandt, for against the latter's variety and pervasive human sympathy Vermeer can set (one or two paintings excepted) only a series of genre paintings remarkably similar in colouring and subject matter, and in which the people depicted are hardly seen as more than objects in the room. Vermeer's genre is interior landscape with the figures little more personalised than the trees in Ruisdael. He is indeed one of the most specialised of all Dutch painters of the century, for whom specialisation was typical.

Johan Vermeer was born at Delft in 1632. His father Reynier Jansz Vos (or Van der Meer or Vermeer) was a citizen of that town with a number of occupations—he was a silk-weaver, an art-dealer, a member of the painters' gild, and also ran a tavern. This list indicates fairly precisely the social position of the family—the craftsman/handworker with diversified interests in the hope of a better living. Whereas the family probably led a comfortable life there is nothing to suggest real prosperity. The young Vermeer married in 1653 and was admitted to the gild of St Luke in the same year. There is no satisfactory evidence about his training, nor is it known who his master was. Probably Vermeer took over his father's art-dealing business after his death in 1655, and it is possible that this occupation, rather than painting, was his chief source of income. It is clear that he worked very slowly and carefully, and it has been argued that most of his known works were still in his possession at the time of his death.[35] At no time does he seem to have been prosperous: he was frequently in difficulties over money— his large family must have been a severe strain on his finances (eight of his children were still minors at the time of his death, and three were adult)—and he died in debt.

Little more than these few facts is known about his life. He had some standing amongst his fellow artists in Delft, for he was elected an official of the painters' gild four times. Also he had a certain reputation outside the confines of the rather quiet town in which he lived and worked. (Delft, although in the past one of the leading towns of Holland, was certainly by the middle of the seventeenth century in decline and had little of the life and activity of the seaport towns Amsterdam and Rotterdam, or of the great textile centres Leiden and Haarlem.) Foreign collectors passing through Delft are known to have visited his studio, e.g. the Frenchman, Balthasar de Monconys, in 1663, who found Vermeer's work overpriced.[36] Vermeer's paintings seem to have fetched reasonably good prices for the time, indeed one is said to have been bought for f.600-, but they were far below the sums which Rembrandt or one of the really fashionable painters could ask for their work.

Vermeer belonged to a later generation than Rembrandt. The latter began his career when Dutch art was only at the start of its great developments and he was himself one of the chief influences in the process. Vermeer began his career in the 1650s when Dutch painters were able to build on the more than solid achievements of the innovators of the preceding decades. He was in fact a representative of the last great flowering of Dutch art before the decline of the late seventeenth and early eighteenth century. The great innovators had done their work and each of the various styles was being brought to perfection. In Vermeer's work, for example, the influence of Carel Fabritius is clear, particularly in its cool tonality. His form of genre painting could only have come as the perfection of a tradition; his was an art of maturity not innovation.

It is perhaps significant that Vermeer's period of activity coincided with those years in which the Dutch economy ceased to expand, population growth slowed notably, and Dutch society in general turned from its dynamic and innovatory phase towards conserving the gains of the past. It may be that the quiet, contemplative mood of Vermeer's paintings, and his concern to perfect an established mode rather than to create a new one reflects the spirit of Dutch society in this period. To attempt to generalise about the mood of a society and then to put forward an individual as the representative of this putative mood is, however, an enterprise of dubious validity.

More immediately relevant to our purpose is the consideration that Vermeer seems to have been typical of most Dutch artists in his lack of social or artistic ambition. What we know of his life, and the nature of the paintings he produced, suggests that he was content to accept the humble station in life which Dutch society allotted to its painters, and that similarly he was ready to accept fully the native tradition in art. Although he was clearly influenced, directly or indirectly, by developments in contemporary European art—the work of the Utrecht Caravaggists is clearly reflected in Vermeer's earliest paintings—he seems to have had no ambition for a European reputation or to achieve the status of a great 'artist' in the sense that was becoming common in Italy and France. If he had had any such ambitions he would have chosen a very different style for his paintings and a very different type of subject —as Rembrandt indeed did in his most ambitious period. But Vermeer stayed firmly in the Dutch tradition and, indeed, developed genre in a direction even less likely to appeal to the tastes of those schooled to appreciate Flemish, French or Italian art.

Yet Vermeer, while accepting the craftsman status of the painter in Dutch society, was able to produce some of the greatest paintings of the Dutch School in the seventeenth century. His art can now be seen as great in an absolute sense. In some ways Vermeer's painting, in its subtleties and in despite of its limitations of range and subject, is the greatest triumph of the Dutch craftsman/painter.

Rembrandt and Vermeer provide a contrast both as artists and men, but to compare either with Jan Steen serves to underline the diversity of Dutch painters in this century, in approach, style and temperament. Steen is one of the most 'Dutch' of painters. His ebullience, lively humanity and humour—even the over-emphasis of his jokes and the frequent crudity of his wit—seem more typical of Dutch life at this period than the greater subtlety and refinement of some of his fellow painters. There is a vitality in his work which is a direct expression of the expansive society in which he lived. He was the great master of the lively scene in genre painting, and such works are the clearest expression of his personality. Even his religious paintings take on the appearance of genre subjects. The sheer number of paintings he produced exemplifies his energy: despite his other occupations, some 800 paintings have been attributed to him and, although all do not show him at his best, the amount alone is impressive.

Jan Steen came from a rather higher level of society than most of his fellow painters—his father was a brewer in Leiden. He was born about 1625 or 1626 and was enrolled as a student at the university of Leiden at the age of 20, but how long he studied there or whether he simply wished to enjoy the privileges of a student is not known. It is also not clear how far Steen was dependent on his art for his livelihood. He is known to have leased a brewery in Delft from 1654 to 1657, and in 1672 he obtained a license to operate a tavern in Leiden. His painting must, however, have taken up a great deal of his time, and one suspects that he could have had only very little to spare for his various businesses. In any event he does not appear to have prospered, and certain anecdotes suggest that his paintings did not command very high prices.[37] Steen is probably the outstanding painter of what Floerke calls national-holl¨ndische works, bought only by 'sailors, peasants and simple burghers' who were not prepared to pay great sums for paintings which they looked upon rather as pieces of furniture.[38]

Jan Steen is another example of the second generation of Dutch painters who began their independent work towards the middle of the century, when the Dutch Republic was at the height of its economic power and political influence. Certainly he was in a position to be able to learn a lot from his first teachers amongst whom were the Haarlem painter of peasant scenes, Adriaen van Ostade, and the great innovator in landscape painting, Jan van Goyen in The Hague. His connection with Van Goyen was very close—he married his daughter in 1649. Steen was also able to learn much from the early work of the Delft school, particularly Pieter de Hoogh and Vermeer, and from the Leiden genre painters, among whom Frans van Mieris the elder seems to have had the greatest influence on him. The influence of the work of Frans Hals on Steen's art was far from inconsiderable, and Steen owned a number of his paintings.

Jan Steen's pictures are about people. Unlike Vermeer, whose people become merely figures or even objects in an interior landscape, in the work of Steen the surroundings of his figures are very much subordinate to the figures themselves. This is especially true of his interior scenes, but even his landscapes—for example, *Skittle players outside an inn* (National Gallery, London) of 1660–63—are dominated by the men, women and children in them. There could be no greater contrast to the *staffage* of so many Dutch landscapists.

However, while Steen's interest in people is clear, there is in his work none of the deep introspection and profound study of human nature to be found in Rembrandt. Steen is a humourist, a painter of the picaresque. In a sense he is the painters' counterpart to Cats, especially in the use he made of old saws and proverbs drawn directly from the language of the common man. Many of his paintings are in this sense literary: they tell a story or make a point, which is often made clear by quoting the relevant saying. An example of this practice is the so-called *Merry Company* (Mauritshuis, The Hague) of about 1663 which has as its motto 'The young ones chirrup as the old ones used to sing'. There is a clear parallel here with emblem books and especially with the use to which Cats put the genre, though with him the emphasis was always on the heavy, banal morality of the accompanying verses rather than on the proverb and its illustration. If Steen had similar roots and perhaps even a similar moral purpose, his morality was much less rigid and didactic and his human sympathy infinitely greater.

Towards the end of his life—he died in 1679—French classicism was beginning to influence Steen's painting, which was a sad foretaste of the general fate of Dutch painting in the last decades of the seventeenth century and throughout the eighteenth. *Two Men and a Young Woman making Music on a Terrace* (National Gallery, London) of about 1670 is an early example of the working of this alien influence. It seems significant that this most Dutch of painters, despite the possession of a developed and mature style of his own, should have shown himself susceptible to this French influence.

The careers of both Vermeer and Jan Steen remind us forcefully of the debt that the great painters of the middle and late century owed to the innovators of the early years of the century, who developed the basic types of Dutch painting—portraiture, landscape and genre. Of the painters we have been especially concerned with thus far, only Rembrandt was not working within a developed Dutch tradition—his inspiration came from outside the Republic, at first mediated through Lastman. Vermeer and Steen largely worked within and extended styles already firmly established by other and earlier Dutch painters. Yet the artists of this earlier generation deserve notice for their own merits and not simply because they made the later great achievement of Dutch art possible.

Of the painters active in the first decades of the century the most prominent is Frans Hals, and this artist is a fine example of the early success of Dutch painting as he must be considered one of the very greatest of the painters of this century. Hals was born sometime between 1581 and 1585 in Antwerp, the son of a textile worker from Mechelin. After the fall of Antwerp to the Spanish in 1585, his parents moved to the North and settled in Haarlem, the centre of linen manufacture in the Republic. Frans was not the only member of his family to turn to painting for a living, his brothers Dirk and Joost also became painters. No works of the latter have been identified, but Dirk was able to establish himself as one of the 'little masters' of Dutch painting specialising in genre both out- and indoors. Frans Hals studied under Karel van Mander (the author of *Het Schilderboek*) but does not show any noticeable sign of being influenced by his style.

Hals' greatest success came in portraiture, in genre treated as portraiture, and in group portraits, where his work is matched only by that of Rembrandt. He enjoyed considerable popularity as a portrait painter and received commissions even from the wealthier and more cultivated sections of Dutch society. His fame was not restricted to Haarlem, and he was even able to steal a civic-guard commission (the *Corporalship of Reynier Real*) from Amsterdam in 1633 from under the noses of the resident painters, who included Rembrandt and the fashionable portraitist Thomas de Keyser. Hals did not in fact finish the painting, but he was to have received f.66– for each man portrayed, which is some indication of the esteem he enjoyed at this point in his career at least.

Despite the high prices he probably received for some of his works, Hals did not prosper through his painting. Indeed he was frequently in debt, and even at the height of his popularity in the 1630s he was being sued for debt by Haarlem shopkeepers. Towards the end of his life, although he was still receiving important commissions, he was almost continuously in financial difficulties. In 1661 he was exempted from his dues to the local gild of St Luke, and in the following year the Haarlem town government made him a gift of f.50– and an award of f.150– for that year. In 1663 this grant was raised to f.200– p.a. and continued to be paid until his death in 1666. Hals continued to paint until his very last years, but this does not appear to have saved him from financial problems. Admittedly, he was not as popular in his last decades as he had been before about 1640, but commissions for portraits continued to come in after this date. Moreover, he was still receiving official commissions until the end—the *Regents of the Old Men's Home* and *Regentesses of the Old Men's Home* (both Frans Hals Museum, Haarlem) both date from 1664.

In landscape, among those pioneers who helped to bring the Dutch School to such perfection, Hercules Seghers has a special place, as he was by far the most original landscapist working in the Republic in the early seventeenth century. Seghers was born in Haarlem about 1589–90 and was thus almost an exact contemporary of Hals—he joined the Haarlem gild of St Luke in 1612, two years after Hals. Unlike the latter, Seghers had not been born in the South, but he was nevertheless able to make use of the work of the Flemish landscape painters of the late sixteenth century. He studied under Gillis Coninxloo in Amsterdam for a while, and in general his work suggests the influence of that group of painters which included Savery and De Momper as well as his master.

In discussing Dutch seventeenth century painters, it becomes tedious to have so often to confess our ignorance of their lives and their social situations, but with Seghers we are again faced by an artist whose life remains obscure. There are stories of his poverty and unhappiness, which follow suspiciously closely the 'misunderstood genius' formula, and his paintings do not appear to have been particularly prized, except by fellow artists. He probably died somewhere about the middle of the 1630s, but his work had an influence totally out of proportion to the number of his paintings—about 15—which have survived. Rembrandt in particular learnt much from Seghers and owned a number of his works.

Perhaps the two most influential landscapists of the earlier generation of Dutch painters were Jan van Goyen and Salomon van Ruysdael, born respectively in 1596 and 1600 (or soon after). Van Goyen was born in Leiden but studied under Esaias van de Velde in Haarlem and spent much of his life in The Hague. Despite the undoubtedly high quality of his work, he did not prosper, was frequently in financial difficulties, and died (in 1656) in debt. Perhaps as a consequence of such problems, he actively pursued other occupations, especially art-dealing. He also became involved in speculation in the great tulip bulb craze of the 1630s, and it was possibly misfortune in this affair and in other chancy investments that kept him in difficulties, rather than the lack of a decent income from his paintings. Ruysdael was born at Naarden (near the border of Holland with Utrecht) but became a member of the gild of St Luke at Haarlem in 1623, and lived there for the rest of his life. He also was influenced strongly by Esaias van de Velde, but he developed an individual style and it is a misfortune for him that his name inevitably reminds one of his greater nephew, Jacob van Ruisdael. He died in 1670.

Of this earlier generation of Dutch painters, one of the most remarkable was Pieter Jansz Saenredam (1597-1665), the first master of realistic architectural painting—one of the most unusual styles to be developed by the Dutch. There had, of course, been a more or less established tradition of architectural painting in the Netherlands in the previous century—one thinks particularly of Hans Vredeman de Vries—but this had been concerned with fantasy buildings, often illustrating some architectural theory, and human figures had normally played a large part in the composition. Saenredam painted portraits of buildings, and was especially interested in church interiors, where it was the space enclosed that was his chief subject. Any human figures in his paintings are of very minor importance, and indeed Saenredam often left it to others to paint them in.

Saenredam was born at Assendelft near Haarlem and was the son of an engraver and draughtsman of some note. He lived in Haarlem for the greater part of his life—it is notable how many of the better Dutch painters of the first half of the century were born or worked in this town—and joined the painters' gild there in 1623. He began to specialise in architectural painting about 1628. He was a hunchback, but there is no need to connect this circumstance with his concentration on buildings rather than people. It was after all a logical step in the development of this type of painting that the figures included should recede into the background and the buildings and the space they contained become more and more clearly the subject of the work. Parallel developments were to take place in landscape and house interiors. Saenredam was probably most successful with his church interiors, where his cool and light colouring suited the bare but well-lit interiors of the churches which had been stripped for Reformed worship.

Of the leading figures of the mature period of Dutch art—the mid-century and the two or three following decades—Jacob van Ruisdael is outstanding among those who have not yet been mentioned. It was perhaps an injustice to this great landscapist not to have dealt with him earlier along with his peers, Rembrandt, Vermeer and Steen, for he was not only one of the greatest of Dutch painters of the century, but also he is arguably the greatest landscape painter in Western art.

Ruisdael was born about 1628/9 in Haarlem—he is yet another great painter from this town—the son of a painter and frame-maker. Thus he was clearly from an artisan background. He became a member of the gild of St Luke in 1648 and, while it is not clear who his first teacher was, the influence especially on his early paintings of his uncle Salomon van Ruysdael is unmistakable.

Few of the artists we have looked at so far spent much time abroad, even if they left the territory of the Republic at all. Only the early mannerists and the Italianate painters made the statutory pilgrimage to Italy. Jacob van Ruisdael, however, did travel abroad for some years in the early 1650s, but in Germany not Italy. It would seem that he was looking for inspiration in different natural surroundings rather than in the art of others. In fact it is certain that at least a great number of his landscapes were imaginary, but Ruisdael's imagination worked on the basis of a close observation of nature. Particularly in his Dutch landscapes, his extraordinary achievement was to produce works with an unmistakably personal stamp and even mood, which nevertheless remained true to the nature of the Dutch countryside.

Soon after his return from Germany Ruisdael settled in Amsterdam, drawn no doubt by the greater market provided by the city. Again it must be confessed that little is known about the details of his life, though stories of poverty and ill-health were made current by Houbraken. What is now known would, however, suggest that he was at least modestly successful and that he received reasonably good prices for his works.

Ruisdael's greatest pupil was undoubtedly Meyndert Hobbema (1638-1709). This gifted artist had an unusual career: he married a servant of an Amsterdam burgomaster in 1668 and was consequently able to gain the post of wine-gauger in the town. This job seems to have left him little time for painting, and his production ceased except for one painting, the *Avenue of Trees at Middelharnis* (National Gallery,

London) which dates from 1689 when Dutch painting had already begun its general decline. It is one of Hobbema's best works, and is perhaps the last of the great Dutch landscapes.

Another landscape painter who deserves a mention at least is Philips Koninck (1619-88), a pupil of Rembrandt highly praised by contemporaries, including Vondel (who, however, characteristically liked his history and genre work and did not mention his landscapes). Koninck was prosperous, but probably through his business interests rather than his painting.[40] Of a rather earlier generation, Aert van der Neer (1603/4-77) was a specialist among specialists, concentrating on winter and moonlit landscapes. Neither type of subject seems to have won a great deal of popularity, and he opened a tavern in Amsterdam in 1657, only to go bankrupt three years later.

Aelbert Cuyp (1620-91) is now possibly one of the most underrated of Dutch seventeenth century painters. In his own time he achieved a certain prosperity, which he owed in a great measure to a successful marriage. He spent most of his life in his native Dordrecht where his father had also been a painter. He was one of the few Dutch painters who allowed animals to figure largely in his works: his landscapes with cows are very numerous, and the cows are very clearly central figures in these paintings. His pictures of river scenes are notable and reflect the interests of an inhabitant of Dordrecht on the busy Maas.

Of the host of fine genre painters produced by the Republic in this century, only one or two can be mentioned here. The names only of such accomplished artists as Gerrit Dou, Gabriel Metsu and Frans van Mieris the elder can be given. Carel Fabritius, however, calls for separate attention both for his originality and for his outstanding talent. He was born in 1622 in the newly-reclaimed Beemster north of Amsterdam and was killed in the explosion of the powder magazine in Delft in 1654. This early death is one of the most tantalising losses in Dutch painting as he had, in a very few years, already made it clear that he was one of the most distinctive and attractive talents at work around the mid-century. Fabritius was the son of a schoolteacher who painted as a hobby. He was originally trained as a carpenter but turned to painting. For a time he was a pupil of Rembrandt (from about 1641), then he returned to the Beemster on the death of his wife in 1643. By 1650 he was living and working in Delft and he joined the painters' gild there in 1652. One or two incidents which have been recorded of his life illustrate well the position of a painter such as Fabritius in Dutch society: when he entered the gild he paid his fee—which was only f.12-

—in two instalments; and in 1653 he accepted the humble task of painting the coat of arms of the town, for which he was paid f.12-. He forms a link between Rembrandt and Vermeer, for the latter was clearly influenced by his work, and it is notable that he painted two of the most revealing self-portraits of the period outside the work of Rembrandt.[41]

Fabritius was one of the creators of the distinct style which marks the Delft school. Besides Vermeer, the other leading painter of this group was Pieter de Hoogh (1629–after 1684). His best work concentrates on the interiors of Dutch houses (e.g. *The Pantry* in the Rijksmuseum, Amsterdam) and was chiefly painted while he was in Delft. After De Hoogh moved to Amsterdam in the early 1660s the quality of his work declined, possibly because the demand in that great cosmopolitan centre was for more pompous and sumptuous pictures along the lines of the French art which was already beginning to makes its influence felt.

Another genre painter, Gerard ter Borch (1617–81), is interesting if only because he is one of the very few leading painters who was not only born outside the province of Holland—in Zwolle—but who spent most of his life away from the great centres of artistic life in the Republic. He lived mainly in Deventer in the province of Overijsel, although he also travelled widely—visiting England, Spain and possibly Italy besides Germany. An interesting picture of his is the *Swearing of the Oath of Ratification to the Treaty of Munster* (National Gallery, London). This work is one of the very few paintings illustrating contemporary events to be produced by a Dutch artist in the seventeenth century. It may be significant of Dutch taste that the painting found no buyer; on the other hand the price Ter Borch asked for it—f.6,000—was extremely high, especially for such a small picture (it measures 18 ins by 23 ins). It was certainly overpriced in terms of the Dutch market. Although he lived outside Holland, Ter Borch sent his paintings there to find the buyers who must have been lacking in Deventer, a town which had long outlived its medieval prosperity. It is clear that it was possible for a painter to live and work outside Holland without losing contact with the taste of the dominant province. That few artists did in fact choose to live outside Holland says much for its peculiar attractions—not only was the market there, but so were the other painters to provide mutual stimulation and inspiration.

In the second half of the century architectural painting became even more specialised than it had been earlier as church interiors, formerly almost the exclusive province of Saenredam, achieved a distinct popularity. Gerard Houckgeest (c. 1600–61) after spending the earlier part of his career painting fantastic church interiors, turned to realistic subjects towards the middle of the century. He worked in Delft and his paintings show certain affinities to the styles of Vermeer and the early De Hoogh. However, architectural painting reached its peak in the work of Emanuel de Witte (1616/18–92). He was born in Alkmaar, worked in Delft in the 1640s, and then moved to Amsterdam. Again he seems only to have begun to specialise in church interiors at about the mid-century. Witte's churches are not realistic in the full sense, as they are often compilations of elements taken from a number of buildings. In this development he seems to have run parallel with the landscape painting of Ruisdael, who also painted imaginative pictures in a realistic style. Towards the end of his life, Witte was in serious financial difficulties and he finally committed suicide.

Another interesting type of subject came to the fore around the middle of the century, the townscape, which can be seen either as an extension of architectural painting or as a specialised form of landscape —the distinction seems hardly important. The outstanding exponent of this subject was Gerrit Berckheyde, who seems to have learnt most from his elder brother, Job, with whom he lived, travelled and worked. The Amsterdam painter Jan van der Heyden was another leading specialist in the townscape. It seems typical of Dutch culture in the seventeenth century that its painters were able to see beauty not only in fairly conventional ways in landscape and architectural monuments, but also in the ordinary streets and canals of a town—that is, in the normal surroundings of the Dutch town dweller. After all, it is hard to think of a Dutch painter of this century who did not live in the town.

Two further subject specialisations should at least be mentioned as they illustrate the range of Dutch painting, and its remarkable ability to innovate through specialisation and concentration. Marine painting— it might be less pompous to call this branch of art seascape—is a specialisation that was to be expected from the Dutch. The Dutch painter of the seventeenth century, with his eye both on nature and the activities of men, could hardly have failed to recognise the important part that the sea and ships played in the life of his country, and be drawn to depict it. Similarly, it is hardly surprising that there was a popular demand for works dealing with the sea and ships. In general terms the development of seascape was from paintings which were little more than portraits of ships to seascapes proper where the sea and the sky are the real subjects. The first specialist in this branch of painting in the Republic was Hendrick Cornelisz Vroom (1566–1640), who was yet another Haarlem painter of the innovatory period of Dutch art. His works are chiefly detailed studies of ships or ships in battle, with the sea and the sky acting purely as background. Jan Porcellis (c. 1584–1632), who was born in Ghent but was chiefly active in the Republic, marks the transition to the seascape proper and he had considerable influence on later painters—Van de Capelle, for example, is known to have collected his works.

During the mature period of Dutch art, the two leading marine painters were Jan van der Capelle (1624–79) and Willem van de Velde the younger (1633–1707), though other major painters, notably Van Goyen, also produced seascapes. Van de Capelle is, as has already been noted, one of the very few masters of the Dutch seventeenth century who was not, socially, a craftsman. His painting was a spare-time activity, and he also collected art. At his death he left more than f.90,000– and one of the outstanding private art collections of his time. Besides seascapes by Simon de Vlieger and Porcellis, he owned works by Van Goyen, Rembrandt, Rubens, Hals, Van Dyck, Brouwer, Seghers and Avercamp.[42] His own paintings are mostly harbour or river scenes, for example *The State Barge saluted by the Home Fleet* (Rijksmuseum, Amsterdam). As in many Dutch landscapes, in his works the sky often seems more important than the ostensible subjects of the paintings.

Van de Velde is generally recognised as the greatest of Dutch marine painters, with more interest in the dramatic than Van de Capelle. After 1672 he moved to England and in 1674 he and his father, Willem the elder (1611–93), began to receive from the crown salaries of £100 p.a. each for painting sea battles. This prosperity, together with the demand to concentrate on giving accurate details of ships and incidents, does not seem to have had a beneficial effect on Van de Velde's art, which showed more freedom before the removal to England.

The other subject specialisation which appears typically Dutch is the still-life. This subject had its origins in sixteenth century Flemish art, but there it normally kept up some appearance of having a more acceptable subject, often by having a Biblical or historical scene in the background. A remnant of such uncertainty is found in the tendency of many Dutch still-life painters to give their work an overt moralising theme—usually with *vanitas* elements included in a fairly rigid iconography. One feels, however, that with the Dutch such elements had become purely conventional, and that the true aim of the artist was to present flowers or other objects in an aesthetically pleasing way. Jan Davidsz de Heem (1606–83/4) can only in part be considered a member of the Dutch School, as he moved to Antwerp as early as 1636 and won an international reputation from there for his exuberant paintings of flowers and fruit. Before his move to the South he had spent some time in Leiden, where his still-lifes of books were seen as a comment on the ephemeral nature of the lives and achievements even of scholars. The greatest Dutch painter of still-lifes, Willem Kalf (1619–93), was born in Rotterdam, spent some years in Paris in the 1640s, and settled in Amsterdam in 1653, where he devoted himself to satisfying the demand which had arisen there among the prosperous for still-lives of banquets and luxury objects. These works reflect very clearly the growing delight of the wealthy in Holland for luxury, and specifically for the ostentatious display of such luxury.

One of the peculiarities of Dutch art in the seventeenth century was the development of distinct and distinctive schools of painting in a number of the towns of Holland. Although Amsterdam was the outstanding centre of wealth in the Republic, and although many painters were finally drawn there by the opportunities it offered in the form of wealthy customers or potential patrons, other towns were far from overshadowed by this city. Haarlem, Delft and Leiden all developed their own schools and styles of painting, and a number of artists—notably Pieter de Hoogh—did their best work in the years before they were sucked in by the temptations of Amsterdam. Delft, where De Hoogh first worked, is one of the towns one would least have expected to produce a thriving and distinctive school of art. It is readily understandable that the bigger, prosperous and growing towns of Holland should be attractive to painters, and that they should prove themselves able to support separate schools of painting, but Delft was not only a relatively small town by contemporary Dutch standards, it was also economically stagnant. Its artists must have relied principally on purchasers outside Delft to provide them with a market and thus a living. However, distances between the towns of Holland were small even by seventeenth-century standards, and it was not too difficult for prospective buyers from The Hague or Rotterdam especially to come into contact with the Delft artists and their work. It was perhaps the quiet and calm atmosphere of Delft, contrasting so sharply with the bustle and pressure of the expanding and economically successful towns of the province, which encouraged the peculiarly meditative mood of such painters as Vermeer, De Hoogh and Fabritius. The Delft style was formed under the influence of gifted artists, and the rôle of these individuals was perhaps paramount, but when we look at a painting such as Vermeer's *View of Delft* (Mauritshuis, The Hague), which sums up so well the restful beauty of the town, it seems plausible that, just as the mood of the town inspired this single masterpiece, so the nature of the whole Delft school was powerfully influenced by the distinctive atmosphere of the town in which these artists lived and worked.

Haarlem was probably the most important centre for painting outside Amsterdam, though there is no style peculiar to Haarlem painters such as those that grew up in Delft or Leiden. The contribution of this town to Dutch seventeenth-century art was the part its painters played in the early decades of the century. It was painters in Haarlem who developed the traditions and styles inherited from the previous century —for example the Haarlem mannerists—aided by immigrants from the South, and they produced a remarkably high proportion of the leading innovators in art, the men who laid the foundations on which the great achievements of Dutch painting in its mature period were built. After Goltzius and Cornelis van Haarlem in the late sixteenth century, there followed such outstanding and influential figures as Esaias van de Velde, Hals, Adriaen van Ostade, Seghers, Pieter de Molijn, Salomon van Ruysdael, Vroom and Saenredam. There is hardly a field of Dutch painting in the development of which Haarlem artists did not play an important and often fundamental rôle.

The Utrecht school, on the other hand, is an oddity. It lay outside the boundaries of Holland, but was near enough to share its wealth and come under the influence of its culture. Yet Utrecht was already at the beginning of the century a centre for Italianate painting, and it remained so throughout the century. The Utrecht style was consequently distinct from anything else produced in the Republic in the seventeenth century—with the possible exception of the Italianate landscapes so much in vogue in the mid- and late-century. The great days of this school were the 1620s, when Terbrugghen and Honthorst were at the peak of their powers and fame, but the town was not without its noted artists at other periods also, as the Utrecht painters included Michiel van Miereveld, Paul Moreelse, Abraham Bloemart and Cornelis Poelenburgh, but the stream of talent did begin to dry up by the middle of the century.

Leiden had its genre specialists and its school of 'fine painters', and it is evident that most of the more important towns were able to build up their own artistic tradition. There were, however, exceptions. The

168   PAINTING—THE ARTIST AS CRAFTSMAN

Hague, despite the market which existed there for elegant portraits, and despite its size, had little independent artistic development. The cultural life of the town was dependent in a great measure on the stadhouders' court and on the entourages of foreign ambassadors, and neither of these groups was particularly appreciative of Dutch art. Rotterdam also produced few and attracted less painters of the first rank, although it was one of the largest and most prosperous of the Holland towns. It must be remembered that Rotterdam only became a major force in the Republic towards the middle of the century—and by that time the great artists had already been born. It remains a little puzzling that more major artists were not attracted by the wealth of the town in the later part of the century.

Thus while, excepting always one or two unusual cases, the province of Holland dominated the artistic life of the Republic, it cannot be said that Amsterdam dominated that of Holland. Despite its wealth and power, this great city was no Dutch Paris and the artistic achievement of the seventeenth century was the work of the province as a whole. Indeed, it could be argued that Dutch art had a better chance of retaining its freshness and originality away from Amsterdam. In general innovation took place elsewhere, and the strength of fashion and foreign influence were great enough in Amsterdam to distort or stultify individual artistic development very often, rather than encouraging the painter to follow his own road. The smaller, but still prosperous, towns of Holland did not offer the same rewards as Amsterdam, but they may very well have provided a more congenial atmosphere for the Dutch painter.

Notes

[1] G. Brom, *Schilderkunst en litteratuur in de 16e en 17e eeuw* (Utrecht–Antwerp 1957), p. 176

[2] For these examples, see H. Floerke, *Studien zur niederländischen Kunst- und Kulturgeschichte. Die Formen des Kunsthandels, das Atelier und die Sammler in den Niederlanden vom 15.–18. Jahrhundert* (Munich–Leipzig 1905), pp. 21–2, 34

[3] J. G. van Dillen, *Van rijkdom en regenten. Handboek tot de economische en sociale geschiedenis van Nederland tijdens de Republiek* (The Hague 1970), pp. 182, 244, 295

[4] H. Floerke, *op. cit.*, pp. 19–20

[5] F. W. Hudig, *Frederik Hendrik en de kunst van zijn tijd* (Amsterdam 1928) (Inaugural lecture, Municipal University of Amsterdam), pp. 12–14

[6] *Ibid.*, pp. 14–15

[7] *Ibid.*, p. 22

[8] *Ibid.*, pp. 27–8

[9] G. Brom, *op. cit.*, p. 183

[10] See above, p. 113

[11] G. Brom, *op. cit.*, p. 212

[12] S. Slive, *Rembrandt and his critics: 1630–1730* (The Hague 1953), pp. 87, 88–9, 91

[13] *Ibid.*, p. 99

[14] K. Fremantle, *The Baroque Town Hall of Amsterdam* (Utrecht 1959), p. 151

[15] H. Floerke, *op. cit.*, p. 180

[16] Quoted in *ibid.*, p. 20

[17] The prices paid for Dutch paintings have been discussed above, p. 121*ff*

[18] H. Floerke, *op. cit.*, p. 89

[19] His *Inleyding tot de Hooge School der Schilder-Konst anders de Zichtbaere Welt* of 1678

[20] Cf. E. H. Gombrich, 'Renaissance artistic theory and the development of landscape painting', *Gazette des Beaux Arts*, 95e année, vie période, vol. 41 (1953), pp. 335–60; reprinted in *Norm and Form* (London 1966)

[21] E.g. V.-L. Tapié, *Le Baroque* (Paris 1961); *Baroque et Classicisme* (Paris 1957), translated as *The Age of Grandeur* (London 1960)

[22] K. Clark, *Rembrandt and the Italian Renaissance* (London 1966)

[23] J. H. Huizinga, *Dutch Civilisation in the Seventeenth Century* (London 1968), p. 13 I have modified the translation slightly

[24] J. A. N. Knuttel, *Bredero* (Lochem 1949), p. 157

[25] *Ibid.*

[26] Cf. A. Dohmann, 'Les événements contemporains dans la peinture hollandaise du xviie siècle', *Revue d'histoire moderne et contemporaine*, tome v (1958), pp. 265*ff*

[27] *Ibid.*, p. 272

[28] J. Rosenberg, *Rembrandt. Life and Work* (London 1968³), p. 7

[29] *Ibid.*, p. 169

[30] See the inventory of his collection and possessions in K. Clark, *op. cit.*, pp. 193–209

[31] B. Haak, *Rembrandt, his life, work and times* (London 1969), pp. 152–3

[32] *Ibid.*, pp. 179a–80

[33] S. Slive, *op. cit.*, p. 54

[34] *Ibid.*, pp. 80–81

[35] L. Goldscheider, *Johannes Vermeer. The Paintings. Complete Edition* (London 1958), p. 13

[36] J. Rosenberg, S. Slive and E. H. ter Kuile, *Dutch Art and Architecture 1600–1800* (Penguin 1966), p. 118

[37] See above, pp. 121–2

[38] H. Floerke, *op. cit.*, p. 180

[39] See below, pp. 221–2

[40] See above, p. 136

[41] One is in the Boymans-Van Beuningen Museum, Rotterdam; the other in the National Gallery, London

[42] A. Bredius, 'De schilder Johannes van de Capelle', *Oud Holland*, x (1892), pp. 32–5

seven

The Fruits of Tolerance

To the modern mind the Dutch Republic of the seventeenth century is remarkable chiefly for the great school of painting which it produced—it is this achievement which probably comes most readily to mind when we think of this notable period of Dutch history. For contemporaries the situation seems to have been very different: most foreign observers felt that the distinctive and surprising feature of Dutch seventeenth-century society was the remarkable degree of freedom of thought and belief which it allowed. There is a good deal to be said for such a point of view for no other state in Europe in the seventeenth century was able, or wished, to grant its subjects so much freedom—of conscience, of speech and, in practice, of the press. There were limits to this toleration, but the authorities in the Republic went much further in practical terms in the direction of an open society than the rest of Europe. Not only was this tolerant attitude the more or less official policy of the central government of the Republic, but individual freedom was further safeguarded, and indeed extended, by the workings of the greatly decentralised political system. In the defence of their privileges local jurisdictions were often prepared to protect individuals against the central courts of the provinces, and the same was true *a fortiori* for the provinces as against the central institutions of the Republic. In consequence, such restrictive laws as existed were often very difficult to enforce, and the application of these laws throughout the Republic was very far from uniform, being largely at the discretion of the local holders of power. As a result the inhabitants of the Republic were able to discuss with great freedom in public and in print important questions in theology, philosophy, politics and science which it was dangerous to voice elsewhere in Europe because of the interests of an established church or of the state. In addition, the Republic became a haven for those who would have been, or had been, persecuted in their own countries for their opinions. Even many thinkers who were not directly threatened with persecution in their own lands found the atmosphere in the Republic more congenial and more conducive to the free exercise of their intellects than that of any other country, as the career of Descartes illustrates. Original and daring thinkers knew that they were less likely to be harassed as a result of their speculations, hindered in their expression, or persecuted by the state than elsewhere, therefore they could feel considerably more at ease in the Republic than, for example, in France or even in England.

The Republic was attractive to intellectual and religious refugees from its very first years. In the first instance, of course, it became a refuge for persecuted protestants, initially those from the Southern Netherlands. The rôle of immigrants from the Spanish Netherlands in the life of the Republic has perhaps been exaggerated, but one field where their importance is undeniable is art: the contribution of artists of Flemish origin to the development of the Dutch school of painting was of primary importance. Other large groups followed in the course of the seventeenth century, including the important colony of Portuguese Jews in Amsterdam, English sectarians and political refugees, and perhaps reached a climax with the great influx of Huguenots after the revocation of the Edict of Nantes in 1685. Some of the greatest figures in the intellectual life of the seventeenth century were members of one or other of these groups, e.g. Locke, Bayle and Spinoza.

A further stimulus to intellectual activity in the Republic was the vitality of printing and publishing, which in itself was in a large measure the consequence of the freedom allowed to them. In the seventeenth century Holland was probably the greatest centre of book production in the whole of Europe, and it was particularly important as a place where books could legally be published which would have been, or had been, banned elsewhere. It was in Holland that the French protestant émigrés found publishers for their polemic and propagandist works, especially after the Revocation—though the imprint was often fictitious, the books purporting to have been published for example in Cologne (a favourite) or even in France. The Dutch presses provided a running commentary on developments in European intellectual and religious life in this century, and contemporary politics did not escape their attention as even in this field censorship was weak. Indeed, the production of pamphlet and other material dealing with political and social problems in the Republic was very considerable throughout the century, and it was often written in notably vigorous, if highly polemical, prose. The licence which it is clear writers and printers felt themselves able to exercise was only partly the result of the considerable legal freedom enjoyed by the Dutch press. Many pamphlets and books were considered—at least by the government of the province or the Republic—to be seditious, as indeed many undoubtedly were, but their authors and printers were very often able to escape punishment. In the first place, they were usually difficult to track down, and even when they were discovered the government of the town in which they lived frequently made it very difficult for the central courts to bring them to trial—either because it sympathised with the views expressed, or simply through jealousy of its own jurisdiction. In practical terms it was almost impossible for the provincial courts of Holland and Zeeland to bring any individual to trial if he enjoyed the protection of the government of his town. Such circumstances, while they did not lead to an uniform system of freedom of publication, meant that the laws limiting this freedom were applied only sporadically and uncertainly.

Also the Republic was the most important country in Europe for the publication of academic and scientific works, and this situation provided a considerable stimulus to Dutch intellectual and cultural activity. Besides the masses of technical works produced by Dutch publishers— one thinks particularly of sea-charts and atlases—Holland was also able to take the lead in publishing books in certain other specialised fields. If Dutch dominance in the printing of works requiring semitic and other unusual typefaces was important only in the limited area of philology and biblical scholarship, the expertise of Dutch publishers in turning out books from classical literature, both in translation and in the original languages, had a much more general importance for the spread of humanist culture in the Republic. An outstanding example of this Dutch success is the so-called 'Elseviers'—cheap editions of classical texts in small format, but in reliable, scholarly versions—produced by the Elsevier publishing house. Nowhere else in Europe at the time were the various branches of intellectual and cultural life so well served by the presses.

It is thus hardly surprising that some of the leading jurists, philosophers, political theorists, theologians and scientists of the century were Dutch or were active in the Republic. Certain figures stand out for the fame they achieved in their own time, or have since won—Grotius, Spinoza, Christiaan Huygens, Leeuwenhoek. Such men must take up the major part of our attention, but others whose names are not so well known must also be considered, especially where they have been robbed of a deserved reputation chiefly because they wrote in Dutch.

The importance of the great religious conflicts within the Republic in the course of the seventeenth century has already been sufficiently stressed, as has the significance of the recurring friction between church and state, which arose partly because of the uncertainty surrounding the relationship of the two, particularly in Holland. Yet there is an interest in the religious history of the Republic quite apart from its political repercussions, for theology was not the least of those areas where the intellectual and spiritual vitality and originality of the Dutch in their Golden Century expressed itself. It was above all in the field of religious controversy that the general tolerance of Dutch society allowed a freedom in the Republic which was unknown in the rest of Europe. The development and expression of ideas on this especially touchy subject which would have brought their authors into danger almost anywhere else in seventeenth-century Europe were allowed, and even encouraged, by the weakness, at least in fact if not in law, of censorship in the Republic.

In this section we are not particularly concerned with Reformed orthodoxy, as this cannot be said to have made any original contribution to theology after the Synod of Dordrecht. As far as the impact which Calvinism, in its most orthodox variant, had on the life of the Republic, the nature of this influence and the form it would take were clear enough by the early years of the century. However, there were currents within Reformed thought, most obviously Arminianism, which were moving in new directions and breaking out of dogmatic rigidity. Within such movements men were rethinking the basic questions of their religion, although such freedom of thought often meant that they were unable to remain within the Reformed Church, either because of the logic of their own convictions, or because of the heresy-hunting tendencies of the grimly orthodox. It is with such movements within Reformed theology as well as those more obviously innovatory in their views and activities that we are here concerned.

The importance of Arminianism, or rather of the Remonstrant movement after its expulsion from the Reformed Church in 1619, in this context is that it gave a respectable base of operations to liberal protestant thinkers, men who could approach new ideas not only as a threat but also as a stimulus towards a re-examination of their beliefs and the consequences of these. Although subject to a more or less severe persecution for a few years after the Synod of Dordrecht, the newly-founded Remonstrant Brotherhood had already begun to open its own independent churches by the early 1630s. Soon the Remonstrants were firmly established as the most important of the many protestant sects in the Republic. The significance of the movement did not lie in the size of its congregation, but in its ability to attract members from the wealthier, better-educated and politically powerful sections of society in the towns of Holland. Whether this situation was a consequence of the 'libertine' attitude towards religion which had been powerful in the Netherlands since the early sixteenth century, of the regents' dislike for a Reformed Church which seemed all too often prepared to trespass into political territory, or of the natural reluctance of such men to submit to the discipline of the Reformed Church, is a question which must be left unanswered here. There is undoubtedly a measure of truth in the first suggestion, but the others are more specific and more convincing perhaps for the seventeenth century. Possibly there was also a certain amount of social antagonism, as the regents and the wealthier groups in general would have been reluctant to accept the authority of ministers from the middle and lower-middle classes, and such was the social origin of most ministers of the Reformed Church.

In any event, it is clear that even regent circles were strongly influenced by the Remonstrants. The peak of their influence on the ruling groups of Holland, after the early years of the century, probably came in the first stadhouderless period. At this time the restrictions on the activities of the regents were less than at any other period of the century, and a large number of Remonstrants, or at least men with connections and sympathies with them, were able to enter the town governments of Holland. The effects of the crisis of 1672 drove most of these religious liberals from government. Some remained even after this date, but open Remonstrants were subsequently excluded from the regent group, although they continued to be influential among the wealthier and better-educated sections of the population of Holland, and exercised an indirect pressure on the regents.

The continued vitality of the movement is sufficiently demonstrated by the rôle Remonstrants played in the development of liberal protestant theology in the later seventeenth century. It was at the Remonstrant academy of Amsterdam that Jean le Clerc taught, and it was with the Remonstrant theologians, Le Clerc and Van Limborch, that the 'enlightened' English theologians corresponded.[1] The Remonstrant movement, however, is perhaps more important as a part of a broader stream of liberal and even radical protestantism. Its existence broke the monolithic structure of Dutch Reformed thought, and the Remonstrant church became a home for moderates, who were prepared to maintain contacts with more extreme groups. The Remonstrant theologians formed part of a lively intellectual and spiritual atmosphere, able to embrace on the one hand followers of the new ideas in philosophy, and on the other the ecumenical and even anti-confessional groups.

The Dutch Republic in the seventeenth century tolerated the growth of radical religious thought, with the very minimum of restriction, from the radical anti-clerical and anti-confessional religious writings of the poet Camphuysen, through the irenism of the Mennonite/ Collegiant Galenus Abrahamsz de Haan, to the extremes of mysticism or of a rational approach to religion.[2] Of all such movements, perhaps the most interesting, if in the long term not the most influential, was that of the Collegiants. This movement had its roots in the *Rijnsburg Vergadering*, founded in the 1620s in a village not far from Leiden. Here assemblies were held twice a year, as well as communion services. The members of the 'assembly' were in the main simple men and the movement had little influence until the 1640s, when 'colleges' began to be set up in the towns of Holland. These colleges were meetings for Bible-study and individual 'prophecy' and had no recognised ministers. They acknowledged Rijnsburg as their spiritual home, but soon developed into something much more adventurous. The Collegiants were not another sect, but attracted adherents from various churches and sects—especially from the Remonstrants, Baptists, Quakers and Socinians. The spiritual and intellectual atmosphere varied greatly from college to college, but what united them was '. . . the desire for simple lay piety, without dogma, ceremonies or church authority'.[3] The dislike of dogma was particularly marked, together with a similar rejection of the idea of the authority of a constituted church, for both these besides being objectionable in theory in practice led to hair-splitting and heresy-hunting, turning the soul away from the essentials of religious experience and concentrating attention on peripheral matters.

The Collegiant movement became important in the intellectual life of Holland just after the middle of the century, chiefly because of its ability to unite, or rather bring into brotherly contact—for it had no confession or even clearly defined membership—people of very different confessions and very disparate social backgrounds. The original Rijnsburg *vergadering* had been composed in the main of artisans, and when the colleges began to spring up they retained their attraction for such people, but also brought in others. Many examples could be given, but perhaps the most prominent figure involved with the Collegiants was Van Beuningen. Coenraad van Beuningen (1622-93) was born into an influential Amsterdam family. He studied law at Leiden, spent some time in Paris as secretary to the exiled De Groot, and then was successively secretary, pensionary, member of the council, and burgomaster of Amsterdam. He was also one of the most important diplomats produced by the Republic in this century, and his influence on foreign policy was great, particularly under De Witt with whom he worked very closely. He led a number of vitally important extra-ordinary embassies during De Witt's period of power, and his diplomatic activities continued under William III until he clashed with the prince in the 1680s. Van Beuningen came into contact with the Collegiants in the 1640s, and was at one stage tempted to withdraw from public life in order to turn to a life of contemplation.[4] Van Beuningen did not take this step, but another regent's son did. Johan Hartigsvelt, the eldest son of a powerful regent family in Rotterdam, could not perhaps have looked forward to as brilliant a career as that of Van Beuningen, but he would certainly have become a member of the Rotterdam *vroedschap* and there the connections of his family would have ensured that his voice carried more than ordinary weight in the deliberations of the council. After he had come into contact with the Collegiants, however, Hartigsvelt experienced a 'conversion' and renounced all secular ambitions and retired to live an ascetic and contemplative existence.

Although no other Rotterdam regent was affected by the Collegiants to the same extent as Hartigsvelt, a number of influential figures in the government of this town were attracted by the movement. Adriaen Paets, a correspondent of De Witt and extra-ordinary ambassador to Spain, though officially a member of the Walloon Church (which was accepted as orthodox by the Reformed Church) was in contact with the Collegiants. He was a typically open-minded and tolerant Dutch intellectual, and he later became the friend and patron of Pierre Bayle when the latter arrived in Rotterdam.[5] Similarly, other regents of the town before 1672, who were Remonstrants or who sympathised with them, maintained contacts with Collegiant circles. Most of these men were forced out of the town government in 1672, though Paets retained his position. It may well be that such a degree of Collegiant influence was peculiar to Rotterdam, but other town governments were touched by the movement to some extent. It was certainly one of the few movements which could bring regents into familiar contact with such figures from the lower orders as the Rotterdam tile-maker—and poet—Joachim Oudaen.

The tolerant attitude of the Collegiants is further witnessed by their readiness to give aid and comfort to Spinoza after his expulsion from the Jewish community of Amsterdam. Here he could feel almost at home, in a circle which embraced Socinians, Quakers and Cartesians—and later the followers of Spinoza himself. In a sense the Collegiant movement can be seen as an exaggerated form of the tolerance so typical of the Republic, and its history illustrates the way in whichthis freedom from dogma could lead to fruitful cross-fertilisation of minds and stimulate philosophers and theologians to re-examine their accepted ideas and assumptions.

If not by birth then certainly by occupation, Spinoza, the greatest philosopher produced by the Republic, belonged to the lower-middle class/artisan section of Dutch society. After being forced to leave the Amsterdam Jewish community because of his heretical views he earned his living by grinding and polishing lenses. Baruch Spinoza (1632-77) was born into a community which had fled to the Republic to escape religious persecution, the Sephardic Jews who had come to Amsterdam in the late sixteenth and early seventeenth century after having been driven first from Spain and then from Portugal. Most had had to accept conversion to Christianity but had maintained in secret their jewish beliefs and practices, and they returned to the open profession of their faith and traditions in the Republic. In Amsterdam, after some hesitation on the part of the town government, they were allowed to found their own synagogue and schools, and their tradition of biblical scholarship began a fresh period of fruitful activity. The Sephardic Jews had been more directly exposed to the influence of Western European philosophy and biblical criticism, and consequently they were, as a community, much less firmly rooted in dogmatic certainty and unchanging ritual than the Ashkenazim of Eastern Europe, who had lived in much more introspective communities. During the first half of the seventeenth century the Amsterdam jewish community was troubled by frequent outbreaks of unorthodox and free-thinking movements, perhaps because it was much less isolated by the intolerance of the surrounding society than most Jewish centres outside the Republic. It is perhaps in this tradition of Jewish free-thought that Spinoza must first be placed.

Spinoza's father was a merchant of modest means in very good standing with the Jewish community. Spinoza was educated in the traditional Jewish manner and was at first viewed as a future intellectual leader of the community. Partly the influence of his father and partly the hopes which had been invested in him caused the leading rabbis to attempt to keep him, after his heterodox views became known, in at least formal obedience to the precepts of their faith. Despite his clear rejection of the fundamental dogmas of their religion, the Jewish community offered him a pension of f.1,000– p.a. if he would conform in public to the jewish rules of life, but Spinoza refused to compromise and was formally cursed and expelled from the community in 1656.

He subsequently lived a very quiet, retired life, working at his craft and his philosophical studies. He was not, however, totally isolated. Even before his expulsion he had been in contact with free-thinking and ecumenical protestant groups, and afterwards his contacts were chiefly with members of such groups and with a number of radical political and philosophical thinkers. He spent some years with the Collegiants at Rijnsburg near Leiden, and was in touch with the leading theorists of the States-party. His *Tractatus Politicus* and *Tractatus Theologico-Politicus* can to a certain extent be regarded as arising out of such contacts. These works were clearly intended to take up and elaborate the political theories contained in the writings of such men as the brothers De la Court,[6] and to support their arguments in favour of religious toleration. However, Spinoza's ideas and his mode of argument were too extreme even for the most radical of his contemporaries, and he was well advised to publish little of his own writings. His ruthless logic and consistent realism brought him into conflict with traditional moral and political philosophy, and theology. He was indeed a subversive thinker: using the tools provided by Christian and Jewish scholasticism he undermined the bases of revealed religion, traditional morality, and the moral interpretation of the state. In particular, his realism led him in political thought to the conclusion that, as a man could have no right to do that which he cannot do, in a strict sense might is right[7]—a conclusion which had dangerous political implications. Again, although a supporter of the De Witt régime in the Republic, it is clear that in theory he believed the most perfect type of constitution to be democracy, and it is a pity that he died before he had written more than a few pages of the section on democracy in the *Tractatus Politicus*. Most dangerous of all was, probably, his concept of God: he argued that all existing things must form a single system, and that this system is God. This view made him an atheist in the eyes of contemporaries, and indeed it is possible that the term 'God' was only used by Spinoza at all to confuse the opposition.

None of his contacts could even approach intellectual equality with

Spinoza, and they showed few signs of any real understanding of his work. He made desultory contact with philosophers outside the Republic, meeting Leibniz during the latter's visit to The Hague in 1676, and he received some recognition from them—he was offered a chair in philosophy at the university of Heidelberg by the Elector Palatine in 1672. He refused the offer, and wisely, for this post would have put him in too exposed a position, and in any case he would not have been able to teach what he thought to be true. His views were not publicly acceptable anywhere in Europe in his time.

Spinoza did not have much influence in his own time, though he won a few disciples who saw to the publication of his works after his death. He was more condemned than read for over a century after his death, but he can now be seen as one of the greatest philosophers of modern times, and certainly the greatest produced by the Dutch Republic. Only in Holland could such a thinker have found the circumstances which would allow him to lead a relatively undisturbed existence. He recognised his own good fortune, 'Now, seeing that we have the rare happiness of living in a republic, where everyone's judgement is free and unshackled, where each may worship God as his conscience dictates, and where freedom is esteemed before all things dear and precious, I have believed that I should be undertaking no ungrateful or unprofitable task, in demonstrating that not only can such freedom be granted without prejudice to the public peace, but also, that without such freedom, piety cannot flourish nor the public peace be secure.'[8] He was not persecuted for his ideas, though he was wise not to make them too generally known, and the atmosphere of free discussion between Christian and Jewish thinkers in the Republic helped to provide Spinoza with the basis for his independent criticism of both traditions. After his break with the Jewish community even such an independent character as Spinoza might have found it difficult to lead a fruitful intellectual life if he had not found acceptance among the radical protestant groups which existed in the Republic. Finally, many of the problems, most notably the political, which Spinoza dealt with in his theoretical writings arose directly out of his experience of Dutch society, and from the controversies over freedom and authority which were such an important part of Dutch intellectual life in the third quarter of the seventeenth century.[9]

A remarkable figure produced by the ecumenical protestant groups was Pieter Cornelisz Plockhoy (1620–94).[10] Born in Zierikzee in Zeeland of Mennonite parents, Plockhoy was living in Amsterdam by the middle of the 1640s and there came into contact with the Collegiants through his Mennonite circle in that town. He was also a member of a group calling itself 'Parnassus on the Y', formed to discuss religious and political problems, and some of the other members of this body were later to encourage Plockhoy in his plans for a cooperative community in America. In 1658 he went to England and attempted to win first Cromwell and then his son Richard over to his scheme for the establishment of an ecumenical church in England. The idea centred round 'one general Christian assembly or meeting-place' with a service consisting of readings from the Bible with free discussion and comment from the congregation. Other churches and sects were to be tolerated and it was to be the duty of the government to keep the country free of religious persecution and constraint.[11] Even more interesting, he also proposed, in a pamphlet entitled *A Way Propounded*,[12] that the problem of poverty be solved by setting up cooperative communities. He started one such community near London and had a plan for another near Bristol, but the restoration of the monarchy brought to an end the times favourable to such experiments in England, and by 1661 Plockhoy was back in Holland.

Now he attempted to realise his ideal in North America. After some bargaining with the burgomasters, he signed a contract with the government of Amsterdam which empowered him to found a community, consisting of himself and 25 families, at Zwaanendaal in New Holland. In 1663 Plockhoy and his followers set out from Amsterdam and in the summer founded the first cooperative community in America. The experiment was brought to an end, however, by the English conquest of New Holland in the following year. Plockhoy spent the rest of his life in America, dying at Germantown in Pennsylvania.

The Reformed Church of the Republic showed in the second half of the century that it was capable of doing more than hang on grimly to the positions established at the Synod of Dordrecht. The leading example of a new direction within the church was the German-born Cocceius (1603–69), who was professor of eastern languages at Leiden from 1650. He restored the emphasis on the Bible and on the necessity of ascertaining the original meaning of the text. Although there was nothing unorthodox in his ideas, he soon found himself the object of bitter attacks from the grimly orthodox, and particularly from the followers of that great champion of orthodoxy, Voetius. Such men saw Cocceius and his teachings as a threat to their cherished dogmatic certainties, especially when he seemed to undermine sabbatarianism by arguing that the observance of the Sabbath should be regarded as an old Christian custom rather than as a command of God. Cocceius died before the storm had fully developed, but the conflict between his followers and those of Voetius lasted for decades and threatened to cause another major split within the church. Though essentially moderate in their ideas, the *Cocceianen* brought out the worst in the orthodox Reformed Church, revealing the strength of obscurantism. They attempted to regain something of the old evangelical spirit, and to put the authority of the Bible above that of any formulated Confession, but they also showed themselves more favourable to some of the newer ideas of the century, and accepted the authority of the state over the church. Such tendencies were sufficient to make them, in the eyes of orthodoxy, little better than Arminians, Cartesians or any of the other heresies the conservatives were so easily able to find in the late seventeenth century.[13]

The notorious case of Balthasar Bekker is a clear example of such obscurantism at work. After the publication of his *Betoverde Wereld*, in which he attacked belief in the devil and witchcraft, Bekker, a minister of the Reformed Church, came under attack from his colleagues and was finally deprived of his position. He was supported by the government of Amsterdam which continued to pay his salary and refused to accept any replacement for him while he lived. It was the rationalist elements in his arguments which aroused the general hostility of the Reformed Church against Bekker, as it was felt that such an approach was also a threat to dogmatic purity.

Of course, one of the greatest weaknesses in the situation of the Reformed Church within the Republic was that it could exercise its machinery of discipline only over its own members. Thus, while it could not touch theologians outside its own ranks, it could easily purge itself of its more original and lively thinkers. Partly as a consequence of this state of affairs, too often during the century the reaction of the Reformed Church to a challenge on any front, whether from the philosophy of Descartes or from the reinterpretation of Biblical texts, was purely negative. Its ministers and professors of theology too often seemed determined to act according to the caricature of themselves given by their opponents, fulminating against the new as a matter of principle, and interpreting intellectual daring as a challenge to the majesty of God.

Given the religious ferment in the Republic throughout the century, the reaction of the Reformed Church can perhaps best be understood as a last, and rather desperate, attempt to maintain a weak, and progressively weakening, position. It is in such a context that its overwhelmingly negative approach should be placed.

A field where the Reformed Church could have considerable influence was music, for public performances took place chiefly in the churches, and religious music had always been one of the peaks of the art. During the fifteenth and sixteenth centuries the Netherlands had been the musical leaders of Europe, especially in polyphony. In the seventeenth century, however, this position was lost—indeed after the death of Sweelinck, although the Republic enjoyed a fairly lively musical life, it produced no composers of any distinction at all. One major reason for this failure was the influence of the Reformed Church. Not only could it not replace the Catholic Church as a major patron of music, it also showed itself to be inimical to the art itself. The early Calvinists were opposed to the playing of music during church services, and this was banned in the Republic at a very early date. However, the church councils were unable to rid their churches of organs, for the organs as well as the fabric of the churches belonged to the local civic authorities. Moreover, the organists were appointed by the town governments, who consequently decided what their duties were to be. The church was able to prevent the use of the organ during services— although in the course of the seventeenth century it was increasingly used to accompany the congregations' singing, which had become unacceptably cacophonous in its absence—but the organ was played at other times on the instructions of the town councils. In most towns the organist was expected to give a public recital a few times a week, so the church was not able completely to inhibit the performance of music within its buildings.

The one major composer produced by the Republic during our period, and then only just within its bounds, was Sweelinck. Born probably in Deventer in Overijsel, Jan Pietersz Sweelinck (1562–1621) was already in Amsterdam by 1566 where his father had become organist of the Old Church. His father died in 1573 and Sweelinck succeeded him after only a few years—he was appointed to this post, which he held until his death, in 1581 at the latest. It is suggestive of the lowly status of the organist and composer in Holland at this time that Sweelinck's salary when he was first appointed was only f.100– p.a. He was one of the truly great composers of his time: not only was he the heir of the great sixteenth-century tradition in the Netherlands, he was also highly

24 Jan Steen, *Merry Company*, c. 1663 (Mauritshuis, The Hague)

25 Carel Fabritius, *Self-Portrait*, 1654 (National Gallery, London)

26 Unknown
Artist, *Baruch
Spinoza* (Herzog
August Library,
Wolfenbüttel)

27 Abraham Lambertsz
van den Tempel, *Pieter
de la Court* (Rijks-
museum, Amsterdam)

28 Adriaen Hanneman, *Johan de Witt* (Boymans—Van Beuningen Museum,
Rotterdam)

29 Rembrandt van Rijn, *The Slaughtered Ox* (Louvre, Paris)

30 Cornelis Troost, *Rumor erat in casa* (Mauritshuis, The Hague)

original and his influence was fundamental to the growth of the great North German school of composers for the organ. It is noticeable, however, that his influence was only fruitful outside the Republic, which was itself marked by the number and not the quality of its organists. The musical scene in the Northern Netherlands was also notable for the excellence of its highly-developed bell-ringing, and for the activities as performers and composers of gifted amateurs such as Constantijn Huygens.

It would be unfair to blame the Reformed Church for this failure in music, but it must be admitted that here as in so many fields of culture its orthodox members tended towards the camp of the philistines. To a considerable extent what we now see as the great achievements of Dutch culture in the seventeenth century were conceived and created in despite of the Reformed Church. That other options were open to the church is sufficiently demonstrated by the existence and fertility of mind of such a man as Pierre Bayle, who was always in the forefront of intellectual activity during his life-time and yet contrived to remain an orthodox Calvinist. There can be little doubt that had Bayle been born a Dutchman his critical freedom would have brought him into conflict with the Reformed Church. If a Bekker was deposed by a Dutch synod, Bayle could hardly have remained in the church with ease.

Any consideration of the intellectual life of Holland, particularly of its impact on contemporary Europe, must include Grotius; perhaps no Dutchman of the seventeenth century was so widely known and admired by the learned community of Europe, and certainly no other can show such a diversity of achievement. It is perhaps now a little difficult to understand the degree of admiration which Grotius won from his contemporaries, but he remains one of the most interesting thinkers of his time, if only because he seemed to personify what it was felt a great jurist, political theorist, historian and theologian should be.

Hugo de Groot (usually known by the latinised form of his name, Grotius) was born in Delft in 1583. His father was a burgomaster of the town who numbered among his friends the great humanist Justus Lipsius and the mathematician Simon Stevin. He was also curator of the university of Leiden, where his brother was a professor of law, from 1594. Thus Grotius' background was very likely to encourage his intellectual development, and was able to provide the contacts to ensure him a successful career. Perhaps more important, Grotius was quite exceptionally precocious intellectually. He went to Leiden in 1594 at the age of eleven and had soon—with the aid of his parents and their friends, who were able to ensure that his talent did not go un-noticed—established a reputation as a child-prodigy of learning. His remarkable success, helped by the social position of his family, brought him to the notice of the highest in the land, and in 1598 he was a member of a special embassy to France led by Justinus of Nassau and Oldenbarnevelt himself. During this expedition he obtained a doctorate in law from the university of Orléans.

The child had been favoured and admired by the leading scholars of the Republic and had been recognised by cultured and intellectual circles throughout Europe; the young man seemed destined to enjoy a notably successful career in almost whatever field he chose. Grotius had decided to concentrate on law, and he began his career as an advocate before the Court of Holland. In 1607, at the age of 24, he gained the important post or advocate-fiscal to this court. His favour with in-fluential politicians and regents continued to grow and in 1613 he became pensionary of Rotterdam—the post which Oldenbarnevelt had held before becoming Advocate of Holland, and which had been held by Oldenbarnevelt's brother, Elias, since that time. Grotius' future seemed assured: he now became one of the closest of Oldenbarnevelt's collaborators and it was believed that he was the chosen successor of the ageing statesman.

Grotius' political convictions made him a determined supporter of the policies pursued by Oldenbarnevelt. He shared the latter's belief that sovereignty lay with the states of the individual provinces and not with the States General or, an idea which had been put forward in the early years of the Revolt, with the people. Grotius' De antiquitate reipublicae batavicae, published in 1610, asserted that from the time of the Batavians onwards sovereignty had belonged to the provincial states, and that the courts of Holland in the medieval period had enjoyed only delegated powers. This argument was historically unsound but, partly through the authority of Grotius, it became an accepted dogma of Dutch history during the course of the seventeenth century. It was a very convenient doctrine for the Holland regents, as it could be used to justify both the rule of the existing oligarchy and the Revolt itself—for according to this version of history there had indeed been no revolt, rather the states had been impelled to use force to prevent Philip II from usurping their legitimate authority.

While his political ideas fitted in very well with those of Olden-barnevelt and his supporters among the regents, Grotius himself was no politician. Not that he had a great deal of opportunity to prove himself in this field. In 1613, when he became pensionary of Rotterdam, the great internal crisis of 1618 was already imminent. Grotius was a leading member of Oldenbarnevelt's party and, moreover, his masters in Rotterdam were among the most fervent and militant supporters of the Remonstrants, so Grotius had to act as the spokesman of the extreme wing of the doomed party. As the crisis approached he was drawn even closer into identification with Oldenbarnevelt—in 1617 he became a member of the Commissioned Council (*Gecommitteerde Raad*), which was a very unusual appointment for a mere pensionary as it made him one of the body which controlled the day-to-day affairs of Holland. Because of his prominent position he was arrested at the same time as Oldenbarnevelt, and was condemned early in 1619 to life-imprisonment and confiscation of all his property.

The rest of his life makes a singular contrast with his early successes. Although he escaped from the castle of Loevestein in 1621—in the famous incident of the book-chest, in which he was smuggled out by his resourceful wife—he was never again able to live in the Republic, nor was he able to find satisfactory employment elsewhere. He lived out the rest of his years—and he was only in his late thirties when he escaped from Holland—in frustrated exile. He received a pension from Louis XIII of France, but it was paid only irregularly, and in 1634 he became Swedish ambassador to France, but was no more successful here than he had been in his previous political employments. He returned to Holland in 1631, but he was still too much the symbol of the vanquished party and was forced to flee again under the threat of renewed imprisonment. Yet it was in these years of frustration and failure that he produced most of the works for which he is still remembered.

Always with a great capacity for work, in his years of exile he seems to have sought solace in yet more concentrated study and literary activity. Even while in prison he was able to work at an astounding pace—to occupy his time he not only translated Euripides into Latin and prepared an apologia for his past conduct (the *Verantwoordinghe* published in 1622), but he also wrote his *Inleyding tot de Hollantsche rechtsgeleerdheit* (Introduction to Dutch Jurisprudence), published in 1631, the first comprehensive study of the civil law of Holland. The production of this work alone, written of necessity largely from memory, was an outstanding achievement, but his expertise was far from limited to the field of law. While he was in prison he also wrote one of his most controversial works, the *Bewijs van den waren Godsdienst*

(Demonstration of the True Religion), first published in 1622. Originally written in verse and intended for the instruction of his children, in a later Latin prose version (*De veritate religionis christianae*) this work achieved great popularity and it was also translated into most European languages. Grotius sprang from the tolerant and theologically liberal section of the Holland regent class and so an irenic tendency was to be expected in his theological writings. Moreover, his direct and painful experience of the Remonstrant/Contraremonstrant conflict, with its attendant bitterness and the subsequent persecution of the losing side, made him even more convinced of the necessity of unity among Christians, and of the sterility of dogmatic hair-splitting. In the *Bewijs* the ecumenical idea is dominant: the stress throughout is laid on those elements of belief common to all Christians, and the basic argument is that these—the belief in Christ and the authority of the New Testament —and these alone are of real importance. The time was not yet ripe for the general acceptance of such ideas, and he was suspected, especially by his orthodox-Reformed opponents, of secret catholic tendencies. Nevertheless his work had considerable influence and was to be an inspiration for the liberal and non-confessional protestant theologians of the later seventeenth century.

During his first years in France, Grotius completed what was probably his greatest work: *De Iure Belli ac Pacis* (Paris 1625). This book, although largely written during these years, was based on an almost incredibly comprehensive knowledge of the writings of jurists from classical times to the great authorities of the preceding century. All Grotius' vast learning was brought to bear on the problem of war between states—the question of peace was, despite the title, hardly raised as it did not seem to constitute a problem. This work, which has been considered one of the great milestones in the development of international law—and has even been seen as having a direct connection with the international law courts of this century—was nevertheless somewhat old-fashioned in design even for its time. The ideas in it were drawn largely from the writings of the great jurists, especially Spanish, of the sixteenth century, and it contains very little that can be seen as original. Moreover, the very plan and nature of the book put it in the sixteenth-century tradition: it contains a host of citations from the most diverse of sources and these are crammed into the work at every possible point, constantly threatening to obscure the argument. Such a compilatory and comprehensive approach gives the work an almost medieval feel; yet it is undoubtedly innovatory, even daring, in its essence. Despite its inevitable failings, it constitutes a remarkably successful attempt to deal with some of the most fundamental problems of international life, and if contemporaries were impressed by Grotius' learning later thinkers were able to build on the foundations he put down. Perhaps the outstanding element is his attempt to base the laws governing relations between states on principles which, though moral, would remain valid even if God did not exist. This effort puts Grotius firmly in the line of the great natural law theorists.

De Iure Belli ac Pacis was also admired, of course, because it seemed to sum up all the preceding work on this problem, and for its systematic and rational nature. With this work Grotius fulfilled all the expectations which he had inspired since his childhood, and triumphantly confirmed his European fame. He died, disappointed in his public career, but celebrated for his scholarship, in August 1645.

This remarkable man was admired by contemporaries for his work in yet another field: the writing of history. Here Grotius satisfied the requirements of his own time rather than those of our own. Not only did he write in Latin, his public being the educated élite of Europe, but like most of the historians of his time he saw the writing of history first and foremost as a literary activity. Perfection of style was more important than a critical investigation of the evidence, and his histories were intended to serve as practical handbooks for statesmen, demonstrating the successes and failures of their like in the past. His work on the history of the Netherlands before the Revolt—*De antiquitate reipublicae batavicae*—has already been mentioned and was important both as summing up the received ideas of the time and for its influence on later generations. However, his major historical works were the *Annales et Historiae* which dealt with the Revolt and the early years of the Eighty Years War. As early as 1601 Grotius had been given the task of writing the history of the Revolt by the States of Holland, and the work was completed in its first version by 1612, but not published. In later years Grotius changed and completely reworked the book and in the event it was only published after his death, in 1657. Grotius' Latin style was greatly admired by contemporaries and the work was a useful summary of earlier writings on the Revolt, especially for readers outside the Republic lacking a knowledge of Dutch. It lacks originality and critical method, however, and can now only be valued as a piece of fine writing. Nevertheless, in his own time Grotius' historical writings were considered to be among the finest achievements of contemporary historiography.

Although important historical works were written in Latin—by Baudius and others besides Grotius—already by the late sixteenth century it had become more usual in the Republic to write history in the vernacular. The history of the Revolt and the early years of the Republic in particular was of too great general interest for it to be hidden away in Latin, accessible only to the highly educated minority. In the first decades of the seventeenth century it is doubtful if a majority of the town regents could read Latin with any ease, though the situation was probably very different by the second half of the century when many regents had read law at Leiden. In the early years of the century at least these regents, who were directly concerned with the running of the state, evidently felt a need for histories in the vernacular, first of the Revolt itself and then on later periods of the Republic's history. Similarly, it is clear that there was a considerable demand from large sections of the population outside the regent groups for accounts in Dutch of recent history. Throughout the seventeenth century there was a fairly large audience for voluminous works on the history of the Republic, and not only of the Revolt.

During the early years of the Eighty Years War, especially in the last decade of the sixteenth and the first of the seventeenth century, the public demand appears to have been chiefly for detailed factual accounts, for chronicles which printed a large number of documents. Whether it was the result of a specific demand or not, this is the type of work which was mainly produced at this time, and only later in the seventeenth century did interpretative works with some pretensions to literary worth begin to appear. During this later stage works concerned both with the Revolt and with the later history of the Republic were often intended as contributions to current political controversies, or were used in this way in any event. Although this function of historical works had its disadvantages, encouraging much distortion and special pleading, it nevertheless gave an urgency and a passion to the study and writing of the history of the Republic, and in consequence much of the historical writing of the seventeenth century makes lively reading. Such relevance and immediacy was in considerable contrast to most of the academic political theory of the age and, in fact, the liveliest political writings of the time very frequently took on an historical form—specifically the works of the brothers De la Court and of Ulric Huber, which will be considered later. Perhaps because history was so useful a weapon in political warfare, nearly all major works were written in Dutch and so could reach a much wider public than books in Latin.

History of this kind was chiefly written by men outside the universities, and was not aimed solely at a learned audience.

Yet historical writing was at a difficult stage in its development in the seventeenth century, and in the Dutch Republic vernacular history was faced with similar problems to other branches of literature through the uncertain state of the Dutch language. Two extremes of historical writing—the chronicle with few literary pretensions and the Latin prose poem—were the dominant forms in the early years of the century. Neither approach could provide very satisfactory history: the chronicle at its worst merely an undifferentiated series of facts in chronological order was at its best only a reliable source of information which still needed to be digested and understood; the Latin works of the official historiographers, who were usually humanists chosen for the excellence of their Latin style, were at their worst plagiaristic, their information plundered from the chronicles and translated into elegant Latin, and at their best were still principally literary exercises, dominated by the demands of style and expressing political and moral lessons drawn from Tacitus. The amalgamation of these two extremes, or rather the combination of the chroniclers' thirst for information with the humanists' clarity of presentation, together with a critical approach to sources and an urge to explain and understand was not fully achieved until after the end of the century. The achievement of the Dutch historians of the seventeenth century was considerable, but was limited by the conception generally held at the time as to the proper concerns of history. 'Au XVIIe siècle, l'Histoire est encore avant tout un genre littéraire et l'historien tout autre chose qu'un érudit spécialisé.'[14] Perhaps even more inhibiting, the historian was debarred from asking the vital questions of causation, or was forced to invoke Fortune, leaving further inquiry to the philosopher and the theologian. There were compensations: 'Telle qu'on la comprend au XVIIe siècle, l'histoire ne peut espérer mettre en lumière que de petites séries causales décousues, décelables dans le champ minuscule de la psychologie individuelle; en revanche, elle s'attribue des prérogatives auxquelles les historiens actuels ont largement renoncé. En effet, selon la conception classique, l'histoire représente le tribune devant lequel la postérité fait comparaître les grandes de ce monde. . . .'[15] It should be added that this idea of the task of the historian was far from completely advantageous for the writing of good history, as the need to pass moral judgements too often hindered (and hinders) the historian in his basic work of understanding the past.

The great chroniclers had themselves lived through the Revolt and the early decades of the Eighty Years War, and their works were a direct reaction to the events which created the Republic. Their own awareness of the importance of the events through which they had lived led them to record as much as they could of the history of their own times. The most important of them were Bor, Van Meteren and Van Reyd: each of these had a very different point of vantage, both geographically and personally, and each had a distinctive personality as a writer.

Pieter Bor (1559–1635) was born in Utrecht and was a public notary there. His great work—*Oorsprongk, begin ende vervolgh der Neder-lantscher Oorlogen* (Origin, beginning and continuation of the Netherlands Wars)—began to appear in 1595, and is a mine of information, particularly through the large number of contemporary pamphlets and official documents included in the text. For this reason it is still useful to the historian, but it does not make easy reading—the work is very long, inchoate and written in a style lacking in sparkle to say the least, though the occasional illuminating comment can be found.

Emmanual van Meteren (1535–1612) was born in Antwerp but lived the better part of his life as a representative of Holland merchants in London. He was in close touch with highly cultivated literary circles and gave much more attention to style and presentation than Bor. Moreover, one of his contacts was Christiaan Huygens the elder (the father of Constantijn), who was secretary to the Council of State and was able to provide him with much useful information. Indeed, his work was at one stage banned by the States General because he had included information which this body would rather have kept secret. His chronicle—*Historie der Nederlandscher ende haerder nabueren oorlogen* (History of the wars of the Netherlands and its neighbours)—first came before the public in 1599, but the definitive edition was only published in 1614. This work contains rather more than the standard descriptions of military and political events, space being given to economic developments, or at least to trade. Van Meteren's occupation must have made him more aware than many others of the importance of such matters in the early history of the Republic.

The last of these interesting writers, Everard van Reyd (1550–1602), was also born outside the province of Holland, at Deventer in Overijsel. From 1584 he was secretary to the stadhouder of Friesland, Willem Lodewijk, and this position gave him an excellent opportunity to observe political developments at close hand. He is perhaps the most interesting and individual of these three chroniclers. The *Voornaamste geschiedenissen in de Nederlanden* (Principal histories of the Netherlands) only appeared after its author's death.

It is worth drawing attention to the fact that none of these three outstanding chroniclers was born or lived in the province of Holland. They were active in the late sixteenth and the first decade of the seventeenth century before Holland had really begun to dominate the intellectual and cultural life of the Republic. The situation was to be very different in later years, also in the field of history—although the lesser provinces continued to produce their historians and histories.[16]

The finest Dutch historian of the seventeenth century was undoubtedly P. C. Hooft, whose work as a poet and dramatist has already been considered.[17] From 1618 Hooft appears to have devoted his life very largely to history with one great aim in mind—to write the history of the Revolt in Dutch. He saw himself faced with two major tasks: to present the crucial period in the life of his country in its full drama and significance, and at the same time to create a Dutch prose style able to express such a theme with the nobility and power of classical Latin. Hooft turned to history under the stimulus of the conflicts which had arisen in the Republic during the Truce; this episode raised fundamental political problems in his mind and he sought the answers to these in the study of history.

Hooft was impressively systematic in the way he prepared for the great task he had set himself. As a first exercise in historical writing, he chose to compose a biography of Henry IV of France, as this king had brought peace and prosperity to a country which had suffered from a period of civil strife even more severe than that which had troubled the Republic during the Truce. Hooft felt that Henry had brought the wars of religion to an end by standing above the warring parties, in a way that Maurice had not been able to do—probably because he had neither the power nor the prestige of a sovereign. Apart from the moral and political value of this work, it was far from negligible as history—it was the first 'life and times' written in Dutch, and Hooft showed a good critical sense in his use of the material available to him—though his first concern was to develop a controlled and concise prose style.

This self-imposed task of improving the Dutch language led him to his next major historical work: the translation of the whole of Tacitus into Dutch. At this period Tacitus was regarded not only as a model historian but also as the great master of Latin prose,[18] therefore he was to be Hooft's mentor not only in the writing of history but also in literary style. In these translations particularly, Hooft modelled his prose very closely on that of Tacitus, both in syntax and in word choice. In so doing he produced a very concise and powerful Dutch, which, however, is occasionally almost as difficult to follow as the Latin of the original—immediate clarity and ease of reading being sacrificed to concision.

Between 1628 and 1638 Hooft not only translated the whole of Tacitus' *Annales et Historiae, Germania* and *Agricola* but also wrote his masterpiece, the *Nederlandsche Historien*, which dealt with the history of the Revolt from 1555 to the death of William the Silent in 1584. This work was published in 1642 and Hooft began a continuation, the *Vervolgh*, probably intended to carry the story on till the end of Leicester's period in the Netherlands and the foundation of the Republic, but this part was unfinished at his death. The *Nederlandsche Historien* has been called 'the most powerful prose-work that the seventeenth century produced'[19] in the Republic, and indeed it might with justice be considered the greatest work of literature produced by a Dutch writer during this century. For it is not only a history but also a drama, as relevant to the politics of his time as Hooft's plays had been. In this great work, Hooft expounds, within the discipline imposed by history, his considered attitude to the problems of government, and William the Silent emerges as the ideal prince, dedicated to the defence of liberty and justice against a tyrant. Moreover, his ideas are expressed in a prose which is as impressive as it is idiosyncratic. Dutch seventeenth-century prose tended to be rambling in structure and overloaded with half-assimilated foreign loan-words, and anyone who has had to read much of it turns with relief and a real pleasure to Hooft's carefully organised, concise and sonorous prose, and is willing to accept the over-artificial elements of his style, such as the alliteration which is used so often as an emphatic device.

Hooft's research for this work was considerable, ranging from the published chronicles written from both the Dutch and the Spanish points of view to unpublished archive material and the oral accounts of participants, but the importance of the history does not lie in the information which it contains. It is an epic account of the Revolt, but an epic based on a critical comparison of the various sources used, with particular emphasis on writers from the catholic or Spanish side as a check on the reliability of the Dutch sources. Hooft's history was a service to his country: by choosing to write in Dutch he sacrificed the chance of European fame, but his service to the Republic and its language was all the greater as a consequence.

However, despite the stature of Hooft's achievement as an historian his approach to the problem of creating a viable Dutch prose proved to be of little help to his contemporaries. His complex Tacitean prose was in the event not imitated by either his own or later generations. Later writers had still to find their own solutions to the problem of language. That such a master as Hooft should have taken what proved to be a sterile direction is a striking indication of the magnitude of the difficulties facing Dutch writers.

The historical work of De Groot, Hooft and the great trio of chroniclers already mentioned was concerned with the Revolt itself and the immediately succeeding decades, but the other outstanding works of history written in the seventeenth century dealt chiefly with later events in the history of the Republic. This circumstance is perhaps further evidence to support the suggestion that the recurring political crises in the Republic were important stimuli in many fields of culture, but especially fruitful for the production of what would now be called contemporary history. The crisis during the Truce, the attempted *coup* by William II, the controversy over the stadhoudership—all were events which brought out fundamental contradictions in the political system of the Republic, contradictions which remained until the state collapsed at the end of the eighteenth century. Histories of such events were at the same time contributions to important political controversies. They not only aroused great interest, they were themselves a product of passionate involvement on the part of their authors. The works of Johannes Uyttenbogaert and Jacobus Trigland on the religious conflicts of the first two decades of the century are clear examples of the fruitful effect of such intense involvement. The former was the leader of the Remonstrants after the death of Arminius, the latter one of the leading Contraremonstrant polemicists; both show the way contemporary history could be put to the service of powerful convictions.

These were polemical works, at least in essence and intention, but the chronicle tradition had not died out. Lieuwe van Aitzema's *Saken van staet en oorlogh, in ende omtrent de Vereenigde Nederlanden* (Affairs of state and war, in and about the United Netherlands), which was published between 1655 and 1671, deals with the years 1621–69 in many volumes. It is a very idiosyncratic work, in which the author does not hesitate to give his own opinion on events or to express his own cynical views of human motivation. It is thus far from dull; however, it is formless and written in an undistinguished Dutch, in this sense resembling the earlier chronicles rather than the work of later writers who gave more attention to form and style.

Aitzema's work is a notable achievement and is still pillaged by modern historians, but the outstanding historian of the later seventeenth century was Gerard Brandt (1626–85). Brandt was a Remonstrant minister with distinct literary pretensions. He took his vocation as an historian very seriously, and produced very readable works in his lives of Vondel and De Ruyter, where he made skilful use of the evidence available to him, taken both from written sources and personal reminiscences, and presented it in a lively style. Moreover, these books are quite short, compact and well-organised. Yet in what should have been his masterpiece—and in many ways still is—Brandt seems to have been overwhelmed by his material. His *Historie der Reformatie* (History of the Reformation)[20] covers four big volumes and, whereas the first volume takes the narrative up to 1600, the last three deal with the religious troubles within the Republic in the early years of the seventeenth century from a Remonstrant point of view in immense detail, ending with the persecution of the Remonstrants after the Synod of Dordrecht. The number of letters, official documents and declarations he felt it necessary to include in the body of the work make it difficult to read, though it remains very useful as a work of reference. Added to the text is a large body of notes, yet he still confessed, 'I had, dear Reader, gathered together besides these Notes also numerous others. For how many events, of works and words, still remain in the History which demand such Notes.'[21] In all, Brandt gives very much the impression that he had lost control of his material. The subject was too important to him to allow the imposition of the strict organisation necessary to give the work a clear shape. For he had a great aim in this work, as he states in the same note—perhaps a rather odd position for such a statement of purpose—'Use meanwhile this work for good; and help to further the peace of the churches, for which God should be prayed to passionately, according to ability.'[22]

Many of the historical works we have just considered—those of Trigland, Uyttenbogaert and Brandt—were primarily concerned with the religious aspect of the problems facing Dutch society, but the difficulties posed by the peculiar nature of the Dutch constitution also gave rise to a particularly lively and continuous discussion similarly stimulated from time to time by the recurring crises of the century. The central problem facing practical Dutch political thinkers was the choice between the republican and the monarchical systems. The conflict between the Orangists and the States-party was mirrored in the disagreements of the theorists. Not that the argument was always carried on in extreme terms, or that the questions at issue were always particularly clear. Normally the Orangist writers kept monarchist ideas at a safe distance and centred their arguments on the necessity for an 'Eminent Head' in the state to provide a focus of loyalty within the political system of the Republic, to provide a generally-accepted leadership, and to minimise the effects of provincial separatism. Such writers tended to see the situation which had existed under the stadhouder Frederick Henry (and earlier, of course, under William the Silent) as the ideal, as he had held in practice a semi-monarchical authority within the Republic. On the republican side the emphasis was commonly placed on the primacy of provincial sovereignty, and on the threat to freedom and prosperity represented by the rule of a prince and thus by the ambitions of the house of Orange. The existence and utility of the stadhoudership itself was rarely attacked, rather republican writers stressed the danger that a stadhouder might employ his power and influence to undermine the constitution and set himself up as a monarch. While the Orangists looked to William the Silent and Frederick Henry as their examples of the benefits which the leadership of a prince of Orange could bring to the state, the Republicans pointed to the actions of Maurice in 1618-19 and to the almost disastrous results of the conduct of William II during his short period of office.

Apart from Spinoza, the Republic of the seventeenth century did not produce any political thinkers of the first rank. Moreover, the political theorists in the Dutch universities showed little sign of any involvement in or even awareness of the peculiar problems created by the Dutch political system. Indeed, it is rather surprising to see just how unrelated the theoretical writings of these academics were to the realities of Dutch political life. In general, the political philosophy taught at Dutch universities and written by their scholars in the seventeenth century was traditional and conservative—in the European not the Dutch sense—and, adopting the Aristotelian schema of possible constitutions, it accepted monarchy as the best of these. Apparently this theoretical preference for monarchy was not a consequence of, nor did it cause, any general attachment to the house of Orange among university professors of politics—some of the leading representatives of this way of thought, for example Burgersdijk, were associated with the Remonstrants in the earlier part of the century and experienced some difficulties as a consequence, yet they continued to uphold the theoretical position of the monarchical system. In fact it is probable that the Republic and its practical problems were far from the minds of these academics as they wrote and taught. As with many Dutch academics, especially in the late sixteenth century and the first decades of the seventeenth century, these men were more citizens of the European intellectual community than of the Dutch Republic, at least as far as their intellectual frame of reference was concerned. Thus they fitted into the general European system of academic political theory in which they had been trained, about which they wrote and lectured, and which formed the essential basis of their thought—it is a more or less accidental misfortune that the teachings of this tradition were so remote from the political realities of the Dutch Republic at the time.

Dutch political theory was able to achieve a measure of originality, and to break loose from the general and traditional European pattern of thought, but this development did not take place in the universities. In the third quarter of the seventeenth century especially, writers began to grapple with the actual problems of Dutch political life and attempted to place them in a theoretical framework. This new approach coincided with the period of Republican supremacy associated with the name of Johan de Witt, when the Republic was enjoying the position of a major power in Europe and when the general prosperity of the country was at its peak. It was at this time that Dutch writers began to lose their sense of inferiority *vis à vis* the established monarchies of the age and to argue in favour of the relative excellence of the constitution of their own country in theoretical terms.

Before about 1650 comment on the politics of the Republic had been largely propagandist in intent and polemic in form, while academic and theoretical discussion of political problems had been unrelated to existing Dutch conditions. During the Wittian period not only did a lively controversy grow up over the relative merits of the Orangist and Republican systems, but from this controversy emerged a number of works which were intended to be more than ephemeral propaganda. These works attempted to provide a universally valid statement of the superiority of republican régimes in general, and more specifically to argue that the political system of the Dutch Republic was both theoretically and practically superior to the monarchical systems in force in most of the rest of Europe.

There had, of course, been some attempts to deal directly with the political system of the Republic before the mid-century, but such writings had been largely unoriginal, and had tended to criticise the

Republic for its divergences from the norms provided by other states. In general terms they offered monarchy as the solution for the political difficulties of the Republic. Such writers arrived at conclusions which were superficially similar to those of the academic political philosophers, but their starting points were as different as their modes of argument. This particular monarchist tendency is well illustrated by P. C. Hooft, who might also be considered its most important representative. In his dramatic work, but more especially in his historical writings, Hooft put forward the concept of the ideal prince, intimating that only in this way could a satisfactory answer to the problem of reconciling power and authority with freedom be found. As has already been indicated, with Hooft this idea was not the consequence of abstract speculation but arose from his consideration of the recent civil disturbances in his own and other countries, which he partly dealt with in his own historical works. In his life of Henry IV he presented the French king as the man who had been able to resolve the internal conflicts of his country; the difficulties which had arisen in the Dutch Republic during the Truce led Hooft to believe that a monarchical system was desirable in order to facilitate the resolution of any such conflicts which might arise in the future. When he dedicated his *Nederlandsche Historiën* to Frederick Henry, Hooft was underlining the parallels he saw between the problems which had arisen during the Revolt and those of his own day. Here again, however, Hooft was being neither particularly original nor particularly Dutch. Just as he was by education and aspirations a member of the international cultured community, so his political attitudes were elaborations of the commonplaces current in this society. He saw the Dutch political crisis during the Truce as a particular example of a problem which was troubling most of Europe, and he adopted the solution which was normally offered by men of similar position and education, of whatever country, at this time. The great influence on Hooft of Montaigne must have encouraged him to adopt a similar attitude to the problems of his own country to that expressed by Montaigne with regard to those of his.

The original element in the political writings which began to appear towards the middle of the century was that, 'Really for the first time in the history of the Netherlands a theory which was republican in principle arose. . . . It meant a revolutionary break with tradition, a sharp rejection of old authorities and obscurities and an occasionally almost snobbish-seeming modernism.'[23] While it would be pointless to deny that the republican writers of this period were strongly influenced by the works of Descartes and Hobbes, nevertheless they were impelled to search for new positions by the demands of the political situation within the Republic and were far from mere disciples of their French and English mentors. William II's attempt at a *coup* in 1650, his arrest of the six deputies to the States of Holland, and his attack on Amsterdam, had threatened the Republic with civil war. It must have been evident to contemporaries that only the death of the young prince in November of that same year had saved the country from further serious conflict. The Republican writers of the next two decades could not forget that a prince of Orange through his ambition and folly had nearly plunged the Republic into civil war. While William II's son was still an infant and the Orangist party crippled by dissension between the widow of Frederick Henry, the widow of William II, and the stadhouder of Friesland Willem Frederik, the problem of the stadhoudership and the position of the house of Orange in the state were not pressing and the Republican régime had no serious challenge to meet. However, as it became increasingly likely that the young prince of Orange would reach maturity, the problem of his future position in the Republic became an ever more real issue in Dutch politics. The difficulties of De Witt and his supporters were only exacerbated when the young prince's uncle, Charles II, established himself on the English throne, for the English king found his nephew a welcome and very effective focus for propaganda against the Dutch Republican régime. In these circumstances the States-party felt an urgent need for theoretical justifications of its rule and policies, founded particularly on an appreciation of Dutch history and the contemporary political situation. The actions of William II in 1650 had convinced the Republicans of the danger which could come from a stadhouder; the resurgence of Orangism in the 1660s provided them with a challenge they could not afford to ignore, even on the theoretical plane.

The most interesting of these Republican political theorists (excepting always the case of Spinoza who defies easy categorisation) were the brothers Johan and Pieter de la Court. Johan (1622–60) was the younger of the two and little is known of his life, but he does seem to have been the more original and powerful thinker. Pieter (1618–85) was less consistent a theorist, and was more concerned with the propaganda value of his publications. The brothers were the sons of a Leiden textile manufacturer who had immigrated from the Southern Netherlands in the early seventeenth century. Pierre de la Court had moved from Ypres to Leiden in 1613 and set himself up as an artisan, but his situation improved rapidly until by 1630 he was one of the most important merchant/manufacturers in the town. He was thus in a position to provide Johan and Pieter with the education proper to the sons of a wealthy Dutch merchant (though their elder brother, Jacob, seems to have been taken straight into the family business), and they finished their education by studying at the university in their home town. At the time, in the 1640s, the philosophy of Descartes was becoming a source of serious controversy at Leiden, its particular champion being the professor of philosophy Heereboord (who married the sister of the De la Court brothers in 1646), and Pieter at least was clearly drawn to the new ideas.

Despite their education, which suited them for positions in government or administration, Pieter and Johan chose to set themselves up as manufacturers and merchants in the Leiden textile industry. Possibly a career in politics was closed to them in any case because their family had not broken through to the circles of the Leiden oligarchy. In addition the political views of the brothers were hardly likely to commend them to the dominant party in the town government, as Leiden had the reputation of being one of the most strongly Orangist of the town governments of Holland. So the brothers built up their position in industry, and devoted their spare time to study. They were able to become the most interesting and original of Dutch political writers—with the exception of Spinoza—of the century, and Pieter became one of the most effective propagandists against the house of Orange during the 1660s.

It is not certain what part of Johan de la Court's published writings is indeed his, for they were all published after his death by Pieter, who not only put his brother's manuscripts in order but added to them copiously. The first edition of the *Politike Weegschaal* was 369 pages long, the third in 1661 572, and by the fourth edition (1662) it had grown to 670 pages.[24] Nevertheless it is fairly clear which works were Johan's and not too difficult to detect the additions made to them by his brother. Johan's political theory was contained in the *Politike Weegschaal* (Political Balance) of 1660,[25] *Politike Discoursen* (Political Discourses)[26] first published in 1662, and *Naeuwkeurige Consideratie* (Accurate Consideration) of the same year.[27] Johan de la Court was unmistakeably a Republican and a supporter of De Witt, but he was far from being a simple propagandist for the existing régime in Holland. His approach was theoretical and immediate practical applications were for him of secondary importance: he was concerned to discover the ideal state-form, or rather the best practicable political system, not to justify the oligarchy of the Republic. Johan, like his brother, was a determined modernist with little more than contempt for the traditional doctrines of political philosophy, particularly as transmitted by the academics of his time. His masters were Descartes, for his psychology, Hobbes and Machiavelli. While he was heavily indebted to these writers, his somewhat disordered and never completely consistent writings contain more than a spark of originality. Basing himself on a pessimistic view of human psychology—drawn from Descartes and Hobbes—Johan considered the various possible political systems from the standpoint of their ability to protect the freedom of the individual citizen from the abuse of power by those in authority. His conclusions were rather startling for the seventeenth century as, although he considered aristocracy to be far preferable to monarchy, he finally chose democracy as the best possible system. In fact, although his works can be read as attacks on monarchy in general and on the pretensions of the house of Orange in particular (the interpolations by his brother often gave his remarks greater contemporary relevance and a stronger polemic tone), his conclusions could hardly have recommended themselves to the Republican regents as they undermined the theoretical basis of the Dutch oligarchy. It may have been some consolation to the Wittian regents that the author of these works clearly did not intend them as blueprints for radical political reform, much less revolution, as he was altogether too distrustful of the anarchic tendencies in human nature, but such men can hardly have been pleased with the general trend of his arguments. The Republicans found the legitimation of oligarchic power in the ill-defined notion of the 'True Freedom'; Johan de la Court, by maintaining that individual freedom would be more efficiently safeguarded by a democratic system, was hitting at the very basis of this justification.

There were other, less modern, aspects to the political philosophy of Johan de la Court, but these are less important to us here than his achievement in breaking out, with the help of Hobbes and Descartes, from the restrictions which had confined political thought to a very conservative tradition since the theories developed to justify the Revolt had gone out of fashion, or rather had become embarrassing to the holders of power in the Republic. Moreover, his theoretical preference for democracy shows that, despite his debts to other writers, he was capable of taking an independent line to an extent that seems to have been almost impossible for most of his Dutch contemporaries.

Pieter de la Court[28] was a writer of much less pronounced theoretical leanings, and he was also much less bold than his brother in advancing original or shocking ideas. He played a central rôle in the political controversy of the 1660s over the stadhoudership, and he was much more obviously a pen in the service of the Wittian system. His chief work, the *Interest van Holland*, was read in manuscript and corrected by Johan de Witt himself, and was later thought to have been written by him. (When the book was translated into English in the early eighteenth century it was attributed to De Witt.[29]) Yet, despite his clear place within the States-party, and despite his support for and close association with De Witt, Pieter de la Court was quite capable of radical formulations, especially when it came to criticisms of the ruling oligarchies of Holland. If he was less abstract than his brother, and if his approach to democracy was much more hesitant, he was still able to argue vigorously for a considerable expansion in the size and social basis of the political nation in the Republic. His list of those who should be excluded from participation in politics is especially interesting. Firstly minors, women and servants; secondly foreigners of only short residence in the country; and

thirdly, all the deaf, dumb, infamous, and poor people living from alms or in poorhouses, must be excluded; together with all others, who, within a certain number of years, had exercised any trade, or worked for a daily wage in anyone's service, whatever that should be: for the same must be presumed to take place through need, and must also be presumed to lack the necessary knowledge for government.[30]

It is clear from this quotation that the great majority of the population was to be excluded from politics, but it is equally clear that, in De la Court's system, the number of men directly involved in political life would have been increased enormously. The similarity of these ideas with those of the Levellers in England is occasionally startling.[31]

The quoted passage occurs in a section of the *Politike Weegschaal* added by Pieter, and his additions to his brother's works are an important source for his ideas, but his major works remain the *Interest van Holland* of 1662,[32] the *Gravelijke Regering* (The Rule of the Counts) of the same year,[33] and the *Aanwijsing* of 1669.[34]

The *Gravelijke Regering* is the most obviously propagandist of his works, being a sustained attack on the powers of the stadhouders and the princes of Orange in Holland. As Geyl has pointed out, this book was in many ways an extension of part of De Witt's *Deductie* of

1654[35]—the official account by the States of Holland of the reasons for its abolition of the stadhoudership. De la Court's polemic against the rule of the counts in Holland was intended as an attack on the house of Orange, and it was read as such by contemporaries. The *Interest van Holland*, although it covered a wider field than the political conflicts of the 1660s, was also a broadside in this pamphlet battle: 'Yet he was also basically concerned to make the excellence of the government of the States clear against the objectionable nature of that of the stadhouders.'[36] Despite his criticisms of the regent oligarchy, De la Court remained a firm supporter of the States Party and seems to have accepted that it would have been impossible to put his anti-oligarchic reforms into practice. Above all he was concerned to stress the disadvantages of rule by the princes of Orange. The increasing weakness of the Wittians before the Orangist resurgence of the years immediately before 1672 only pushed him more firmly into the Republican camp.

De la Court's second marriage in 1661 allied him to the Amsterdam merchant family Van der Voort, and in 1666 he moved to Amsterdam and entered into partnership with his brothers-in-law. They were involved, among other enterprises, in supplying the Dutch fleet with provisions and munitions during the second Anglo-Dutch war. It is possible that he began to consider a political career about this time, for in 1670 he was enrolled at the university of Orléans and in 1672 he became an advocate before the Court of Holland. The fall of theWittian régime, however, ended the possibility of any such career for De la Court: he found that he was one of the men most threatened by popular violence and was forced to flee to the Southern Netherlands for safety.

Although the emphasis has so far been placed on the political content of De la Court's writings, much of his work was in fact concerned with the economic 'interest' of the Republic. It would be better perhaps to say that he was concerned with the prosperity of his own province—his intense particularism is shown by his use of the term 'the republic of Holland and West-Friesland' (the official name of the province being Holland and West-Friesland). For De la Court political questions were inseparable from questions of economic policy. If Johan had been concerned to discover the political system which would best protect the freedom of the individual, for Pieter a political system was expected to provide both freedom and prosperity. In this attitude he reflected very clearly the interests of the wealthy and active merchants of Holland, who were probably in favour of his economic, if not political, ideas.

The De la Courts worked outside the universities and reacted strongly against the political philosophy which still held sway there. Spinoza, who was clearly influenced by their works, was also outside the somewhat stifling atmosphere of the Dutch universities. He, however, was a philosopher concerned to construct an abstract system, and he wrote in Latin, and a very abstract and impersonal Latin at that. The De la Court brothers, although giving their works a theoretical foundation, were very much involved in the practical political problems which faced the Dutch Republic, and Pieter in particular tied his discussions very closely to the economic and social realities of his country. They were both specifically concerned with Holland and the reforms they suggested were designed to correct what they felt to be weaknesses in the Dutch system of government. It is entirely typical of them that they chose to write in Dutch, and not in the Latin of the learned. They aimed at a Dutch audience and were involved in Dutch problems, and this direct response to particular problems gives their work an immediacy that much other political theory of the time lacked.

After the fall of the Wittian régime and the rise to power of William III, political controversy lost much of its life and originality. Political theory returned to the universities and became an academic game played with varying degrees of conviction and written in Latin. To use Latin in the later seventeenth century, however, had very different implications than it had had in the first decades of the century. In the early years of the century Latin was still the universal language of academic and intellectual intercourse, and original Latin literature was still flourishing, in quantity if not in quality. Constantijn Huygens, Heinsius, Grotius—to mention only some outstanding figures—all wrote a considerable amount of Latin verse. The position of Latin was, of course, not unchallenged, but it was dominant in the universities and powerful outside, for instance the historical work of Grotius. By the later years of the century Latin had already been pushed decisively into the background in most fields: Latin literature had almost died out except as an exercise for schoolboys, and even in the field of thought the vernaculars had begun to triumph with the French of Descartes and the English of Hobbes and Locke. Christiaan Huygens used French rather than Latin for many of his scientific works, though in this area the victory of the vernacular was far from complete. Only in the universities was the supremacy of Latin still unchallenged, and this was especially true of the universities of the Dutch Republic. Dutch political theorists, by writing in Latin, cut themselves off to a large degree from many of their contemporaries and most of posterity. Kossmann asks[37] why Willem van der Muelen (1659–1739) has been forgotten while Locke, 'no more profound or original than he', is regarded as one of the most important thinkers of his age. Whatever the comparative merits of their works, it may well be that the fact that Van der Muelen wrote in Latin while Locke wrote in English has more than symbolic importance in bringing out the differences between the two writers and in explaining the disparity in the influence that each was able to exert.

The most important political philosopher in the Republic in the last quarter of the seventeenth century was Ulric Huber (1636–94). He was born in Dokkum in Friesland, studied in Marburg, Heidelberg and Strassburg, then spent most of his adult life as professor of law at the university of Franeker in his native province. His chief political work was *De jure civitatis libri tres*, which was first published in 1672, but only reached its definitive form in the edition of 1694. Huber was an academic writing in Latin, but his grasp of traditional theory did not blind him to the realities of the Dutch situation. His analysis of the Revolt was acute. He concluded that before the Revolt the Netherlands had been a constitutional monarchy, but that the people had since then, albeit tacitly, abdicated their political rights in favour of the provincial states and that, in consequence, the Republic was an absolute aristocracy. He went on to argue that an aristocracy was the best form of government, especially if tempered by a constitution and if the aristocracy were as broadly based as possible. His theory was founded on a close, careful and realistic analysis of the Dutch political system. Moreover, he indicated how the Republic could move in the direction of the liberal state by expanding the ranks of those who could take part in government as much as possible, and by providing carefully for the protection of the rights of the individual. Huber in this way developed a political theory which sounds remarkably modern through his consideration of the Dutch political system.[38] Yet his work was in Latin and was very largely lost in the moribund circles of late seventeenth-century academics, having little influence on later thinkers.

The Dutch Republic of the seventeenth century also produced a notable crop of scientists working, like most of the interesting historians and political thinkers, outside the universities. Here one of the Republic's advantages, in science as in politics and theology, was the absence of an established church powerful enough to hinder the expression and development of new ideas which seemed a threat to the intellectual bases or religious orthodoxy. Galileo experienced the consequences of the Catholic Church's fear of innovatory ideas which challenged the accepted orthodoxies in science and philosophy, and similar attitudes were strong in the Reformed Church in the Republic. In the latter case, however, Reformed orthodoxy lacked the power to impose its views on society as a whole. On the other hand, the Dutch universities were much more open, as public institutions, to pressure from the Reformed Church than were individual scientists, and this circumstance may help to explain why most of the original scientific work, except in the case of medicine, carried out in the Republic in the seventeenth century took place outside the universities.

Of the leading Dutch scientists, Christiaan Huygens won international fame for his work, but this celebrity was achieved by turning his back to a great extent on his own land and making himself part of the European learned community. Huygens made a major contribution to the development of scientific method as well as making particular discoveries and putting forward theories which proved fruitful, but he did not owe his training to any institution in the Republic, nor was his own country especially forward in recognising his merits in any tangible way.

Christiaan Huygens was the son of Constantijn, secretary to the princes of Orange, who has already been discussed as a poet and as the epitome of the cultivated renaissance man. Christiaan's family connections meant that he was only partly rooted in Dutch society, his father's circle comprising courtiers and cultivated aristocrats from most western European countries. Yet the young Huygens can also be seen as a member of that generation of Dutchmen who produced the last great fruits of Dutch civilisation before the relative sterility of the eighteenth century. Huygens was born in 1629, within a few years of Spinoza (1632), Vermeer (1632), Johan de Witt (1625) and Leeuwenhoek (1632). Huygens was educated by private tutors at home—his father's wealth was by this time considerable—and was then sent to study law, first at Leiden then at the newly-opened academy at Breda (where his father was one of the curators). Constantijn clearly aimed at an official career for his sons, preferably in the service of the house of Orange (Christiaan's elder brother, Constantijn, did in time find a place in the household of William III), but circumstances defeated these plans. After the death of William II and the subsequent eclipse of the house of Orange, prospects of preferment through the service of that house were poor, and public office would be very difficult to obtain for the sons of a man as attached to the defeated party as the elder Huygens. In 1655, incidentally on a visit to Paris, Huygens took his doctorate in law at the protestant university of Angers, but this was his last step on the road to a public career. (Later in life, however, attempts were made to persuade William III to grant Huygens an official post, more in recognition of his achievements in science than because of any presumed administrative ability, but William was not interested.)

Huygens lived the life of a gentleman of independent means, devoting his time and energies to science. Mathematics and science were acceptable occupations for the well-born amateur at this time, and many of his correspondents were similarly gentlemen with a dilettante interest in such subjects. Given his background and education, Huygens could as easily have become a scholar or a man of letters, but his talents and interests lay elsewhere. He lived and corresponded in an international *milieu* which included very many men of high social status, whose work nevertheless was almost as important to science as the poetry of similar men had been to the literature of an earlier generation. Yet while his father's poems had won for him a respectable place in the literary world, Huygens' work placed him among the very greatest scientists of the seventeenth century, his achievement surpassed perhaps only by those of Galileo and Newton. In astronomy he discovered the ring of Saturn, using a telescope whose lenses he had ground himself; his application of the pendulum to clocks in the 1650s was the most important step forward in accurate time-keeping in this century;[39] and his theory of the wave-motion of light was one of the most significant developments in seventeenth-century physics. There can be no place here even for a cursory glance at Huygen's scientific work; suffice it to say that his greatness was recognised by his contemporaries, and confirmed by later commentators.

Huygens spent much of his life in Paris, living there almost continuously from 1661 to 1681, and it was from Louis XIV that he received the most tangible recognition of his merit—a gift of 1,200 livres in 1663 (in return Huygens dedicated his *Horologium oscillatorium*, which appeared in 1673, to the French king) and the same amount in the following two years. More, Huygens drafted the first programme for the projected *Académie des Sciences*, and in 1666 he became a member of this new body with a pension of 6,000 livres a year, together with living quarters in the Bibliothèque Royale. Only in 1683 did he finally lose this position, after the French government had begun to put pressure on the Huguenots and consequently on foreign protestants living in France as well. It is an interesting comment on his attitude to his own country that Huygens did not find the outbreak of the war between the Republic and France in 1672 a reason for him to leave his lucrative and scientifically fruitful work in Paris. As he wrote to his brother, Lodewijk, when war threatened, '. . . je ne suis emploié en rien qui aie quelque chose de commun avec la guerre'.⁴⁰ He was an international man, wrote his correspondence, even to his own family, largely in French or Latin, and his only important vernacular writings were also in French. Here he presents a sharp contrast to those very Dutch scientists Swammerdam and Leeuwenhoek. By birth Huygens belonged to a section of Dutch society that was culturally more European than Dutch, and it is also not without significance that he could find a more congenial—and financially rewarding—work-place in Paris than anywhere in the Republic. Culturally Holland was already beginning to lose ground to its bigger neighbours.

The other Dutchmen who made important contributions to the growth of scientific knowledge during the seventeenth century came from very different sectors of society. Like Huygens they also worked outside the universities, but for rather different reasons. If a university chair was too humble a position for a man of Huygens' social background—university professors were on the whole not drawn from the wealthier social groups, and their salaries were relatively modest—men such as Leeuwenhoek and Swammerdam were cut off from the possibility of a university post by their lack of a particular type of education, or by the lack of a certain expertise. Teaching at Dutch universities was carried on in Latin, and both these men felt themselves insufficiently competent in this language to use it as their mode of expression. Swammerdam had enjoyed a university education but he preferred to write in Dutch and have his work translated for the benefit of a European audience; Leeuwenhoek knew little or no Latin. Moreover, Dutch universities in the seventeenth century were little likely to recognise the merits of experimental or observational science.

Jan Swammerdam (1637–80) was the son of an Amsterdam apothecary famous for his collection of natural curiosities, who was sufficiently well-off to send his son to university at Leiden, but who was not prepared to support him in his disinterested studies for very long. Swammerdam, with his passion for entomology and anatomy, seems to have been unable to settle to any occupation which would have earned him a living. He graduated in medicine, but seems never to have practised. Moreover, he was both physically weak and mentally unstable—towards the end of his life he experienced a conversion, under the influence of Antoinette Bourignon,⁴¹ to a sort of mysticism, associated with powerful feelings of guilt over his own dedication to his studies, which were vanities from the point of view of his religious convictions. Swammerdam's situation was aggravated by constant clashes with his father, who resented having to support his son after he had become an adult, and who finally refused to give him any more help. The only serious offer of support Swammerdam received was from the Grand Duke of Tuscany who offered him f.12,000– for his collection of insects, but only on condition that he move to Florence and accept conversion to catholicism. Swammerdam could not accept this last condition. The last years of his life were unhappy in the extreme, but he preserved the record of his researches though these were only published long after his death by his admirer, the physician Herman Boerhaave. His studies, in particular of the anatomy and physiology of insects, not least his beautifully accurate drawings of his observations, and considering the defective instruments of his time, made him the most important and original entomologist of his century, and indeed his work was not superseded before the nineteenth century.[42]

Anthonij van Leeuwenhoek (1632–1723) also came from a modest level of society and he shared Swammerdam's passion for knowledge of things small as well as his capacity for minute observation and concentrated effort. Unlike Swammerdam, however, he did not have a university education and he did all of his research in his spare time, as he had no independent income. For nearly 40 years he was chamberlain to the *schepenen* of Delft, an unimportant post but one that was neither ill-paid nor demanding. Such posts were much in demand and Leeuwenhoek must have considered himself lucky to have found such an agreeable appointment. It allowed him to lead a comfortable life and left him time for the research which made him famous, at least in scientific circles. He was perhaps appreciated more outside the Republic than at home, although he wrote only in Dutch. He corresponded with the Royal Society, of which he was made a member, and by the end of his life this modest man was known and respected throughout the European scientific world. His discovery of 'little animals' in water was one of the most exciting events of the century in science and determined the course of microscopy for over a century. His observations of protozoa and even bacteria were a remarkable achievement, but as seventeenth-century biology lacked the concept of the cell such unicellular organisms were impossible for Leeuwenhoek and his contemporaries to understand.[43]

These two notable scientists are further examples of the cultural and intellectual vitality of the Dutch artisan and lower-middle classes. From this same area of society had sprung almost all the leading painters and the greatest poet, Vondel. The social groups which provided political and economic leadership were distinctly less productive in art and science, though their contribution in literature, history and political thought was considerable.

Notes

[1] See R. L. Colie, *Light and Enlightenment. A study of the Cambridge Platonists and the Dutch Arminians* (Cambridge 1957)

[2] See especially, L. Kolakowski, *Chrétiens sans Église. La conscience religieuse et le lien confessionnel au XVIIe siecle* (Paris 1969), a great part of which is concerned with figures active in the Dutch Republic

[3] C. W. Roldanus, *Zeventiende-eeuwse geestesbloei* (Utrecht/Antwerp 1961), p. 98

[4] For Van Beuningen, see C. W. Roldanus, *Coenraad van Beuningen, staatsman en libertijn* (The Hague 1931); M. A. M. Franken, *Coenraad van Beuningen's politieke en diplomatieke aktiviteiten in de jaren 1667–1684* (Groningen 1966)

[5] E. Labrousse, *Pierre Bayle*, vol. I: *Du pays de Foix à la cité d'Erasme* (The Hague 1963), pp. 165–6, 172 n., 217

[6] See below, pp. 198–203

[7] R. J. McShea, *The Political Philosophy of Spinoza* (New York/London 1968), p. 71

[8] Spinoza, *Chief Works*, vol. I (Dover ed., New York 1951), p. 6

[9] E. H. Kossmann, *Politieke theorie in het zeventiende-eeuwse Nederland* (Verhandelingen der Koninklijke Nederlandse Akademie van Wetenschappen, afd. Letterkunde, nieuwe reeks—deel lxvii—no. 2) (Amsterdam 1960), esp. p. 50

[10] For the best account of his life and ideas, see J. Séguy, *Utopie Coopérative et Oecuménisme. Pieter Cornelisz. Plockhoy van Zurik-zee 1620–1700* (Paris/The Hague 1968)

[11] *Ibid.*, p. 39

[12] *A Way Propounded to make the poor in these and other Nations Happy by Bringing together a fit, suitable and well qualified people unto one Household-government, or little Commonwealth, wherein every one may keep his property, and be employed in some trade or other, as shall be fit, without being oppressed* (1659)

[13] C. W. Roldanus, *op. cit.*, p. 73

[14] E. Labrousse, *Pierre Bayle*, vol. II: *Hétérodoxie et rigorisme* (The Hague 1964), p. 29

[15] *Ibid.*, p. 33

[16] For example, see E. H. Waterbolk, *Twee eeuwen Friese geschiedschrijving. Opkomst, bloei en verval van de Friese historiografie in de zestiende en zeventiende eeuw* (Groningen/Djakarta 1952), with a summary in English

[17] See above, pp. 90–1

210 THE FRUITS OF TOLERANCE

E.-L. Etter, *Tacitus in der Geistesgeschichte des 16. und 17. Jahrhunderts* (Basel/Stuttgart 1966), esp. pp. 1, 9–11

G. Knuvelder, *Nederlandse letterkunde*, vol. 2, p. 205

Historie der Reformatie, en andere Kerkelyke Geschiedenissen, in en ontrent de Nederlanden. Met eenige Aentekeningen en Aenmerkingen (Amsterdam 1671–1704)

Ibid., vol. 1 (Amsterdam 1677²), p. 52 n

Ibid.

E. H. Kossmann, *op. cit.*, p. 30

Ibid., p. 36 n. 3

The original title was *Consideratien en exemplen van staat. Omtrent de fundamenten van allerly regeringe*, but this was changed in later printings to *Consideratien van staat ofte Politike Weegschaal* from which the usual short title is taken

Politike discoursen handelende in ses onderscheide boeken van steeden, landen, oorlogen, kerken, regeeringen, en zeeden

Naeuwkeurige consideratie van staet wegen de Heerschapye van een vrye en geheymen staets-regeering over de gantsche Aertbodem

For his career and ideas, see Th. van Thijn, 'Pieter de la Court. Zijn leven en zijn economische denkbeelden', *Tijdschrift voor geschiedenis*, 69e jaargang (1956), pp. 304–70

The True Interest and Political Maxims of the Republick of Holland and West-Friesland (London 1702)

Th. van Thijn, *art. cit.*, pp. 323–4

Cf. C. B. Macpherson, *The Political Theory of Possessive Individualism. Hobbes to Locke* (Oxford 1962), chap. III

Interest van Holland, ofte gronden van Hollands-Welvaren

Historie der gravelijke regering in Holland

The *Aanwijsing der heilsame politike Gronden en Maximen van de Republike van Holland en West-Vriesland* was a revised edition of the *Interest van Holland*. It deserves separate mention as it is nearly twice as long as the original

P. Geyl, *Het stadhouderschap in de partij-literatuur onder De Witt* (Amsterdam 1947) (Mededelingen der Koninklijke Nederlandsche Akademie van Wetenschappen, afd. Letterkunde, nieuwe reeks, deel 10, no. 2), p. 6

Ibid., p. 21

E. H. Kossmann, *op. cit.*, p. 71

Ibid., p. 103

C. M. Cipolla, *European Culture and Overseas Expansion* (Penguin 1970), pp. 133–4

C. Vollgraaf, *Biographie de Christiaan Huygens* (in *Oeuvres Complètes de Christiaan Huygens*, vol. 22 (The Hague 1950), p. 661

For Antoinette Bourignon, see L. Kolakowski, *op. cit.*, chap. x

A. R. Hall, *From Galileo to Newton 1630–1720* (London 1963), pp. 168–9

Ibid., pp. 171–3

eight

Decline

The eighteenth century in Dutch history is a concept as well as a chronological period. It refers to a time of decline and lack of vitality on all fronts of national life—and especially in the field of culture. Taken in this sense, the 'eighteenth century' started around 1670 or 1680 in the Republic. The political and even the economic decline of the Dutch Republic can be regarded with some sense of inevitability, for a country as small as the Republic could not hope to compete in the long run on equal terms with France and England, whose resources both in material and men were vastly superior. However, the cultural decline which can be seen in the late seventeenth and eighteenth century is a much more disturbing phenomenon, and one which is much less easy to explain. Moreover, there are certain nuances which have to be taken into account—for example, the decline is much less apparent in intellectual activities where the dominant rational spirit of the eighteenth century could act as a stimulus, and a certain vitality is evident in some of the arts as well. In a discussion of the aftermath of the Republic's Golden Century one is tempted to be too dramatic, and hence to underestimate the modest but real achievements of the eighteenth century. Nevertheless, it is clear that in the seventeenth century the Dutch Republic produced a civilisation of quite remarkable vigour, originality and diversity, while in the following century it became a minor power culturally, very much under French influence, and with very little of its own to offer the rest of Europe.

The flourishing civilisation of the Republic during the seventeenth century was made possible by its economic dominance in Europe, and the accompanying boom of the Dutch economy. The wealth of the Republic gave it the opportunity to develop a rich and diverse culture, and the relatively wide distribution of this prosperity over the upper and middle classes enabled the culture which evolved to be less dominated by the example and ideals of an aristocracy than any other country in Europe. The changes which took place in the Dutch

economy in the late seventeenth and early eighteenth century help to
explain the social and cultural changes which at least in part were
caused by them.

One important change was that the Dutch share in European trade
fell decisively, but only at a fairly late date. Although Dutch trade never
again reached the peak of the 1640s and came under heavy attack in the
second half of the seventeenth century, nevertheless the Republic
retained its leading position in Europe until the second quarter of the
following century. Even after this lead had been lost to England and
France, the Dutch decline was largely relative—the total value of
European trade had grown while the fall in the value of Dutch trade
was negligible. The need for a staple market had gone, and a process of
external contraction took place in Dutch trade, with an increasing
emphasis on trade with neighbours and a fall in the importance of
commercial relations with more distant areas. Also trade in colonial
goods became relatively more important in the total trade of the
Republic.

The situation was very different for industry—whereas trade had
shown only a relative decline, in industry the decline was absolute, and
in the textile industry disastrous. The production of the Leiden industry
fell from a peak of 139,000 pieces in 1671, to 85,000 in 1700, 54,000 in
1750, and to 29,000 in 1795.[1] Similarly, shipbuilding suffered severely
—the most important yards were in the area around Zaandam and
while there were 306 ships on the stocks here in 1707, after 1750 there
were less than five a year.[2] Some industries held their ground, e.g.
dyeing, tobacco-curing, the distilling of gin and brandy, but the
overall picture was of a steady and serious decline. The reasons for this
lay partly in the mercantilist policies of surrounding countries, in the
lack of raw materials within the boundaries of the Republic, and in the
small size of the internal market. Two further reasons, however, might
be put forward: firstly the wages paid in Holland were much higher
than in most other European countries; and secondly the Dutch failed
to keep in the forefront of technological change. The high wages seem
to have been made necessary by the taxation system in the Republic,
and in Holland in particular, with the heavy excises on food and other
necessities of life. The dominant political groups refused, from motives
of self-interest, to shift the burden of taxation from indirect to direct
taxes and thus helped to price Dutch products out of the European
market. For example, the weekly wage of a cotton-printer in Switzer-
land was f.3– to f.3.50 in 1766, in Augsburg f.3– in 1760, while in

Holland at the same period it was f.9– to f.10–.[3] The technological
stagnation which is evident in the eighteenth century is yet another
example of what might be termed a general ossification in Dutch life,
and we shall meet similar resistance to necessary change repeatedly in
this chapter.

The fisheries, which had played such an important rôle in the early
stages of the Dutch boom, were also in full decline by the eighteenth
century. There had been about 500 herring busses in Holland around
1630, but a century later the number had dropped to 219.[4] This fall
continued throughout the eighteenth century; but not only were there
fewer boats employed in the fishery, the average catch per boat also
fell considerably—it would seem that there were fewer herring available. There was a similar decline in whaling and in the less-important
cod-fishery. For both these branches the eighteenth century was a
period of depression with little or no profit to be made. (This situation
was less important in cod-fishing as the chief function of this branch of
the industry was to keep the herring busses and their crews employed
during the winter.) Probably the most important cause of decline in all
these activities was the great rise in competition from other countries,
especially England.

The decline in trade, industry and fishing was balanced to a slight
extent by a steady if slow increase in agricultural production and
profits. This was a development of considerable importance for 'it is
not impossible, though it cannot be proved, that this (i.e. agriculture)
even contributed the biggest part of the national income and that
relatively the most inhabitants were directly involved in it. This can be
taken as certain for the land provinces.'[5] This improvement in the state
of agriculture, which took place especially in the second half of the
eighteenth century, probably brought with it a slight decline in the
economic importance of Holland vis à vis the other provinces.

The social consequences of these economic changes are difficult to
assess, but some suggestions can be made. The decline in trade and
industry was accompanied by an increase in financial activity, particularly in the field of foreign investment. There was a surplus of capital
available for investment in the Republic, therefore interest rates were
low and investors looked abroad to find better returns from their
money. Dutch financiers were especially attracted by the British
National Debt, the English East India Company, and the Bank of
England. The increasing importance of the financial sector of the Dutch
economy seems to have brought with it an increased concentration of

wealth in the hands of a small group of wealthy *rentiers*. Moreover, the heavy involvement of the wealthier classes in foreign investment led to a certain dissociation from the national interest, as the interests of these groups were often as closely bound up with those of foreign countries as with the Republic's. This situation may be one explanation of the complacency with regard to the position of the Republic in Europe which became so characteristic of the Dutch regents in the course of the eighteenth century.

The growth of large-scale structural unemployment was also a consequence of these changes in the Dutch economy, especially because of the decline in labour-intensive industries. The fall in the numbers involved in fishing also led to serious unemployment. There may not have been a serious fall in *per capita* real income, though there would appear to have been some decline, but there was a marked change in its distribution. Poverty and unemployment increased significantly, while a greater proportion of the country's wealth came into the hands of financiers and *rentiers*.

The weakness of the Dutch economy in the eighteenth century should not be too heavily emphasised. On the whole the economic decline was relative rather than absolute; Holland remained prosperous but lost its lead in European trade. The qualitative changes in the economy which accompanied this relative decline were, nevertheless, important. The increasing polarisation in society between rich and poor had important consequences, especially in the towns of Holland. The importance of these economic changes is reflected in the demographic history of the period. The population of Holland grew rapidly in the first half of the seventeenth century, and then the growth began to slow down until a peak was reached in the 1670s or 1680s. Subsequently the population fell in the province as a whole, and this fall was most marked in some of the towns. The demographic peak of the late seventeenth century was not reached again before the nineteenth century. The development seems to have been very different in the land provinces, which saw a rise in population during the eighteenth century, particularly in its second half. Overall the population of the Republic may have grown a little in these years of demographic difficulties for Holland.[6]

It must be concluded that for Holland, if not for the rest of the Republic which was more concerned with agriculture, the eighteenth century was a period of economic difficulties and even distress for the majority of the population, especially the lower classes in the bigger towns. Such problems, however, were hardly felt by the Dutch regents who were chiefly involved in the financial sector and thus had no reason to complain of the situation or wish to change it.

The economic decline of the Republic was relative, but the decline of its international influence was rapid and absolute. After 1715 the Republic ceased to play any rôle of significance in European affairs. Indeed for long periods it seemed to play no active part whatsoever. The rise of France and England to predominance in Europe after their troubles in the earlier seventeenth century, states with far greater potential resources than the Republic, meant that the latter could no longer hope to exercise as much influence as it had done in the middle years of the seventeenth century. That this would be the case had already become apparent by the closing decades of this century, though the situation had been confused to some extent by the internal problems of England, which prevented it from acting powerfully in Europe until after the fall of James II.

Similarly, both Austria and Prussia were able to play major rôles in the measured military and political conflicts of the eighteenth century, while Russia had for almost the first time begun to enter into the calculations of western European statesmen. In these new conditions the Republic could only hope to be a power of the second rank. It had been able to act as a great power in the previous century partly through its economic strength, partly because of the efficiency of its tax system, but largely as a consequence of temporary weaknesses in so many of the other countries of Europe. In the eighteenth century the Dutch economy was relatively weaker, its tax system much less efficient in tapping the wealth of the country, and so the ability of the Republic to make its presence felt in Europe declined much more than might have been expected. Moreover, even the regents of Holland seem to have accepted this decline with something approaching complacency. Complaints were voiced, but dissatisfaction was not sufficient to lead to the internal reforms which were necessary to increase the administrative and financial efficiency of the Republic. The dominant groups in Dutch politics preferred to accept the fall in the international influence of the Republic, which did not directly threaten their own financial interests, rather than embark on reforms which would have undermined their vested interests.

This apathy with regard to the Republic's position in Europe was accompanied by an even greater complacency in respect to the political system within the state. The oligarchies in the voting towns of Holland had remained fluid in their composition throughout the seventeenth century because a number of peculiar circumstances had kept in check the natural tendency of all oligarchies to become closed orders within society. Firstly and most obviously, the recurrent crises in Dutch political life—in 1618, 1650 and 1672—had periodically disrupted the oligarchies, bringing new men and families in to the political élite. Further, the expansion of the Dutch economy in at least the first half of the century brought a rapid change in the relative distribution of wealth, and introduced new families into the wealthiest section of the population. Such families were slowly able to force their way into regent circles. The stagnation of the Dutch economy in the late seventeenth and eighteenth century removed to a great extent this force for change. Also after 1672 the occasions on which the personnel of the town governments was changed as a result of political crisis were less frequent. In consequence, by the first decades of the eighteenth century the urban oligarchies had become very stable, and it had become very difficult for an outsider to break into the privileged circle of the regents.

Again, in the seventeenth century the stadhouder had been an important factor in balancing to a certain degree the power of the Holland regents, but for a good part of the eighteenth century—1702 to 1747—there was no stadhouder for any of the provinces outside Friesland and Groningen, and even when William IV was made hereditary stadhouder of all the provinces in 1747 he found that his interests were closely allied with those of the regents. Whereas in the previous century the stadhouders had looked for support outside the regent group, leaning heavily on the Orangism of the ministers of the Reformed Church and the traditionally Orangist sentiments of the lower classes, and had usually seen their interests as opposed to those of the Holland regents, after the middle of the eighteenth century the stadhouders found that they had more to gain by cooperating with the regents than by opposing them. The stadhouder was no longer a threat to the power and stability of the oligarchy, he had become its guarantor.

Thus changes in both political and economic conditions encouraged the transformation of the oligarchy in Holland into a distinct social order with a monopoly of power. This process was also aided by the increasing importance of the financial sector for the Dutch economy, as most regents were heavily involved in investments. A consequence of this concentration on finance seems to have been that the regents became less responsive to the needs of the country as a whole and more concerned to secure the safety of their investments at home and abroad. The fluidity of the regent élite in the seventeenth century had meant that new men and families directly involved in trade or industry steadily found their way into the oligarchy. Such seems no longer to have been the case in the eighteenth century, despite the new men introduced, for example in Amsterdam, by William IV in 1748. As fewer and fewer new families made their way into the oligarchy the *rentier* element became increasingly predominant.

This consolidation of the oligarchy can be seen as a major cause of the ossification of the Dutch political system. As the eighteenth century progressed, the need for internal reform became increasingly clear, but it is also clear that the regents themselves were unwilling to carry through the necessary changes. 'The weakness of Holland's situation in the eighteenth century was more that the state appeared completely unable to act according to the demands of the changed circumstances.'[7] This was written with economic problems particularly in mind, but it would seem to be as relevant for the attitude of the political élite to the weaknesses of the political system. Probably the most pressing need was for a stronger central authority in the Republic, bringing with it a limitation of the independence of the provinces and towns. Even in the years of the Republic's greatest power, the political system had worked slowly and had required great skill in management for it to operate efficiently. In the eighteenth century it became even more difficult to achieve effective cooperation between the provinces, and it occasionally seemed as if the state was drifting apart. Necessary reforms were held up or blocked by the opposition of one or other of the provinces, and constitutional changes were clearly necessary by the early years of the century. Simon van Slingelandt (grand pensionary 1727–36) had recognised this fact, and while secretary to the Council of State had prepared a series of reforms which would have brought greater efficiency at the expense of a part of the sovereignty of the individual provinces. This cost was evidently too high and, despite the clear and expressed need, the reforms could not be carried through.

Similarly, the oligarchic system, especially in Holland, required modification. It had worked remarkably well in the seventeenth century; inefficiency and corruption were present, of course, as in every seventeenth-century system of government, but the regents had to act with the knowledge that there was an independent power within the state—the stadhouder—which could be used against them. Further, the regent élite remained very much an integral part of the wealthier classes of the Republic, and its actions were influenced, and to some extent determined, by the interests and opinions of this section of society. That the system worked less well in the following century was partly a result of the closing up of the oligarchy, but some of the responsibility should also be borne by William III. The latter was only concerned to ensure that his foreign policies were supported by the Holland voting towns, and not with the means used to obtain this support. Consequently, instead of using his authority to check regent corruption and malpractices, he was prepared to support corrupt political managers in the towns—for example, the *baljuw* of Rotterdam, Van Zuylen van Nievelt—as long as such men were ready to use their power to provide support for his policies.

Such an attitude on the part of the stadhouder could only encourage that weakening of initiative and public spirit which is exemplified by the proliferation of 'friendships' and 'contracts of correspondence'. In their eighteenth-century form the effect of such formal agreements between the regents was to create an oligarchy within the oligarchy by excluding a substantial proportion of the regents from offices of power, profit and prestige. Also these agreements arranged for the equal distribution of such offices among the members of the inner circle according to fixed rota systems. The emphasis was on equality rather than on rewarding ability. In the words of Geyl: 'A dissolving levelling, somewhat corrected by nepotism—such was the reality which men tried to give an ideal appearance by the lavish use of the word Liberty (*Vrijheid*). . . . Indeed, valuable Dutch traditions, which, as a stiff sense of privilege and sturdy individualism, we have seen help to build the greatness of earlier generations, were here transformed into their opposites.'[8] For it had now become the accepted opinion in the Republic that, whatever its faults, the Dutch political system was far superior to that of any other state. The De la Courts and the other seventeenth-century republican theorists who had struggled so hard to reach a fresh understanding of the nature of the state, to point out the advantages of the Dutch system, and to defend this against the received pro-monarchical prejudices of the age, had laid the foundations for the uncritical worship of the Republican system which became predominant in the following century. The Republican spirit degenerated into a complacent acceptance of the existing system as the best that was practically possible. A hard-won appreciation of the virtues of the Dutch polity was replaced by a series of clichés, and 'Freedom' for the eighteenth-century regents was confused with the preservation of their own privileges.

The financial system of the Republic also gave rise to very serious problems, and lack of revenue certainly weakened the state's ability to carry on an active and vigorous foreign policy. This financial weakness was in part a consequence of the circumstances already mentioned—disagreement between the provinces made changes difficult and also led to serious delays in the payment of provincial quotas; and the regents tended to regard administration as a legitimate source of profit for themselves, so much of the revenue collected in taxes failed to reach the points where it was needed.

More important, however, were the imperfections in the tax system itself, with its emphasis on excises and other taxes on consumption. The burden was placed on those least able to support it and the resources of the wealthier sections of society were hardly tapped at all. In 1748 William IV himself proposed the substitution of a poll-tax for the excise, but he rapidly capitulated before pressure from the regents, and the tax system remained essentially unchanged until the end of the Republic.

Similarly, the *convooien en licenten*, the import and export duties which were used to finance the navy, proved impossible to reform effectively. The chief problem here was the amount of evasion which took place, with the connivance of the town governments who effectively controlled the imposition and collection of these duties. Although the need to end evasion was generally recognised, real reform was inhibited by the mutual rivalry and mistrust of the individual towns and provinces. Each hoped to lure trade and shipping away from its competitors and one way of achieving this aim was to allow easier evasion of duties. Consequently, no town could contemplate cutting down evasion unless it was assured that its rivals were doing likewise. The administrative independence of the towns meant that this condition was never met, and so evasion continued despite the number of *placaten* issued on the matter and despite the number of declarations of good intent which were made. Rivalry between province and province, town and town, ensured that no matter how clearly defects were demonstrated no effective reforms could be carried out.

The political and social system of the Republic, despite its obvious weaknesses, lasted until the last decades of the eighteenth century. Only the Patriot movement of the 1780s seriously threatened the power of the entrenched oligarchies, and even at this stage the old system was able to reassert itself, partly through Prussian intervention, and partly because of the split between moderates and democrats within the Patriot movement itself. In effect it took the French invasion to shatter the power of the regents allied to the house of Orange. Yet even here it has recently been argued[9] that the social and political dominance of the regent oligarchy was not effectively broken at this time, as the French found it convenient to work with and through the existing ruling groups. Whether the regent oligarchy or aristocracy was defeated in 1796 or 1848 is, however, a question beyond the scope of this work.

The preceding pages may have exaggerated somewhat the weaknesses of both the Dutch economy and the political system of the Republic, for the country still appeared to be wealthy—if the growing numbers of the unemployed were overlooked—and its naval and military incapacity only became unmistakable in the 1740s. It would be difficult on the other hand to exaggerate the decline of Dutch culture in this century. The failure was not quantitative—poems and paintings were produced in large numbers accompanied by a good deal of self-congratulation—but qualitative. One quick way to characterise the eighteenth century would be to say that while the French invasion of 1672 failed militarily and politically, it succeeded almost completely on the cultural plane. In the seventeenth century foreign influences, especially Italian and French, had been powerful but had stimulated rather than inhibited a vigorous and individual cultural life, though the difficulties facing Dutch literature in its attempt to use the imported modes were great. In the following century Dutch writers and painters did little more than imitate French models as faithfully as they were able. Perhaps even more indicative of the nature of the Dutch decline is the fact that on the whole Dutch writers and painters were unaware of the mediocrity of their works. In painting the change was especially swift and complete—not only did eighteenth-century Dutch artists fail to build on the great achievements of the previous century, they were unable to appreciate the works of their predecessors. Despite the lifelessness of their own imitations of the dominant French style, they felt that only with themselves had the Republic produced artists whose work could stand comparison with that of their French and Italian contemporaries. Such self-satisfaction with so little justification was all too typical of the Dutch Republic in the eighteenth century, and such inability to recognise the greatness of the Dutch School of the previous century underlines how far the Dutch had gone in rejecting their own cultural heritage in favour of that of France.

It was, of course, in painting that the most striking decline took place, and it was here that French influence was most pernicious. By the end of the seventeenth century the standards by which art was judged and the rules according to which it should be created had been taken over from the French. The system elaborated by Le Brun[10] was accepted as the key to the understanding of true art. The great seventeenth-century painters had worked from and within a native tradition in art and had thus been able to create a style distinct from those dominant in the rest of Europe. They had used the innovations, technical and stylistic, of Italian and Flemish painters and made them serve their own ends. Even Rembrandt, the most international of all the great Dutch artists of the period, retained a powerful personal and stylistic independence even when clearly following Italian or Flemish models; despite the marked differences between his works and those of the great majority of his Dutch contemporaries he remains unmistakably Dutch. This ability to absorb and transmute foreign influences had been lost by the end of the seventeenth century. In fact, this decline must probably be dated from the 1670s. After this time no fresh major talent emerged in the Republic, and Dutch painters began to produce undistinguished imitations of the works of the French school.

This sad transformation was in part a consequence of the lack of major painters, but also of a change in the nature of the market for art in the Republic. The French influence over Dutch painters was only one aspect of a general surrender by the wealthy and educated to the dictates of French taste—or what they understood this to be. The regents as they developed into a separate social order, increasingly removed from that direct contact with the rest of Dutch society which the oligarchy had maintained for most of the seventeenth century, began to adopt the tastes and style of life of European aristocratic society. In their turn the wealthier sections of Dutch society began to ape the borrowed manners and cultural pretensions of their political masters, and so a significant proportion of the potential market for Dutch paintings turned away from the indigenous traditions in art. The demand was increasingly for works composed according to French precepts, and specifically for works in the style of the masters of French classicism. The Dutch painters naturally attempted to answer the demands of their market. They were particularly susceptible as they could turn to no theoretical works justifying the sort of art produced by the Dutch School in the seventeenth century. The great Dutch artists had been men of practice, with little or no interest in theory. Most of them had in any case lacked the education, and certainly the motivation, to write theoretical treatises on their art. The literary élite, which might have supplied this deficiency, had throughout the century failed to recognise the greatness of the Dutch School and had preferred the work of Italian, Flemish and, later, French artists, or of those Dutch painters who most nearly approximated to these models. French classicism, in contrast, not only answered the needs of an aristocracy of increasing self-consciousness and with a desire for works of art to express and reflect its dignity, it also had the support of the French theorists of art. In this way French literature lent some of its prestige to French painting.

The decline of Dutch painting was not immediate, and traces of the seventeenth-century approach to painting lingered on into the eighteenth, but after the deaths of the great artists of the mature period no painters of a similar individuality or quality appeared. Rembrandt died in 1669, Vermeer in 1675, Jan Steen in 1679, and Jacob van Ruisdael in 1682. Hobbema lived on until 1709, but painted very little after 1668. Even during the later years of these masters Dutch taste had begun to swing away from them, favouring a lighter tonality and a greater conscious elegance, particularly in portrait and genre. This movement in taste became predominant in the last two decades of the century, though one or two painters remained as reminders of the older approach. The most notable of these was probably Aert de Gelder (1645–1727) who continued to paint in the manner of the late Rembrandt until his death. He had considerable talent and in as late a work as the *Family of Herman Boerhaave* (Paris, Louvre) the liveliness of the painting and the naturalness of the poses stand out very favourably from the dull, affected and contrived portraiture of his contemporaries. Less important was the after-life of the Leiden school of genre painting. This style of carefully-painted interior scenes, usually concerned with the daily lives of the wealthy, was carried on through to the nineteenth century by such competent craftsmen as Nicolaas Verkolje (1673–1746), the sons of Frans van Mieris—Jan (1660–90) and Willem (1662–1747)— and by his grandson Frans the younger (1689–1763).

The Republic was, however, able to produce one painter of some originality and ability in the eighteenth century. Cornelis Troost (1697–1750) specialised in satirical genre works which have been compared with those of Hogarth, though his humour is less biting and more indulgent of human frailty. One artist of Troost's stature is little enough to place alongside the long list of great and very talented artists working in the Republic in the seventeenth century. Perhaps it is more surprising that the Republic should have produced so many outstanding artists in the one century, than that it should have produced so few in the next.

Dutch literature in the eighteenth century also presents an unexciting picture, but here the difficulties facing Dutch writers are apparent and the achievements of the preceding century much less impressive. Dutch literature had always been threatened with dominance by foreign or international modes, and even the best writers of the seventeenth century had failed to resolve the contradictions between the borrowed styles and the peculiar society for and about which they were writing. Hooft, Bredero, Huygens and Vondel had at least in part succeeded in controlling their renaissance models and produced works of lasting value, but the ability of Dutch writers to break through the limitations imposed by the styles they borrowed decreased as the century wore on. At first they had taken their models from the late renaissance, and in particular from French and Italian vernacular poetry; in the later seventeenth century the literature of French classicism presented a challenge which the Dutch were unable to overcome.

As with painting, the strength of French influence came not only from the greatness of the literature produced by the French in this period but also from the ability of the French to provide reasoned theoretical, yet elegant, expositions of the rules of the 'classical' style. The precepts for literary composition produced by such theorists as Boileau[11] were perhaps as important as the works of Corneille, Racine and Molière in spreading French influence in the Republic. An important stage in the French conquest of Dutch letters was marked by the foundation of the society *Nil volentibus arduum* at Amsterdam in 1669. The aim of this group was the promotion of philosophy and literature in the Republic, though in practice their emphasis was heavily on the latter. They were consciously inspired by the Académie Française and sought to apply in Holland the formulae for the composition of poetry and drama which were being elaborated by their French contemporaries. The spirit represented by the circle around *Nil* rapidly became dominant in the Republic, with the result that: 'Smoothness and mellifluousness, the smoothly polished verse, external elegance and fineness of form, the result of *polissez, repolissez toujours*, became the *summum* of poetic art. They applied their standards also to the poems of the greatest writers of the seventeenth century, which were "corrected" by the men of *Nil*.'[12] Not only were the French rules accepted, but French works either in the original or in translation became the ideal in literature. Consequently, it is difficult to point to any works until the late eighteenth century with much individuality or vitality. The rule of polished mediocrity, imitative of French models, was established by the early eighteenth century.

An even more destructive phenomenon was the progress made by the French language itself. As early as 1673 Pieter de Groot could write: 'Enfin Monsieur, vous verres s'il est besoing qu'on s'en server (sc. serve) dans le francois, qui est fait pour les intelligents, aussy bien que dans le Flament, qui n'est que pour les ignorants. . . .'[13] Admittedly these lines were written while De Groot was in exile in the Southern Netherlands, and they seem a little early for the establishment of such attitudes in the Republic—but 50 years later such a statement would have appeared a commonplace. The stadhouders' court had always had a strong French orientation, and towards the end of the seventeenth century this attitude began to spread to the regents. These latter were becoming increasingly aware of themselves as aristocrats, and so were attracted to those styles and ways of behaviour common to the international aristocratic world. In this world the tone was set by France, and the French language was its chosen medium, so the regents and the wealthier classes in the Republic began to use French not only as a literary language but also in their ordinary conversation.

The belief that French was the proper language for intelligent and cultured people was encouraged by the presence of large numbers of gifted Huguenot refugees in the Republic, most of whom refused to learn Dutch—or rather do not even appear to have thought of doing so. Men of the quality of Pierre Bayle, especially because of his great ability as an intellectual publicist, encouraged their hosts to regard French as the civilised language par excellence. The use of French did not, of course, spread far down the social scale, nor was resistance to it lacking, but it was a very real weakness for Dutch literature that many of the leading figures in Dutch intellectual and social life considered it beneath their dignity to show any interest in what was being written in Dutch. Even Justus van Effen, whose Hollandsche Spectator, inspired by the English spectatorial writings, was such an important phenomenon in Dutch literature in the early eighteenth century, published a number of his works in French rather than in Dutch.

Yet there were some positive aspects to Dutch literature in this period, notably towards the end of the century. Certainly, the quality of Dutch prose improved markedly, and thus one of the great problems

which the writers of the previous century had failed to solve was
dealt with satisfactorily by their less gifted successors. One of the most
notable literary events of the century was the publication in 1782 of the
novel *Sara Burgerhart* which not only marked a new vitality in Dutch
literature, but was also remarkable for having been written by two
women, Betje Wolff and Aagje Deken. A good novel written by
women was a sign that at last Dutch literature was producing something
of independent value.

The situation was rather more favourable in science and in intellectual
fields. Here at least something was retained of the remarkable vitality
of the seventeenth century. In science there was the great Herman
Boerhaave (1668–1738) whose medical and chemical work won for him
a European reputation. Boerhaave was a professor at Leiden, thus
presenting a contrast with the leading scientists of the preceding century,
all of whom had worked outside the universities. In fact, in the eighteenth century the Dutch universities showed a sustained intellectual
vigour, especially in those fields where they already had a record of
substantial achievement—for example, in the study of the classics and of
eastern languages. However, the education provided by the universities
seems to have deteriorated, partly because teaching was still carried on
in Latin while the ability of the majority of students to understand this
language declined steadily.

One field in which the eighteenth century was able to improve on the
work of the seventeenth was the writing of history. Not only were there
the assiduous antiquarians and the meticulous publishers of letters and
documents—the correspondence of Johan de Witt was published in six
volumes from 1723 to 1725—but in narrative history the century can
boast of the great work of Wagenaar. This continued interest in history
was perhaps largely a consequence of its continued usefulness in contemporary political controversy. Indeed many works which purported
to be history can best be read as commentaries on the political situation
in the Republic when they were written.

Jan Wagenaar (1709–73) wrote his great work on Dutch history in
support of the political views of the Republicans. He began his working life as a clerk and worked his way up to become a merchant in
wood. In the meantime he was able to write an almost unbelievable
quantity of reliable and firmly-documented history. The most important of his works was the *Vaderlandsche Historie* (History of the Father-
land) published in no less than 20 volumes between 1749 and 1759.
Wagenaar was far from being one of the greatest of historians, yet as

Geyl remarks, '. . . the *Vaderlandsche Historie* is nevertheless an achievement which compells respect and in the development of Dutch culture
an occurrence of importance'..[4] He goes on to praise Wagenaar's
knowledge, his critical approach, and his ability to organise and present
his material. Moreover, his prose-style is effective and careful, so over
all the history is a quite outstanding achievement, and it is still useful
for modern scholars—the volumes on the seventeenth century in
particular retaining considerable value.

Towards the end of the century the spur of political crisis again
brought an upsurge in historiography. Of particular importance was
the work of Adriaan Kluit on the history of the Netherlands in the
Middle Ages, intended to undermine the historical foundation of the
claims of the provincial states to sovereignty. In general, in this important aspect of culture at least the Republic can be said to have kept pace
with the rest of Europe.

The guiding lights of the intellectual life of the Republic in the
eighteenth century were the ideas of reason and tolerance. This spirit
was triumphant even in the Reformed Church: the grimly orthodox
who had been so powerful at the beginning of the century as the cases
of Balthasar Bekker and Frederick van Leenhoff show,[15] lost ground
steadily and the more flexible and rationalistic approach of the *Cocceianen* became increasingly characteristic of the church. In philosophy
the thinkers of the English and French Enlightenment were able to
express better than any Dutch writer the spirit predominant in the
Republic. The Dutch had played their part in preparing the way for
the Enlightenment in the seventeenth century, and they had little
further of note to contribute. At the Dutch universities a considerable
proportion of the chairs in philosophy were occupied by Germans—
the most prominent of these being Christian Wolff at Utrecht.

For the greater part of the century the development of political
thought in the Republic was inhibited by an abiding complacency with
regard to the political system of the Republic, and by the terms in
which political debate was conducted. The continuing debate between
Orangists and Republicans was carried on largely in terms of conflict-
ing versions of Dutch history. This may well have been fruitful as a
stimulus to historical writing, it was clearly not conducive to any
reappraisal of actual or theoretical political problems. Again, the satis-
faction of so many commentators with the political system is surprising
considering the weaknesses which it continued to reveal. Despite such
drawbacks it was felt that property and 'Freedom' were safeguarded

more effectively in the Republic than anywhere else. Only towards the
end of the century did new ideas and new approaches to political life
become important, especially through the Patriot movement in its
various forms. In these years the ideological deadlock between Orangists and Republicans was broken as new problems came to the surface
which made the old political divisions irrelevant. The democratic ideas
of the late years of the century were a sign that the Republic in its old
form was nearing its end.

In an overall view of the history of the Republic in the eighteenth
century two leading characteristics emerge—impotence and complacency. The state proved unable to deal effectively with the problems
which it had to face not only in foreign affairs but also internally. In
addition Dutch culture lost its independence and vitality to a marked
degree; yet the Dutch not only showed no awareness of any decline but
they welcomed the acceptance of French cultural criteria as a step
forward in civilisation. In some ways the Republic in the eighteenth
century might be regarded as an 'underdeveloped' country—its
economy was generally stagnant, and the relative or absolute declines
in trade, industry and fishing caused a chronic structural unemployment.
The population had lost its buoyancy, in Holland at least, declining early
in the century and only making up its losses in the later years. The
political and social system ossified, leaving the regents and their
wealthy supporters in a social position somewhat resembling that of
colonial exploiters in their own country.

It is hardly surprising that this complacent and stagnant society could
in culture show little to compare with the greatness of the previous
century; or that it should prove content to accept French cultural
leadership, even to the extent—in some of the socially dominant groups
—of preferring the French language to their own. Even the Dutch
imitations of French models lacked life, copying the form with quite
admirable application but filling it with clichés—moral, intellectual
and emotional.

The acceptance of the cultural norms of French classicism led to the
rejection of their own seventeenth century culture to a large extent.
The rules and attitudes which the Dutch as a whole adopted in the
eighteenth century clashed fundamentally with most that was original
and vital in the artistic production of the previous century. This opposition was most clear in painting where the acceptance of French criteria
made it impossible for the Dutch to understand or appreciate the
nature and quality of the Dutch School of the seventeenth century. In

consequence they were unable to use the native tradition as a basis for further development; Dutch artists were cut off from their roots.

It may well be that this failure to value the work of the seventeenth century in the face of the inimical attitudes of the rest of Europe was inevitable—such a small country as the Republic could not perhaps in the long run be expected to maintain an independent cultural tradition. In the seventeenth century the Republic could not be termed a small country in contemporary European terms: the relative size of its economy was much greater than in the eighteenth century. Moreover, a combination of special circumstances gave it the opportunity to play the part of a major power politically, and to a certain extent culturally also. Before the second decade of the following century had passed it had become clear that the Republic had become a minor power, and thus it perhaps inevitably came under the influence both politically and culturally of its more powerful neighbours. The Republic had played an important part in the creation of Enlightenment Europe, but after the end of its Golden Century it no longer had the strength to maintain an independent course.

Notes

[1] J. de Vries, *De economische achteruitgang van de Republiek in de achttiende eeuw* (Amsterdam 1959), p. 84

[2] *Ibid.*, p. 87

[3] *Ibid.*, p. 107; but cf. the criticism of this argument in J. G. van Dillen, *Van rijkdom en regenten. Handboek tot de economische en sociale geschiedenis van Nederland tijdens de Republiek* (The Hague 1970), p. 653

[4] J. de Vries, *op. cit.*, p. 137

[5] *Ibid.*, p. 150

[6] J. A. Faber *et al.*, 'Population changes and economic developments in the Netherlands: a historical survey', *Afdeling agrarische geschiedenis, Bijdragen* 12 (Wageningen 1965), p. 110

[7] P. Geyl, *Geschiedenis van de Nederlandse stam* (Amsterdam/Antwerp 1961-2), vol. IV (1701-51), p. 991

[8] *Ibid.*, p. 1002

[9] See C. H. E. de Wit, *De strijd tussen aristocratie en democratie in Nederland 1780-1848* (Heerlen 1965)

[10] E.g. C. Le Brun, *Méthode pour apprendre à dessiner les passions proposée dans une conférence sur l'expression général et particulière* (Paris 1698)

[11] N. Boileau, *Art poétique* (Paris 1674)

[12] G. Knuvelder, *Nederlandse letterkunde*, vol. 2 ('s-Hertogenbosch 1967), p. 378

[13] F. J. L. Krämer, *Lettres de Pierre de Groot à Abraham de Wiquefort* (The Hague 1804), p. 401

[14] P. Geyl, *op. cit.*, p. 1039

[15] For Bekker, see above, p. 181; for Van Leenhoff, see L. Kolakowski, *Chrétiens sans Eglise* (Paris 1969), pp. 315-41

Bibliography

This is far from a comprehensive bibliography. It contains those works which the author feels to be particularly interesting, or which he found useful himself. Others are included because they are the only treatments of important topics, or because they are in English, French or German.

Introductory

1. J. Huizinga, *Dutch Civilisation in the Seventeenth Century* (London 1968). This brilliant essay is still indispensable.
2. P. Zumthor, *Daily Life in Rembrandt's Holland* (London 1962).
3. C. Busken Huet, *Het Land van Rembrandt* (Haarlem 1882–4, many later editions). Still a classic.
4. H. A. Enno van Gelder, *Cultuurgeschiedenis van Nederland in vogelvlucht* (Antwerp 1965).
5. P. L. Muller, *Onze gouden eeuw*, 3 vols (Leiden 1896–8).
6. J. and A. Romein, *Erflaters van onze beschaving* (Amsterdam 1938–40). A series of biographical essays, always stimulating often brilliant, on figures from six centuries of Dutch history.

Also for general comments on Dutch society see:

7. J. Bientjes, *Holland und die Holländer im Urteil deutscher Reisender (1400–1800)* (Groningen 1967).
8. R. Murris, *La Hollande et les Hollandais au XVIIe et XVIIIe siècle vus par les Français* (Paris 1925).

General Histories

9. *Algemene geschiedenis der Nederlanden*, 12 vols (Antwerp/Utrecht 1949–58). A collaborative work, covering all the Low Countries.
10. P. J. Blok, *A History of the Netherlands*, 5 vols (London 1898–1912).
11. G. J. Renier, *The Dutch Nation* (London 1944).
12. J. and A. Romein, *De lage landen bij de zee*, 4 vols (Amsterdam 1934).
13. B. H. M. Vlekke, *The Evolution of the Dutch Nation* (New York 1945).

14. P. Geyl, *Geschiedenis van de Nederlandse stam*, 6 vols (Amsterdam/ Antwerp 1961–2³).

On the Republican period:

Sections of 14 have been translated into English as

15. P. Geyl, *The Revolt of the Netherlands 1555–1609* (London 1958²), and

16. *The Netherlands in the Seventeenth Century*, 2 vols (London 1961–4). These works devote considerable space to cultural history.

16 (a). K. H. D. Haley, *The Dutch in the Seventeenth Century* (London 1972). Now the best short introduction in English to Dutch history in this period.

17. J. Presser, *De Tachtigjarige Oorlog* (Amsterdam 1948³).

18. C. Wilson, *The Dutch Republic* (London 1968).

The Dutch Republic and Europe

On Dutch diplomacy:

19. J. Heringa, *De eer en hoogheid van de staat. Over de plaats der Verenigde Nederlanden in het diplomatieke leven van de zeventiende eeuw* (Groningen 1961).

Other works:

20. A. Th. van Deursen, *Honni soit qui mal y pense? De Republiek tussen de mogenheden (1610–1612)* (Mededelingen der Koninklijke Nederlandse Akademie van Wetenschappen, afd. Letterkunde, nieuwe reeks, deel 28, no. 1) (Amsterdam 1965).

21. S. Elzinga, *Het voorspel van den oorlog van 1672. De economisch-politieke betrekkingen tusschen Frankrijk en Nederland in de jaren 1670–72* (Haarlem 1926).

22. W. J. M. van Eysinga, *De wording van het Twaalfjarig Bestand van 9 april 1609* (Verhandelingen der Koninklijke Nederlandse Akademie van Wetenschappen, afd. Letterkunde, nieuwe reeks, deel LXVI, no. 3) Amsterdam 1959).

23. M. A. M. Franken, *Coenraad van Beuningen's politieke en diplomatieke aktiviteiten in de jaren 1667–1684* (Groningen 1966).

24. M. A. M. Franken, 'The General Tendencies and Structural Aspects of the Foreign Policy and Diplomacy of the Dutch Republic in the Latter Half of the 17th Century', *Acta Historiae Neerlandica*, vol. III (1968), pp. 1–43.

25. A. van der Essen, *Le Cardinal-Infant et la politique européenne de l'Espagne, 1609–1641* (Louvaine 1944).
26. P. Geyl, *Orange and Stuart, 1641–1672* (London 1969).
27. C. van der Haar, *De diplomatieke betrekkingen tussen de Republiek en Portugaal, 1640–1661* (Groningen 1961).
28. G. Mitsukuri, *Englisch-niederländische Unionsbestrebungen im Zeitalter Cromwells* (Tübingen 1891).
29. E. C. Molsbergen, *Frankrijk en de Republiek der Vereenigde Nederlanden 1648–1662* (Rotterdam 1902).
30. J. J. Poelhekke, *'T Uytgaen van den Treves* (Groningen 1960).
31. J. J. Poelhekke, *De Vrede van Munster* (The Hague 1948).
32. S.-M. Arnauld de Pomponne, *Relation de mon ambassade en Hollande, 1669–71*, ed. H. H. Rowen (Utrecht 1955).
33. J. Römelingh, *De diplomatieke betrekkingen van de Republiek met Denemarken en Zweden, 1660–1675* (Amsterdam 1969).
34. H. H. Rowen, *The Ambassador prepares for war* (The Hague 1957).
35. F. Shriver, 'Orthodoxy and diplomacy: James I and the Vorstius affair', *English Historical Review* 85 (1970), pp. 449–74.
36. A. Waddington, *La république des Provinces-Unies, la France et les Pays-Bas Espagnols de 1630 à 1650*, 2 vols (Paris 1895–7).
37. C. Wilson, *Profit and Power. A Study of England and the Dutch Wars* (Cambridge 1957).

Internal History

(i) Political History and biography:

38. S. B. Baxter, *William III* (London 1966). Rather weak on the Dutch side.
39. R. Belvederi, 'Oldenbarnevelt e Maurizio d'Orange', *Studi di storia medievale e moderna in onore di Ettore Rota* (Bari 1956), pp. 205–46.
40. P. J. Blok, *Frederik Hendrik, prins van Oranje* (Amsterdam 1926).
41. J. D. M. Cornelissen, *Johan de Witt en de Vrijheid* (Nijmegen/Utrecht 1945). A lecture.
42. A. Th. van Deursen, 'De Raad van State en de Generaliteit', *Bijdragen voor de Geschiedenis der Nederlanden*, 19 (1964), pp. 1–48.
43. J. G. van Dillen, 'Amsterdam's Rôle in Seventeenth Century Dutch Politics and its Economic Background', *Britain and the Netherlands*, vol. II (Groningen 1964), ed. J. S. Bromley and E. H. Kossmann, pp. 137–48.
44. J. G. van Dillen, 'De West Indische Compagnie, het Calvinisme en de politiek', *Tijdschrift voor geschiedenis*, 74 (1961).

45. S. J. Fockema Andreae, *De Nederlandse staat onder de Republiek* (Verhandelingen der Koninklijke Nederlandse Akademie van Wetenschappen, afd. Letterkunde, nieuwe reeks, deel LXVIII, no. 3) (Amsterdam 1969³).

46. R. Fruin (ed. H. T. Colenbrander), *Geschiedenis der Staatsinstellingen in Nederland* (The Hague 1901).

47. R. Fruin, *Tien jaren uit den Tachtigjarigen oorlog, 1588–1598* (Amsterdam 1861). Despite its age still well worth reading.

48. H. Gerlach, *Het proces tegen Oldenbarnevelt en de 'Maximen in den Staet'* (Haarlem 1965).

49. N. Japikse, *Johan de Witt* (Amsterdam 1915).

50. N. Japikse, *Prins Willem III, de Stadhouder-koning*, 2 vols (Amsterdam 1930–33).

51. G. W. Kernkamp, *Prins Willem II* (Amsterdam 1943).

52. G. H. Kurtz, *Willem III en Amsterdam* (Utrecht 1928).

53. A. Lefèvre-Pontalis, *Vingt années de république parlementaire au dix-septième siècle. Johan de Witt, grand-pensionnaire de Hollande*, 2 vols (Paris 1884).

54. J. C. Naber, *Calvinist of Libertijnsch? (1572–1631)* (Utrecht 1884).

55. J. C. Naber, *De staatkunde van Johan de Witt* (Utrecht 1882).

56. J. C. H. de Pater, *Maurits en Oldenbarnevelt in den strijd om het Twaalfjarig Bestand* (Amsterdam 1940).

57. G. J. Renier, *William of Orange* (London 1932).

58. J. V. Ripperda Wierdsma, *Politie en Justitie: een studie over Hollandschen staatsbouw tijdens de Republiek* (Zwolle 1937).

59. L. W. G. Scholten, *De vrijheidsgedachte en Johan de Witt* (Assen 1948).

60. Sir W. Temple, *Observations upon the United Provinces of the Netherlands*, ed. G. N. Clark (Cambridge 1932).

61. J. den Tex, *Oldenbarnevelt*, 4 vols (Haarlem 1960–70). Despite its length, a very readable work. The fourth volume consists of documentation and a further similar volume is promised.

62. J. den Tex, 'Le procès d'Oldenbarnevelt (1618–1619) fut-il un meurtre judiciaire?' *Tijdschrift voor rechtsgeschiedenis*, vol. xxii, no. ii.

63. M. Th. Uit den Bogaard, *De Gereformeerden en Oranje tijdens het eerste stadhouderloze tijdperk* (Groningen 1954).

64. J. Th. de Visser, *Kerk en staat*, vol. II (Leiden 1926).

65. J. A. Wijnne, *De geschillen over de afdanking van 't krijgsvolk in de Vereenigde Nederlanden in de jaren 1649 en 1650* (Utrecht 1885).

(ii) Particular problems:

66. J. Bax, *Prins Maurits in de volksmening der 16e en 17e eeuw* (Amsterdam 1940).

67. A. C. Carter, *The English Reformed Church in Amsterdam in the seventeenth century* (Amsterdam 1964).

68. E. Conring, *Kirche und Staat nach der Lehre der Niederländische Calvinisten in der ersten Hälfte de 17. Jahrhunderts* (Neukirchen–Vluyn 1965).

69. H. A. Enno van Gelder, *Vrijheid en onvrijheid in de Republiek*, vol. 1 (Amsterdam 1947).

70. R. B. Evenhuis, *Ook dat was Amsterdam. De kerk der hervorming in de gouden eeuw*, 2 vols (Amsterdam 1965–7).

71. J. A. Faber, 'De oligarchisering van Friesland in de tweede helft van de zeventiende eeuw', *Afdeling Agrarische Geschiedenis* Bijdragen 15 (Wageningen 1970).

72. C. J. Guibal, *Democratie en oligarchie in Friesland tijdens de Republiek* (Groningen 1934).

73. P. W. Klein, 'De heffing van de 100e en 200e penning van het vermogen te Gouda, 1599–1722', *Economisch-Historisch Jaarboek*, 31 (1967), pp. 41–62.

74. J. Melles, *Ministers aan de Maas. Geschiedenis van de Rotterdamse pensionarissen met een inleiding over het stedelijk pensionariaat 1508–1795* (Rotterdam/ The Hague 1962).

75. Ch. Mercier, 'Les théories politiques des Calvinistes dans les Pays-Bas', *Revue d'histoire ecclésiastique*, vol. 29 (1933), pp. 25–73.

76. B. E. de Muinck, *Een regentenhuishouding omstreeks 1700. Gegevens uit de privé-boekhouding van mr. Cornelis de Jonge van Ellemeet. Ontvanger-Generaal der Verenigde Nederlanden (1646–1721)* (The Hague 1965).

77. D. Nobbs, *Theocracy and Toleration. A Study of the disputes in Dutch Calvinism from 1600 to 1650* (Cambridge 1938).

78. W. H. F. Oldewelt, 'De beroepsstructuur van de bevolking der Hollandse stemhebbende steden volgens de kohieren van familiegelden van 1674, 1715 en 1742', *Economisch-Historisch Jaarboek*, vol. xxiv, pp. 80 *ff*; vol. xxv, pp. 167 *ff*.

79. J. K. Oudendijk, *Johan de Witt de zeemacht* (Amsterdam 1944).

80. W. van Ravesteyn jr., *Onderzoekingen over de economische en sociale ontwikkeling van Amsterdam gedurende de XVIe en het eerste kwart der XVIIe eeuw* (Utrecht 1906).

81. I. Schöffer, 'Protestantism in Flux During the Revolt of the Netherlands', *Britain and the Netherlands*, vol. II, eds J. S. Bromley and E. H. Kossmann (Groningen 1964), pp. 67–84.

82. A. C. J. de Vrankrijker, *Het maatschappelijk leven in Nederland in de Gouden Eeuw* (Amsterdam 1937).

(iii) The regents:

83. P. J. Blok, *Geschiedenis eener Hollandsche stad onder de Republiek* (The Hague 1916). A study of Leiden.
84. H. van Dijk and D. J. Roorda, 'Sociale mobiliteit onder regenten van de Republiek', *Tijdschrift voor geschiedenis*, 84e jaargang (1971), afl. 2, pp. 306–29.
85. J. E. Elias, *De Vroedschap van Amsterdam 1578–1795*, 2 vols (Haarlem 1903–5). A pioneer work, largely genealogical.
86. J. E. Elias, *Geschiedenis van het Amsterdamsche regentenpatriciaat* (The Hague 1928). A revised version of the lengthy introduction to 85.
87. H. A. Enno van Gelder, *De levensbeschouwing van Cornelis Pieterszoon Hooft* (Amsterdam 1918).
88. R. Fruin and N. Japikse, 'De Dordtsche regeringsoligarchie', *Bijdragen voor Vaderlandsche Geschiedenis en Oudheidkunde*, VI (1924).
89. P. Geyl, 'Historische appreciaties van het zeventiende-eeuwse regenten-regiem', reprinted in *Studies en strijdschriften* (Groningen 1958).
90. A. Merens, *De geschiedenis van een Westfriese regentenfamilie, het geslacht Merens* (The Hague 1957).
91. D. J. Roorda, *Partij en factie: De oproeren van 1672 in de steden van Holland en Zeeland, een krachtmeting tussen partijen en facties* (Groningen 1961).
92. D. J. Roorda, 'Een zwakke stee in de Hollandse regentenaristocratie. De Hoornse vroedschap in opspraak, 1670–75', *Bijdragen voor de Geschiedenis der Nederlanden*, XVI (1961).
93. D. J. Roorda, *Eeuw tegen eeuw* (Groningen 1971). Public lecture.
94. D. J. Roorda, 'The Ruling Classes in Holland in the Seventeenth Century', *Britain and the Netherlands*, vol. II (Groningen 1964), eds J. S. Bromley and E. H. Kossmann, pp. 109–33.
95. D. J. Roorda, 'Party and Faction', *Acta Historiae Neerlandica*, vol. II (1967), pp. 188–222. A summary of 91.
96. I. Schöffer, 'La stratification sociale de la République des Provinces-Unies an XVIIe siècle', in *Problèmes de stratification sociales*, ed. R. Mousnier (Paris 1968), pp. 121–33.
97. I. Vijlbrief, *Van anti-aristocratie tot democratie. Een bijdrage tot de politieke en sociale geschiedenis der stad Utrecht* (Amsterdam 1950).
See also 23, 43, 44, 60, 71, 72, 74, 76.

Economic History

(i) General surveys:

98. J. A. van Houtte, *Een economische en sociale geschiedenis van de Lage Landen* (Antwerp/Zeist 1966). Sketches the economic history of the whole of the Low Countries.

99. J. G. van Dillen, *Van rijkdom en regenten. Handboek tot de economische en sociale geschiedenis van Nederland tijdens de Republiek* (The Hague 1970). A somewhat old-fashioned economic (*not* social, despite the title) history of the Republic.

(ii) Specialised works:

100. V. Barbour, *Capitalism in Amsterdam in the 17th Century* (Baltimore 1950).

101. H. E. Becht, *Statistische gegevens betreffende den handelsomzet van de Republiek der Vereenigde Nederlanden gedurende de 17e eeuw* (The Hague 1908).

102. E. Beins, *Die Wirtschaftsethik der Calvinistischen Kirche der Niederlande 1565–1650* (The Hague 1931).

103. P. M. Bondois, 'Colbert et la question de sucre. La rivalité franco-hollandaise', *Revue d'histoire économique et sociale*, XI (1923), pp. 12–61.

104. J. van Beylen, *Schepen van de Nederlanden. Van de late middeleeuwen tot het einde van de 17e eeuw* (Amsterdam 1970).

105. C. R. Boxer, *The Dutch Seaborne Empire 1600–1800* (London 1965).

106. G. van Brakel, *De Hollandsche handelscompagnieën der 17e eeuw* (The Hague 1908).

107. I. J. Brugmans, 'De Oost-Indische Compagnie en de welvaart in de Republiek', *Tijdschrift voor geschiedenis*, 61 (1948).

108. R. Bijlsma, *Rotterdams welvaren 1550–1650* (The Hague 1918).

109. A. E. Christensen, *Dutch trade to the Baltic about 1600. Studies in the Sound toll register and Dutch shipping records* (Copenhagen/The Hague 1941).

110. J. E. Elias, *Het voorspel van den eersten Engelschen oorlog* (The Hague 1920).

111. J. A. Faber, 'The decline of the Baltic grain-trade in the second half of the 17th century', *Acta Historiae Neerlandica*, vol. 1 (1966).

111 (a). J. A. Faber, *Drie eeuwen Friesland. Economische en sociale ontwikkelingen van 1500 tot 1800*, 2 vols (Afdeling Agrarische Geschiedenis, Bijdragen 17, Wageningen 1972).

112. S. C. van Campen, *De Rotterdamse particuliere scheepsbouw in de tijd van de Republiek* (Assen 1953).

113. P. W. Klein, *De Trippen in de 17e eeuw. Een studie over ondernemersgedrag op de Hollandse stapelmarkt* (Assen 1965).

114. T. P. van der Kooy, *Hollands stapelmarkt en haar verval* (Amsterdam 1931).

115. H. A. H. Kranenburg, *De zeevisscherij van Holland in den tijd der Republiek* (Rotterdam 1946).

116. C. te Lintum, *De Merchant Adventurers in de Nederlanden* (The Hague 1905).

117. N. W. Posthumus, *De geschiedenis van de Leidse lakenindustrie*, 3 vols (The Hague 1908–39).

118. N. W. Posthumus, *Inquiry into the history of prices in Holland*, 2 vols (Leiden 1946–64).

119. J. C. Riemersma, *Religious Factors in early Dutch Capitalism* (The Hague 1967).

120. M. P. Rooseboom, *The Scottish staple in the Netherlands* (The Hague 1910).

121. H. Schoorl, *Isaäc le Maire, koopman en bedijker* (Haarlem 1969).

122. B. H. Slicher van Bath, *Een samenleving onder spanning. Geschiedenis van het platteland in Overijsel* (Assen 1957).

123. F. Snapper, *Oorlogs invloeden op de overzeese handel van Holland 1551–1719* (Amsterdam 1959).

124. Z. W. Sneller, *Geschiedenis van den steenkolenhandel van Rotterdam* (Groningen/Djakarta 1946).

125. J. C. Westerman, 'Statistische gegevens over den handel van Amsterdam in de zeventiende eeuw', *Tijdschrift voor geschiedenis*, 61 (1948), pp. 3–15.

125 (a). A. M. van der Woude, *Het Noorderkwartier. Een regionaal historisch onderzoek in de demografische en economische geschiedenis van westelijk Nederland van de late middeleeuwen tot het begin van de negentiende eeuw*, 3 vols (Afdeling Agrarische Geschiedenis, Bijdragen 16, Wageningen 1972).

See also 37, 43, 73, 78, 80, 330.

(iii) Colonies and extra-European trade:

126. S. Arasaratnam, *Dutch Power in Ceylon, 1658–1687* (Amsterdam 1958).

127. V. C. Bachman, *Peltries or Plantations. The economic policies of the Dutch West India Company in New Netherland, 1623–1639* (London/Baltimore 1969).

128. C. R. Boxer, *The Dutch in Brazil, 1624–1654* (Oxford 1957).

129. C. R. Boxer, *Jan Compagnie in Japan, 1600–1850. An essay on the cultural, artistic and scientific influence exercised by the Hollanders in Japan from the 17th to the 19th centuries* (The Hague 1950).

130. T. J. Condon, *New York Beginnings, the commercial origins of New Netherland* (New York/London 1968).

131. W. P. Coolhaas, *A Critical Survey of Studies on Dutch Colonial History* (The Hague 1960).
132. K. Glamann, *Dutch-Asiatic Trade, 1620–1740* (Copenhagen/The Hague 1958).
133. W. J. van Hoboken, 'The Dutch West India Company, the political background of its rise and decline', *Britain and the Netherlands*, vol. 1, eds J. S. Bromley and E. H. Kossmann (London 1960).
134. M. A. P. Meilink-Roelofsz, *Asian Trade and European Influence in the Indonesian Archipelago between 1500 and about 1630* (The Hague 1962).
135. T. Raychaudhuri, *Jan Company in Coromandel, 1605–1690. A study in the interrelations of European commerce and traditional economies* (The Hague 1962).
136. B. H. M. Vlekke, *Nusantara. A History of the East Indian Archipelago* (Cambridge, Mass. 1945).
See also 44, 105, 107, 110.

(iv) Demography:

137. J. A. Faber, H. K. Roessingh, B. H. Slicher van Bath, A. M. van der Woude and H. J. van Xanten, 'Population changes and economic developments in the Netherlands: a historical survey', *Afdeling Agrarische Geschiedenis* Bijdragen 12 (Wageningen 1965).
138. G. J. Mentink and A. M. van der Woude, *De demografische ontwikkeling te Rotterdam en Cool in de 17e en 18e eeuw* (Rotterdam 1965).
See also 111 (a), 125 (a).

Literature

139. A. G. H. Bachrach, *Sir Constantine Huygens and Britain, 1596–1687: a pattern of cultural exchange*, vol. 1: *1596–1619* (London/Leiden 1962).
140. A. J. Barnouw, *Leven van Vondel* (Haarlem 1926).
141. A. Beekman, *Influence de Du Bartas sur la littérature néerlandaise* (Poitiers 1911).
142. L. van den Branden, *Het streven naar verheerlijking, zuivering en opbouw van het Nederlands in de 16e eeuw* (Ghent 1956).
143. G. Brom, *Schilderkunst en litteratuur in de 16e en 17e eeuw* (Utrecht 1957).
144. H. G. van der Doel, *Daar moet veel strijds gestreden zijn. Dirk Rafaelsz Camphuysen en de Contraremonstranten. Een biografie* (Meppel 1967).
145. J. van Dorsten, *Poets, Patrons and Professors: Sir Philip Sidney, Daniel Rogers and the Leiden Humanists* (London 1962).

146. G. A. van Es, *Barokke lyriek van protestantsche dichters in de 17e eeuw* (Groningen 1946). An inaugural lecture.

147. G. A. van Es and G. S. Overdiep, *De letterkunde van Renaissance en Barok in de zeventiende eeuw*, I (*Geschiedenis van de Letterkunde der Nederlanden*, IV) (Antwerp/'s-Hertogenbosch 1948).

148. L. W. Forster, *Die Niederlande und die Anfänge der Barock-lyrik in Deutschland* (Groningen 1967). A lecture.

149. A. M. F. B. Geerts, *Vondel als classicus bij de humanisten in de leer* (Tongerloo 1932).

150. P. L. M. Grooten, *Dominicus Baudius. Een levensschets uit het Leidsche humanistenilieu* (Nijmegen 1942).

151. A. G. van Hamel, *Zeventiende-eeuwsche opvattingen en theorieën over literatuur in Nederland* (The Hague 1918).

152. K. Heeroma, *Protestantse poëzie der 16e en 17e eeuw* (Amsterdam 1940).

153. D. J. H. ter Horst, *Daniel Heinsius (1580–1655)* (Utrecht 1934).

154. C. Huygens, *De jeugd van Constantin Huygens, door hemzelf beschreven* (Translated into Dutch by A. H. Kan) (Rotterdam 1946).

155. G. Kalff, *Literatuur en tooneel te Amsterdam in de 17e eeuw* (Haarlem 1895).

156. G. Kalff, *Geschiedenis van de Nederlandsche letterkunde*, 7 vols (Haarlem 1906–12). A general history of Dutch literature.

157. E. Kern, *The Influence of Heinsius and Vossius upon French Dramatic Theory* (Baltimore 1949).

158. G. Knuvelder, *Handboek tot de geschiedenis der Nederlandse letterkunde* 4 vols ('s-Hertogenbosch 1967[4]). Vol. 2 covers the period 1567–1766.

159. J. A. N. Knuttel, *Bredero* (Lochem 1950).

160. W. Kramer, *Vondel als barokkunstenaar* (Antwerp/Utrecht 1951).

161. J. Melles, *Joost van den Vondel. De geschiedenis van zijn leven* (Utrecht 1957). Especially useful for his account of the economic and social situation.

162. J. P. Naeff, *De waardering van Gerbrand Adriaensz Bredero* (Gorcum 1960).

163. G. S. Overdiep et al., *De letterkunde van de Renaissance tot Roemer Visscher en zijn dochters* (*Geschiedenis van de Letterkunde der Nederlanden*, III) (Antwerp/'s-Hertogenbosch 1944).

164. J. C. H. de Pater, *Jan van Hout. Een levensbeeld uit de 16e eeuw* (The Hague 1946).

165. E. du Perron, *De Muze van Jan Compagnie. Overzichtelijke verzameling van Nederlands-Oostindiese belletrie uit de Compagniestijd, 1600–1780* (Bandoeng 1948).

166. H. J. A. Ruys, 'Heiman Dullaert (1636–1684)', *Oud-Holland*, XXXI (1913).

167. H. Scherpbier, *Milton in Holland. A study in the literary relations of England and Holland before 1730* (Amsterdam 1933).

168. G. Schönle, *Deutsch-Niederländische Beziehungen in der Literatur des 17. Jahrhunderts* (Leiden 1968).

169. P. R. Sellin, *Daniel Heinsius and Stuart England* (Leiden/London 1968).

170. L. Simons, *Het drama en het tooneel in hun ontwikkeling*, 5 vols (Amsterdam 1921–30).

171. W. A. P. Smit, *Dichters der Reformatie in de zestiende eeuw* (Groningen 1939).

172. W. A. P. Smit, *De dichter Revius* (Amsterdam 1928).

173. W. A. P. Smit, *Van Pascha tot Noah. Een verkenning van Vondels dramas naar continuiteit en ontwikkeling in hun grondmotief en structuur*, 3 vols (Zwolle 1956–62).

174. W. A. P. Smit and P. Brachin, *Vondel (1587–1679). Contribution à l'histoire de la tragédie au XVIIe siècle* (Paris 1964).

175. H. W. van Tricht, *P. C. Hooft* (Arnhem 1951).

176. F. Veenstra, *Bijdrage tot de kennis van de invloeden op Hooft* (Assen 1946).

177. T. Weevers, *Poetry of the Netherlands in its European Context 1170–1930* (London 1960).

178. J. Wille, *Heiman Dullaert, zijn leven, omgeving en werk* (Zeist 1926).

179. J. A. Worp, *Geschiedenis van het drama en het tooneel in Nederland* (Groningen 1904).

180. J. A. Worp (ed.), *De Briefwisseling van Constantijn Huygens (1608–1687)*, 6 vols (The Hague 1911–17).

181. C. Ypes, *Petrarca in de Nederlandse letterkunde* (Amsterdam 1934).

See also the relevant sections in 1, 3, 15, 16, 17, 206, 245, 246, 252, 304.

Education

182. P. Dibon, *La philosophie néerlandaise au siècle d'or*, vol. 1: *L'enseignement philosophique dans les universités à l'époque précartésienne (1575–1650)* (Amsterdam 1954).

183. A. Eekhof, *De theologische faculteit te Leiden in de 17e eeuw* (Utrecht 1921).

184. E. Garin, *L'éducation de l'homme moderne. La pédagogie de la Renaissance (1400–1600)*, translated from Italian (Paris 1968). For humanist educational ideas and practice.

185. D. Grosheide, 'De kerken en de Schoolordre voor de Hollandse Latijnse scholen van 1625', *Gereformeerd Theolo isch Tijdschrift*, 59 (1959), pp. 86–92.

186. G. J. Heering and G. J. Sirks, *Het Seminarium der Remonstranten* (Amsterdam 1934).

187. E. J. Kuiper, *De Hollandse 'schoolordre' van 1625* (Groningen 1958).

188. H. Schneppen, *Niederländische Universitäten und deutsches Geistesleben von der Gründung der Universität Leiden bis ins späte 18. Jahrhundert* (Münster 1960).
See also 150, 153.

The Arts

(i)   Painting:

The fundamental work for this section is:

189. J. Rosenberg, S. Slive and E. H. ter Kuile, *Dutch Art and Architecture 1600–1800* (Penguin 1966), with a more than useful bibliography.

190. K. Bauch, *Der frühe Rembrandt und seine Zeit* (Berlin 1960).

191. I. Bergström, 'Rembrandt's Double-Portrait of Himself and Saskia at the Dresden Gallery', *Nederlands Kunst-Historisch Jaarboek*, XVII (1966), pp. 143 ff.

192. W. von Bode, *Die Meister der holländischenund vlämischen Malerschulen* (Leipzig 1919).

193. A. Bredius, 'De schilder Johannes van de Capelle', *Oud-Holland*, X (1892).

194. K. Clark, *Rembrandt and the Italian Renaissance* (London 1966).

195. A. Dohmann, 'Les événements contemporains dans la peinture hollandaise du XVIIe siècle', *Revue d'histoire moderne et contemporaine*, V (1958).

196. H. Floerke, *Studien zur niederländischen Kunst- und Kulturgeschichte. Die Formen des Kunsthandels, das Atelier und die Sammler in den Niederlanden von 15.–18. Jahrhundert* (Munich/Leipzig 1905).

197. J. Gantner, *Rembrandt und die Verwandlung Klassischer Formen* (Bern/Munich 1964).

198. H. E. van Gelder and J. Duverger, *et. al.*, *Kunstgeschiedenis der Nederlanden van de Middeleeuwen tot onze tijd*, 3 vols (Antwerp/Utrecht 1954–6³).

199. H. Gerson, *Ausbreitung und Nachwirkung der holländische Malerei des 17. Jahrhunderts* (Haarlem 1942).

200. H. Gerson, *Het tijdperk van Rembrandt en Vermeer* (Amsterdam 1952).

201. L. Goldscheider, *Johannes Vermeer. The Paintings. Complete Edition* (London 1958).

202. E. H. Gombrich, 'Renaissance Artistic Theory and the Development of Landscape Painting', *Gazette des Beaux Arts*, XLI (1953); reprinted in *Norm and Form* (London 1966).

203. L. Gowing, *Vermeer* (London 1952).

204. B. Haak, *Rembrandt, his life, work and times* (London 1969).

205. A. Heppner, 'The Popular theatre of the Rederijkers in the Work of Jan Steen and his contemporaries', *Journal of the Warburg and Courtauld Institutes*, III (1939-40).

206. G. J. Hoogewerff, *De geschiedenis van de St.—Lucasgilden in Nederland* (Amsterdam 1947).

207. G. J. Hoogewerff, *De Noord-Nederlandsche schilderkunst*, 5 vols (The Hague 1936-47).

208. A. Houbraken, *De Groote Schouburgh der Nederlantsche Konstschilders en Schilderessen*, 3 vols (Amsterdam 1718-21).

209. F. W. Hudig, *Frederik Hendrik en de kunst van zijn tijd* (Amsterdam 1928). Inaugural lecture.

210. H. Kauffmann, 'Rembrandt und die Humanisten vom Muiderkring', *Jahrbuch der preussischen Kuntsammlungen*, XLI (1920).

211. E. Lotthé, *La pensée chrétienne dans la peinture flamande et hollandaise (1432-1669)*, 2 vols (Lille 1947).

212. W. Martin, 'The Life of a Dutch Artist in the Seventeenth Century', *The Burlington Magazine*, VII (1905); VIII (1905-6); X (1906-7).

213. W. Martin, *De Hollandsche schilderkunst in de 17e eeuw*, 2 vols (Rotterdam 1935-6).

214. N. Pevsner, *Academies of Art Past and Present* (Cambridge 1940). With a section on Holland.

215. J. Rosenberg, *Rembrandt. Life and Work* (London 1968³).

216. F. Schmidt-Degener and H. E. van Gelder, *Jan Steen* (London 1927).

217. K. E. Schuurman, *Carel Fabritius* (Amsterdam 1947).

218. S. Slive, *Rembrandt and his Critics, 1630-1730* (The Hague 1953).

219. S. Slive, *Frans Hals*, 2 vols (London 1970).

220. S. Slive, 'Notes on the Relationship of Protestantism to Seventeenth Century Dutch Painting', *The Art Quarterly*, XIX (1956).

221. W. Stechow, *Dutch Landscape Painting of the Seventeenth Century* (London 1966).

222. P. T. A. Swillens, *Pieter Jansz Saenredam* (Amsterdam 1935).

223. P. T. A. Swillens, *Johannes Vermeer* (Utrecht 1950).

224. W. R. Valentiner, *Pieter de Hooch* (Stuttgart 1929).

225. W. R. Valentiner, *Rembrandt and Spinoza: a study of the spiritual conflicts in 17th century Holland* (London 1957).

226. C. White, *Rembrandt and his World* (London 1964).
227. F. Würtenberger, *Das holländische Gesellschaftsbild* (Schramberg im Schwarzwald 1937).
See also 1, 3, 129, 143, 166, 178, 228, 230.

(ii) Architecture:

228. K. Fremantle, *The Baroque Town Hall of Amsterdam* (Utrecht 1959).
229. D. F. Slothouwer, *De paleizen van Frederik Hendrik* (Leiden 1945).
230. P. T. A. Swillens, *Jacob van Campen, Schilder en Bouwmeester* (Assen 1961).
231. F. A. J. Vermeulen, *Handboek tot de geschiedenis der Nederlandsche bouwkunst*, 3 vols text, 3 vols plates (The Hague 1928–41).
232. J. J. Vriend, *De bouwkunst van ons land*, 3 vols (Amsterdam 1949–50).
See also 189, 210.

(iii) Sculpture:

233. E. Neurdenburg, *De zeventiende eeuwsche beeldhouwkunst in de Noordelijke Nederlanden* (Amsterdam 1948).
234. E. Neurdenburg, *Hendrik de Keyser* (Amsterdam n.d. (1929)).
See also 189, 228.

(iv.) Music:

235. D. J. Balfoort, *Het muziekleven in Nederland in de 17e en 18e eeuw* (Amsterdam 1938).
236. Ch. van den Borren, *Geschiedenis van de muziek in de Nederlanden*, 2 vols (Antwerp 1948).
237. S. Groenveld, 'Constantijn Huygens en het orgelgebruik in zijn tijd (1640/41)', *Tijdschrift voor geschiedenis*, 79e jaargang (1966), afl. 3, 260–79.
238. P. Nuten, 'Niederländische Musik. Die 2 Hälfte des 16. Jahrhunderts', in F. Blume, *Die Musik in Geschichte und Gegenwart*, vol. ix (Kassel 1961).
239. B. van den Sigtenhorst-Meyer, *Jan P. Sweelinck en zijn instrumentele muziek* (The Hague 1934).
240. R. L. Tusler, *The organ music of Jan Pieterszoon Sweelinck* (Bilthoven 1958).

Intellectual Developments

(i) General:

241. A. Barnes, *Jean Le Clerc (1657–1736) et la République des Lettres* (Paris 1938).

242. F. F. Blok, *Nicolaas Heinsius in dienst van Christina van Zweden* (Delft 1949).
243. H. Bonger, *Dirck Volckertsz Coornhert* (Lochem 1942).
244. H. Bonger, *De motivering van de godsdienstvrijheid bij Dirck Volckertszoon Coornhert* (Arnhem 1954).
245. C. C. de Bruin, *Joachim Oudaan in de lijst van zijn tijd* (Groningen 1955).
246. G. Cohen, *Ecrivains Français en Hollande dans la première moitié du XVIIe siècle* (Paris 1920).
247. R. L. Colie, 'Constantyn Huygens and the Rationalist Revolution', *Tijdschrift voor Nederlandse Taal-en Letterkunde*, 72 (1955), pp. 193–209.
248. W. J. M. van Eysinga, *Hugo Grotius. Eine biographische Skizze* (Basle 1952).
249. G. Güldner, *Das Toleranzproblem in den Niederlanden im Ausgang des 16. Jahrhunderts* (Lübeck 1968).
250. H. C. Hazewinkel, 'Pierre Bayle à Rotterdam', in P. Dibon (ed.), *Pierre Bayle, le philosophe de Rotterdam* (Amsterdam/Paris 1959).
251. E. Labrousse, *Pierre Bayle*, 2 vols. (The Hague 1963–4).
252. J. Melles, *Joachim Oudaan, heraut der verdraagzaamheid* (Utrecht 1950).
253. G. Oestreich, 'Politischer Neustoizismus und Niederländische Bewegung in Europa und besonders in Brandenburg-Preussen', in G. Oestreich, *Geist und Gestalt des frühmodernen Staates* (Berlin 1969).
254. P. Polman, *Godsdienst in de Gouden Eeuw* (Utrecht 1947).
255. L. J. Rogier, *Geschiedenis van het Katholicisme in Noord-Nederland in de 16e en 17e eeuw* (Amsterdam 1947).
256. C. W. Roldanus, *Coenraad van Beuningen, staatsman en libertijn* (The Hague 1931).
257. C. W. Roldanus, *Zeventiende-eeuwse geestesbloei* (Utrecht/Antwerp 1961[2]).
258. C. W. Roldanus, 'Adriaen Paets, een republikein uit de nadagen', *Tijdschrift voor geschiedenis*, 50e jaargang (1935), pp. 134 *ff.*
259. W. Rood, *Comenius and the Low Countries. Some aspects of the life and work of a Czech exile in the seventeenth century* (Amsterdam 1970).
260. C. L. Thijssen-Schoute, *Uit de Republiek der Letteren. Elf studiën op het gebied der ideëngeschiedenis van de Gouden Eeuw* (The Hague 1967).
261. P. N. Winkelman, *Remonstranten en Katholieken in de eeuw van Hugo de Groot* (Nijmegen 1945).
See also 69, 87, 139, 150, 153, 169, 175, 188, 225, 268, 292.

(ii) *Theology:*

262. R. L. Colie, *Light and Enlightenment. A study of the Cambridge Platonists and the Dutch Arminians* (Cambridge 1957).

263. K. Dijk, *De strijd over Infra- en Supralapsarisme in de Gereformeerde Kerken in Nederland* (Amsterdam 1912).
264. A. H. Haentjens, *Hugo de Groot als godsdienstig denker* (Amsterdam 1946).
265. L. and M. Harder, *Plockhoy from Zurick-Zee. The study of a Dutch Reformer in Puritan England and Colonial America* (Newton, Kansas 1952).
266. W. I. Hull, *Benjamin Furly and Quakerism in Rotterdam* (Swarthmore 1941).
267. C. B. Hylkema, *Reformateurs. Geschiedkundige studiën over godsdienstige bewegingen uit de nadagen onzer Gouden Eeuw*, 2 vols (Haarlem 1900–2).
268. W. P. C. Knuttell, *Balthasar Bekker, de bestrijder van het bijgeloof* (The Hague 1906).
269. L. Kolakowski, *Chrétiens sans Eglise. La conscience religieuse et le lien confessionnel au XVIIe siècle* (Paris 1969).
270. C. Krahn, *Dutch Anabaptism. Origin, spread, life and thought* (The Hague 1968).
271. J. Lindeboom, *De confessioneele ontwikkeling der reformatie in de Nederlanden* (The Hague 1946).
272. W. Rex, *Essays on Pierre Bayle and religious controversy* (The Hague 1965).
273. C. W. Roldanus, *Hugo de Groot's Bewijs van den waren godsdienst* (Arnhem 1944).
274. J. Séguy, *Utopie coopérative et oecumenisme. Pieter Cornelisz Plockhoy van Zurik-Zee 1620–1700* (Paris/The Hague 1968).
275. J. C. van Slee, *De Rijnsburgsche Collegianten* (Haarlem 1895).
276. J. C. van Slee, *De geschiedenis van het Socinianisme in de Nederlanden* (Haarlem 1914).
See also 35, 54, 68, 77, 102, 144, 183, 185, 186, 241, 243, 244, 245, 249, 251, 252, 254, 256, 257.

(iii) Political and economic thought:

277. P. Geyl, *Democratische tendenties in 1672* (Mededelingen der Koninklijke Nederlandse Akademie van Wetenschappen, afd. Letterkunde, nieuwe reeks, deel 13, no. 11) (Amsterdam 1950).
278. P. Geyl, *Het stadhouderschap in de partij-literatuur onder De Witt* (Mededeelingen der Koninklijke Nederlandsche Akademie van Wetenschappen, afd. Letterkunde, nieuwe reeks, deel 10, no. 2) (Amsterdam 1947).
279. D. Grosheide, *Cromwell naar het oordeel van zijn Nederlandse tijdgenoten* (Amsterdam 1951).

280. E. H. Kossmann, *Politieke theorie in het zeventiende-eeuwse Nederland* (Verhandelingen der Koninklijke Nederlandse Akademie van Weten-schappen, afd. Letterkunde, nieuwe reeks, deel LXVII, no. 2) (Amsterdam 1960).

281. E. Laspeyres, *Geschichte der volkswirthschaftlichen Anschauungen der Niederländer und ihrer Litteratur zur Zeit der Republiek* (Leipzig 1863, reprint Nieuwkoop 1961).

282. G. L. Liesker, *Die staatswissenschaftlichen Anschauungen Dirck Gras-winckels* (Freiburg 1901).

283. R. J. McShea, *The Political Philosophy of Spinoza* (New York/London 1968).

284. Ph. van Praag, 'Un populationniste hollandais: Pieter de la Court (1618–1685)', *Population* (1963), no. 2, pp. 349–58.

285. H. P. G. Quack, *Plockhoy's sociale plannen* (Verslagen en Mededeelingen der Koninklijke Nederlandsche Akademie van Wetenschappen, afd. Letterkunde, 3e reeks, ix).

286. Th. van Tijn, 'Pieter de la Court. Zijn leven en economische denk-beelden', *Tijdschrift voor geschiedenis*, vol. LIX (1956), pp. 306–70.

287. A. C. J. Vrankrijker, *De staatsleer van Hugo de Groot en zijn Nederlandsche tijdgenooten* (Nijmegen 1937).

See also 41, 48, 63, 64, 68, 75, 87, 102, 175, 176, 248, 274, 288.

(iv) Philosophy:

288. R. A. Duff, *Spinoza's Political and Ethical Philosophy* (Glasgow 1903).

289. M. Francès, *Spinoza dans les pays néerlandais de la seconde moitié du XVIIe siècle* (Paris 1937).

290. S. Hampshire, *Spinoza* (Penguin 1962).

291. K. O. Meinsma, *Spinoza en zijn kring* (The Hague 1896).

292. P. H. van Moerkerken, *Adriaan Koerbagh 1633–1669. Een strijder voor het vrije denken* (Amsterdam 1948).

293. I. S. Révah, 'Spinoza et les hérétiques de la communauté judéo-portugaise d'Amsterdam', *Revue de l'histoire des religions*, 77e année (1958), vol. 154, pp. 173–218.

294. W. G. van der Tak, *Bento de Spinoza, zijn leven en gedachten over de wereld, den mensch en den staat* (The Hague 1928).

295. C. L. Thijssen-Schoute, *Nederlands Cartesianisme* (Amsterdam 1954).

296. A. Vloemans, *Spinoza, de mensch, het leven en het werk* (The Hague 1931).

297. A. Wolf (ed.), *The Correspondence of Spinoza* (London 1928).

See particularly 182 and 283; also 247, 251, 260.

(v) Science:

298. A. E. Bell, *Christian Huygens and the development of science in the 17th century* (London 1947).
299. E. J. Dijksterhuis, *Simon Stevin. Science in the Netherlands around 1600* (The Hague 1970).
300. A. Schierbeek, *Antoni van Leeuwenhoek. Zijn leven en zijn werken*, 2 vols (Lochem 1950–55).
301. A. Schierbeek, *Jan Swammerdam* (Lochem 1947).
302. C. Vollgraf, *Biographie de Christiaan Huygens* (in *Oeuvres complètes de Christiaan Huygens*, vol. 22) (The Hague 1950).

(vi) History:

303. J. C. Breen, *P. C. Hooft als schrijver der Nederlandsche Historiën* (Amsterdam 1894).
304. J. D. M. Cornelissen, *Hooft en Tacitus* (Nijmegen 1938).
305. E.-L. Etter, *Tacitus in der Geistesgeschichte des 16. und 17. Jahrhunderts* (Basle 1966).
306. R. Fruin, 'De historiën van E. van Meteren', in *Verspreide Geschriften*, vol. VII (The Hague 1903), pp. 383–410.
307. H. Kampinga, *De opvattingen over onze vaderlandsche geschiedenis bij de Hollandsche historici van de XVIe en XVIIe eeuw* (The Hague 1917).
308. H. C. A. Muller, *Hugo de Groot's 'Annales et Historiae'* (Utrecht 1919).
309. S. B. J. Silverberg, 'Gerard Brandt als kerkhistoricus', *Nederlandsch Archief voor Kerkgeschiedenis*, 49 (1968/9), pp. 37–58.
310. W. D. Verduyn, *Emanuel van Meteren* (The Hague 1926).
311. B. A. Vermaseren, *De Katholieke Nederlandsche geschiedschrijving in de 16e en 17e eeuw over den Opstand* (Maastricht 1941).
312. E. H. Waterbolk, 'Zeventiende eeuwers in de Republiek over de grondslagen van het geschiedverhaal. Mondeling of schriftelijke overlevering', *Bijdragen voor de geschiedenis der Nederlanden*, vol. 12 (1957/8), pp. 26–40.
313. E. H. Waterbolk, *Twee eeuwen Friese geschiedschrijving. Opkomst, bloei en verval van de Friese historiografie in de zestiende en zeventiende eeuw* (Groningen/Djakarta 1952).
See also 66, 150, 175, 176, 248.

(vii) Publishing:

314. C. Clair, *Christopher Plantin* (London 1960).
315. D. W. Davies, *The World of the Elzeviers* (The Hague 1954).

316. F. J. Dubiez, *Op de grens van Humanisme en Hervorming. De betekenis van de boekdrukkunst te Amsterdam in een bewogen tijd* (Nieuwkoop 1962). Deals with printing and publishing in Amsterdam up to 1578.

317. I. H. van Eeghen, *De Amsterdamse boekhandel 1680–1725*, 4 vols (Amsterdam 1960–67).

318. W. Hellinga *et al.*, *Kopij en druk in de Nederlanden* (Amsterdam 1962).

319. M. M. Kleerkooper and W. P. van Stockum, *De boekhandel te Amsterdam in de 17e eeuw, biographische en geschiedkundige aantekeningen*, 2 vols (The Hague 1914–16).

320. A. Willems, *Les Elzevier* (Brussels 1880, reprint Nieuwkoop 1962). See also 69, 260.

The 18th Century

(i)   General:

See the relevant sections of 9, 10, 14.

(ii)   The Dutch Republic and Europe:

321. N. A. Bootsma, *De Hertog van Brunswijk 1750–1759* (Assen 1962).

322. A. C. Carter, *The Dutch Republic in Europe in the Seven Years War* (London 1971).

323. P. Geyl, *Willem IV en Engeland* (The Hague 1924).

324. R. M. Hatton, *Diplomatic Relations between Great Britain and the Dutch Republic 1714–1721* (London 1950).

325. J. G. Stork-Penning, *Het grote werk; vredesonderhandelingen gedurende de Spaanse Successie-oorlog* (Groningen 1958).

(iii)   Economic decline:

326. A. C. Carter, 'Dutch Foreign Investment, 1738–1800', *Economica*, November 1953, pp. 322–40.

327. A. C. Carter, 'The Dutch and the English Public Debt in 1777', *Economica*, May 1953, pp. 159–61.

328. P. W. Klein, 'Stagnation économique et emploi du capital dans la Hollande des XVIIIe et XIXe siècles', *Revue du Nord*, LII (1970), pp. 33–41.

329. M. Morineau, 'La balance du commerce franco-néerlandais et le resserrement économique des Provinces-Unies au XVIIe siècle', *Economisch-Historisch Jaarboek*, 30 (1965).

330. J. de Vries, *De economische achteruitgang der Republiek in de achttiende eeuw* (Amsterdam 1959). The standard work.

331. C. Wilson, *Anglo-Dutch Commerce and Finance in the Eighteenth Century* (London 1941).

332. C. Wilson, 'The economic decline of the Netherlands', *Economic History Review*, IX (1939).

333. C. Wilson, 'Taxation and the decline of empires, an unfashionable theme', *Bijdragen en Mededelingen van het Historisch Genootschap te Utrecht*, vol. 77 (1963), pp. 10–26; reprinted in *Economic History and the Historians: collected essays* (London 1969).

See also 98, 99, 105, 114, 115, 117, 118, 122, 137, 138, 346.

(iv) Political, social and cultural history:

334. J. S. Bartstra, *Vlootherstel en legeraugmentatie 1770–1780* (Assen 1952).

335. M. G. de Boer, 'Oligarchische uitwassen te Haarlem in het midden der 18e eeuw', *Bijdragen voor Vaderlandsche Geschiedenis en Oudheidkunde* (1944).

336. L. Brummel, *Frans Hemsterhuis, een philosophenleven* (Haarlem 1925).

337. J. R. Bruijn, *De admiraliteit van Amsterdam in rustige jaren, 1713–51. Regenten en financiën, schepen en zeevarenden* (Amsterdam 1970).

338. H. T. Colenbrander, *De Patriottentijd, hoofdzakelijk naar buitenlandsche bescheiden*, 3 vols (The Hague 1897–9).

339. A. Th. van Deursen, *Leonard Offerhaus. Professor historiarum Groninganus (1699–1779)* (Groningen 1957).

340. A. Th. van Deursen, *Jacobus de Rhoer, 1722–1813. Een historicus op de drempel van een nieuwe tijd* (Groningen 1970).

341. J. L. F. Engelhard, *Het generaalplakkaat van 31 juli 1725 op de convooien en licenten en het lastgeld op de schepen. Een studie over de heffing der in- en uitvoerrechten van de Republiek der Vereenigde Nederlanden, hoofdzakelijk tijdens de achttiende eeuw* (Assen 1970).

342. P. Geyl, *Revolutiedagen in Amsterdam (Augustus–September 1748), Prins Willem IV en de Doelistenbeweging* (The Hague 1936).

343. P. Geyl, *De Patriottenbeweging, 1780–1787* (Amsterdam 1947).

344. P. Geyl, *De Wittenoorlog. Een pennestrijd in 1757* (Mededelingen van de Koninklijke Nederlandse Akademie van Wetenschappen, afd. Letterkunde, nieuwe reeks, deel 16, no. 10) (Amsterdam 1953).

345. J. Hartog, *De Spectatoriale geschriften van 1741 tot 1800. Bijdrage tot de kennis van het huiselijk, maatschappelijk en kerkelijk leven onder ons volk in de tweede helft der achttiende eeuw* (Utrecht 1889²).

346. J. Hovy, *Het voorstel van 1751 tot instelling van een beperkt vrijhavenstelsel in de Republiek* (Groningen 1966).

347. G. A. Lindeboom, *Herman Boerhaave* (London 1968).

348. C. H. E. de Wit, *De strijd tussen aristocratie en democratie in Nederland 1780–1848* (Heerlen 1965).

349. J. de Witte van Citters, *Contracten van Correspondentie* (The Hague 1873).

Many of the general works already cited have relevance for the eighteenth century but particular attention is drawn to the following: 9, 14, 72, 78, 84, 158, 188, 189; and also 7, 8, 231, 236.

Index